Road Biking™ Ohio

HELP US KEEP THIS GUIDE UP TO DATE

Every effort has been made by the author and editors to make this guide as accurate and useful as possible. However, many things can change after a guide is published—roads are detoured, phone numbers change, facilities come under new management, etc.

We would love to hear from you concerning your experiences with this guide and how you feel it could be improved and kept up to date. While we may not be able to respond to all comments and suggestions, we'll take them to heart and we'll also make certain to share them with the author. Please send your comments and suggestions to the following address:

Globe Pequot Press
Reader Response/Editorial Department
P.O. Box 480
Guilford, CT 06437

Or you may e-mail us at: editorial@GlobePequot.com

Thanks for your input, and happy riding!

Road Biking™ Series

WITHDRAWN

Road Biking™
Ohio

A Guide to the State's Best Bike Rides

Celeste Baumgartner

FALCONGUIDES

GUILFORD, CONNECTICUT
HELENA, MONTANA

AN IMPRINT OF GLOBE PEQUOT PRESS

FALCONGUIDES®

Copyright © 2010 Morris Book Publishing, LLC

FalconGuides is an imprint of Globe Pequot Press.

Falcon, FalconGuides, and Outfit Your Mind are registered trademarks and Road Biking is a trademark of Morris Book Publishing, LLC.

Photos by Celeste Baumgartner unless otherwise indicated.
Maps by Trailhead Graphics Inc. © Morris Book Publishing, LLC
Layout: Sue Murray
Project editor: John Burbidge

Library of Congress Cataloging-in-Publication data
Baumgartner, Celeste.
  Road biking Ohio : a guide to the state's best bike rides / Celeste Baumgartner.
    p. cm.
  Includes index.
  ISBN 978-0-7627-3963-9
 1. Cycling—Ohio—Guidebooks. 2. Bicycle touring—Ohio—Guidebooks. 3. Ohio—Guidebooks.
I. Title.
  GV1045.5.O3B38 2010
  796.609771—dc22
                              2010003374
Printed in the United States of America
10 9 8 7 6 5 4 3 2 1

Contents

The Rides

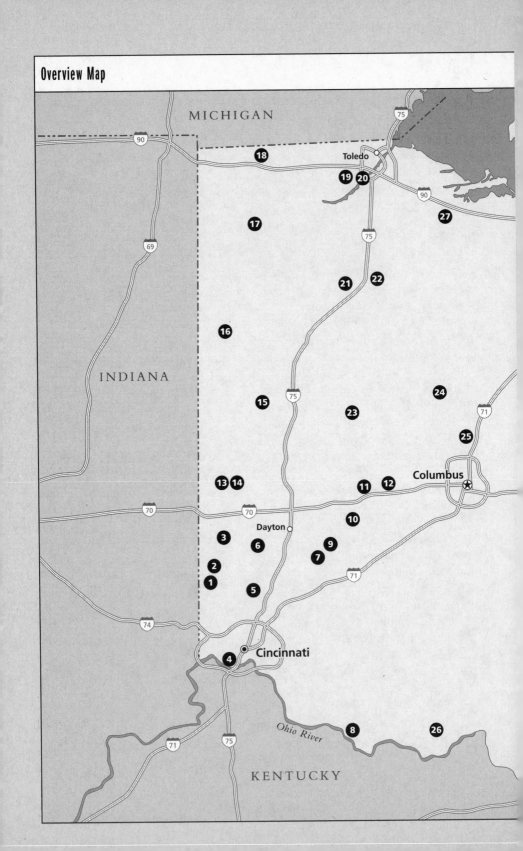

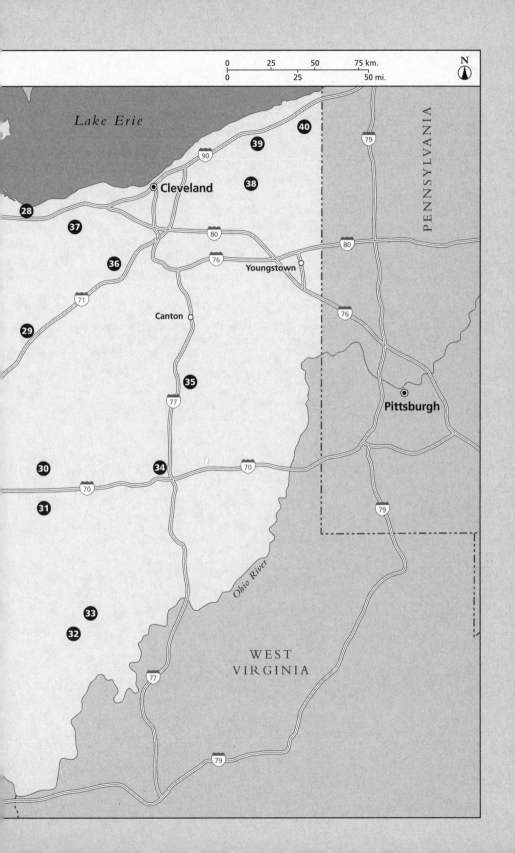

Preface

Thanks for green grass, blue skies, hills and valleys, a smooth road on which to ride, a friend to ride with, and being pleasantly tired at the end of the day.

Ohio and biking make a match. Good roads, multi-use trails, plentiful bike clubs and shops, the Buckeye State's got what it takes. Finding good routes for this book was easy. I have written a bicycling column for the *Journal-News* in southwestern Ohio for more than fifteen years. The roads there are like my backyard. For the rest of the state, I sought the advice of bicycle clubs and shops. Funny, the people there, wherever, were always convinced that their territory was absolutely the best in the state for biking. Convention and visitors bureaus were also helpful in finding bike routes. Several came up with a route of their own; others put me in contact with a bicyclist who could help. The challenge was in choosing the best forty rides. I went for low traffic, high scenery. They're spread over Ohio. I want to thank all of those people for their help. Is it just me or are bicyclists really a friendly, helpful lot? And what is it with bicyclists and eating?

- We contacted a bike club in Mansfield asking if they could suggest a route. They rode and mapped a route before we arrived, and then the whole gang went along with us just for fun and to show us where to get the best apple pie.
- We had a problem while on the road, called a bike shop in Geauga County; could we stop in? They stopped what they were doing, met us at the door, carried our bikes up the steps, fixed the problem, and suggested a route to ride and where to eat lunch.
- At another shop in Delaware, they mapped routes for us and most importantly directed those routes around the best ice cream shops and the restaurant with the best fried baloney sandwiches anywhere.

Many bike clubs and shops sent maps, offered to ride along, and gave us cell phone numbers in case we got lost. They include the Cincinnati Cycle Club, Cycle Path Bike Shop (Athens), Flatlanders Bicycle Club (Fremont), Hancock Handlebars (Findlay), Licking County Bicycle Club, Medina County Bicycle Club, Mid-Ohio Bikers (Mansfield), Toledo Area Bicyclists, and Michael Hart at Mycle's Cycles (Ripley). Extremely helpful were recommendations from convention and visitors bureaus in Ashtabula County, Lorain County, Cambridge/Guernsey County (thanks for introducing me to Tom Davey), Carroll County, Van Wert County and Licking County, and the chamber of commerce in New Bremen. Thank you, Charley Conley at DeLorme, who spent patient hours on the phone helping me learn to use my GPS.

Thank you to Scott Adams, John Burbidge, and everyone at Globe Pequot Press for their help and patience in turning my meanderings into something very organized and nice.

Thanks to John, my husband, who encouraged me to do this from day one and made sure I always had air in my tires. Thanks to Penny Westrick, who immediately said "Let's go" when she heard the idea. She biked from one end of the state to the other with me, our bike bags stuffed with her Sunny Morning Muffins (recipe included). She also introduced me to fried dill pickles. Thanks to John and to Penny's husband Pat for taking care of the dogs while we were gone. And to my kids Eric, Amy, Tim, and Jenny, who inspired me to get on a bike again when I was a grown-up and convinced me that I could go down the Darrtown Road hill without braking, and to my long-gone parents, who stirred in me a love of being outside, birds, trees, flowers, and quiet nonmotorized things.

I hope that you enjoy these rides as much as I did.

Introduction

About fifteen years ago many of my friends were taking vacations to far-distant places. Being a little light in the pocket, I was staying home and feeling sorry for myself. Then some little spark suggested I explore my own territory on a shoestring in the form of a bicycle. I've been doing that ever since, and what a wealth I have discovered. Ohio is one cool state, varying from corner to corner, with the Lake Erie region being its own environment. You want hills? The southeast has unabashed hills and breathtaking scenery. You like flat? Go northwest. The graceful wheat, bean, and corn fields stretch on until you feel dizzy. You like anything in between? Try almost anywhere else in the state.

I like to put in my biking miles. It's a fitness thing. Going fast, especially downhill, is fun. Yet I am not a macho-dude biker who has to go as far and as fast as possible. I relish seeing well-tended farmsteads, gardens, and great old barns. I stop to look at flowers and birds and always carry a camera and binoculars. I hope that the routes in this book accommodate those interests yet can still be enjoyed by those who like going as far and as fast as possible.

Ohio has some of the most picturesque farm country anywhere. We raise mostly corn, soybeans, and wheat, and there are wineries, especially in the northeastern part of the state. There are dairy farms, hogs, and beef cattle operations; we have one of the largest horse populations in the country. Besides farms, Ohio has great forests, some prairie, a Great Lake, the Ohio River, and a good number of covered bridges.

These bike routes will often bring you face to face with Ohio history, especially as related to:

- Covered bridges—many routes traverse one or more. Most were built between 1825 and 1875, according to Rickie Longfellow, who knows because she is with the Federal Highway Administration. The cover was originally used to protect the bridge's trusses and decks from snow and rain—an uncovered bridge would last about twenty years, but a covered one could last a hundred. The cover also kept horses from being spooked by the water underneath.
- The Underground Railroad, which was a loose network of antislavery folks and safe houses that helped thousands of slaves escape to the North and Canada. Traveling at night, the slaves followed the "drinking gourd" (Big Dipper) on hidden paths that became quiet country roads.
- Canals—between 1825 and 1847, 1,000 miles of navigable canals were built in Ohio. These canals gave Ohio farmers and businessmen access to the Ohio River and Lake Erie. They were the state's first transportation system and opened markets for agricultural and industrial products. But then came the railroads; canals were mostly abandoned, only to make a comeback years later as a tourist attraction. The towpaths tend to be flat and transpose into excellent bike trails.

On Silver Hart Road

- The "Indian Wars," as they're called, delayed the settlement of the Northwest Territory. England (the former owner of that territory) used Native Americans to create havoc, which made settlers reluctant to buy land. Generals Arthur St. Clair and "Mad" Anthony Wayne built a series of forts, and the battles raged until the Battle of Fallen Timbers in 1794 convinced the English and the Native Americans to yield. That led to the signing of the Treaty of Greenville and settlement. Many of the rides in this book are in and around places connected to that struggle.
- Johnny Appleseed, aka John Chapman, was a real person who developed into a folklore legend. You may not meet his presence often—but think of him when you see an apple orchard. He was a kind man and a successful nurseryman who gained fame by distributing apple trees all over the Midwest. It is said that he wore his cooking pan as a hat when he traveled.

I don't know if Johnny Appleseed traveled over the entire state, but if he did, he experienced a wide variety of terrain. Glaciers entered Ohio several times during the last two million years, but they did not cover the entire state. Generally, the glaciated portions of the state tend to be flatter—but nothing is simple. Those glaciated regions have their share of hills and valleys. The southeast portion of Ohio is part of the unglaciated Appalachian Plateau. The highest place in the state is Campbell Hill in Bellefontaine, at 1,549 feet above sea level; this hill is one of several in the region atop a geologic island called the Bellefontaine Outlier. Then there's the northwestern part of the state; eons ago it was covered by a large lake. When the lake receded to become Lake Erie as we know it today, it left behind the Great Black Swamp. Settlers avoided the swamp because the mud and mosquitoes made travel difficult. Eventually, when all of the surrounding area was settled, the swamp was tamed with drainage tile. Funny how things go; now people are taking out the drainage tile and restoring the wetlands. Yet the northwest, although it has some big cities, is still sparsely settled. All of this is a way of saying that bicycling in Ohio is never boring. You can find nice spells of flat road, challenging hills, and pleasant rolling land almost anywhere in the state.

As far as Ohio weather, we have a saying: If you don't like it, wait a while and it will change. Summers are glorious—warm and sunny with pleasant temperatures. If those temperatures climb into the 90s for a few days, we will probably say, "It's not the heat, it's the humidity." That's when nothing beats a crisp bike ride at dawn. In April and May the temperature range is 37 to 70 degrees F in the northeast and 41 to 72 in the southwest. A day in spring when the oak leaves are the size of squirrels' ears and spring beauties are peeping through is amazing. Fall is the sunniest season, with warm September days running at 52 to 71 degrees, resulting in some of the most beautiful fall foliage you can imagine. Winters can be cold, 17 to 43 degrees in the dead of it. Sissy that I am, I rarely bike in the winter, but some diehards go at it year-round.

Ohio is becoming more and more urbanized. We lived in farm country for a long time. Now there's a Wal-Mart and Applebee's down the road, with fields sprouting more houses than corn, and that's typical of most of the state. Some roads where I once biked are now too busy. Riding a route in Springfield on quiet roads suggested by local bikers, we came upon a detour; construction crews were building a subdivision and a mall and rearranging the roads. We changed the route. Yet many pleasant, one-lane rural roads remain. We asked a man in Prospect how busy the roads were and he said, "There's nothing out there but farmers and cows," and he was right. When we looked for bike routes in some northwestern counties, we were told repeatedly that you could ride anywhere; all the roads were flat and all had low traffic. That was pretty much the case. Also, multi-use trails seem to follow development. Many are a pleasant ride on their own. Oftentimes we used multi-use trails to get out of busy cities and onto quiet rural roads.

It's interesting that the roads in the northwestern part of the state are laid out in a grid. A county engineer told me that early surveyors experimented with many surveying systems before finally settling, in northwest Ohio, on the grid. They continued to use that system as they traveled west. In other parts of the state, roads seem to follow the lay of the land. As far as road signs go, I find it interesting that different counties have the signs facing different directions. It can be a tad off-putting until you figure out the local system. Also, some counties have every road carefully signed and some—well, some seem to have come up short on road signs. At intersections without road signs, I have done my best to include landmarks or other indicators. I know there are also times when the view of roads from your bike seat does not look like the map. I tried to be specific in those instances.

The publishers and I have done our best to provide accurate, up-to-the-minute maps in this book. Yet detours, road closings, and new subdivisions happen. Carrying a local county map is a good backup; it also enables you to leave the route and go exploring on your own should you choose. Maps are available from the county engineer's office in the seat of each county, and some counties have maps with bicycling routes highlighted. There is no general phone number for engineers' offices, but if you have Internet access you can do a Web search. You can pick up the map or have it mailed. Some are free, some cost a dollar or two—money well spent if you come face to face with a bridge that's out.

Basic Equipment

The only thing worse than, or at least as bad as, a bridge out is a flat tire or other bicycle malfunction while you're on the road. A good, well-maintained bicycle is a joy to ride and can increase your biking safety. Buying one at a good bike shop instead of the local box store will cost a few more dollars but is worth the expense. Folks at a bike shop will take time to help you find the right bike for your style of riding. They'll fit you to your bicycle, making any necessary adjustments to the cranks, handlebar stem, handlebars, and saddle; saddles are incredibly important, and in recent years manufacturers have made vast improvements. Finally, a bike shop will establish a regular maintenance program. For any bike, an annual tune-up is important whether you do it yourself or take it to the shop. It's a critical aspect of safe and happy riding.

I have a bicycling friend who will not ride with anyone not wearing a helmet. He doesn't want to see their brains scattered all over the road, he said. A high percentage of cyclists' brain injuries can be prevented by a helmet; estimates range from 45 to 88 percent. To do its job, a helmet must be fitted securely, level on your head, and have the straps carefully and properly fastened. Helmets should be replaced every couple of years—suggestions on exactly how often vary. They must be replaced if you crash, even if the helmet looks fine. Higher prices are mostly for style and pizzazz. As long as a helmet has the U.S. Consumer Product Safety Commission (CPSC) seal and is properly fitted, it will do the job.

When I first got back into biking as an adult, I took an organized ride—maybe 30 miles. I drank water at all of the stops, but I did not carry a water bottle. That evening I almost passed out in the grocery store. The next time I rode, I had a frame-mounted water bottle. Now I carry two. Keeping hydrated is critical. One rule of thumb is to take a big drink every fifteen minutes, and obviously, drink more if it's hot. On the flip side, when it's cool you still need water but may need to remind yourself to drink. Another bicycling rule of thumb is to eat before you're hungry and drink before you're thirsty. Even on a short ride, you can get amazingly hungry and that will sap your energy. Keep your bike bag stuffed with a supply of commercial energy bars, bananas, Penny's Sunny Morning Muffins, or whatever tickles your fancy. I have included restaurants or places where food is available on or near the route.

PENNY'S SUNNY MORNING MUFFINS

2 tsp. baking soda

2 cups flour (you could use half whole wheat)

1 cup sugar

2 tbsp. honey (or skip the honey and use 1¼ cups sugar total)

½ cup old-fashioned oatmeal

1 tbsp. cinnamon

½ tsp. salt (optional)

1½ cups finely shredded carrots

1½ cups peeled and shredded apple

½ cup raisins (try golden)

¼ to ½ cup pecans (optional)

2 Egg Beaters® or the equivalent

1 egg, beaten

¼ cup apple butter

¾ cup nonfat plain yogurt

1 tbsp. vanilla

In a large mixing bowl, combine baking soda, flour, sugar, honey, oatmeal, cinnamon, and salt. In another bowl combine carrots, apples, raisins, pecans, beaten eggs, apple butter, yogurt, and vanilla. Add to dry ingredients and stir until moistened. Use paper muffin cups and spray them with Pam. Bake at 350° to 375° for 18 to 20 minutes. Makes 24 muffins.

For trips of any distance, a bike bag of some type is helpful. I carry food, maps, a first-aid kit (Adventure Medical Kits, 800-324-3517, has waterproof Pocket Medic™ kits that will fit in your pocket), a lightweight windbreaker, a bike lock, and tools—you can now find handy-dandy *little* tool kits or multipurpose tools that will do everything except change a flat for you; you need to be able to fix a flat. For this you will need a tire patch kit, tubes, and an air pump, and you need to know how to use them. Except in the heat of summer I carry a balaclava and full-finger gloves. It's a good idea to take your credit card and cell phone. Hope you will never need it but carry identification and carry a cell phone with an ICE (In Case of Emergency) phone number. Enter "ICE" followed by the name of the person to be contacted in case of emergency.

I have had a few scares but have never been too concerned about dogs. If I hear barking, I pedal faster—once you're out of a dog's territory, it will usually stop. I carry

Bicycle/pedestrian bridge over US 24

a can of mace but have never used it. Other ideas are squirting water from your water bottle into the dog's face or carrying a plastic bottle filled with coins or rocks or something that will make a lot of noise if you shake it. Or maybe throw it.

If you ride a recumbent bike as I do, you don't really need bicycling-specific clothing—just no pant legs that would catch in the chainring. On an upright bicycle, bike shorts or tights definitely make a long day in the saddle seem a little shorter. Fingerless gloves provide cushioning comfort against road shock from the handlebars and protection in case of a spill. You can find a great selection of rain gear; I use a water-resistant windbreaker that I keep in my bike bag. The one caveat is to be sure your rain gear will not catch in your wheels. Some things are worse than getting wet.

Road Safety and Rules of the Road

Road biking is fun and healthy—no question. Learn the rules, use common sense, and then ride correctly and confidently to increase your safety level. In Ohio most of the motor vehicle rules apply to bicyclists as well as motorists. Some rules apply to bicyclists only. For a paraphrased list of those rules, get a copy of *Ohio Bicycling Street Smarts*, an all-round helpful book available online or in hard copy. Contact the Ohio Department of Transportation, 1980 West Broad St., Columbus, 43223; (614) 752-4685; www.dot.state.oh.us/bike.

If you ride in violation of traffic laws, you increase your risk of a crash and you may give up your rights. If you get into a crash, the courts will almost always find it was your fault. Stop at stop signs, signal your turns, and ride with the traffic flow—studies show that is safer than riding against traffic. Stay in the right lane unless you need to turn left. Then, when it's clear, move into the left lane, signal your turn, be certain that everyone who needs to know is aware that you're turning by making eye contact or moving the hand with which you are signaling, and then go.

When you're in the right lane, don't stay too far right. If you are riding next to parked cars on the right, someone may open a door into your line of travel. Also, cars passing on the left may try to crowd you. Take up your space. It makes you more visible. Motorists will know you're there and be less likely to sideswipe your knee. Use common sense about riding side by side with another cyclist; it's fine on quiet roads, but on narrow, winding, or busier roads it can be rude and dangerous.

In towns with busy roads, I have mentioned where sidewalks are available for riding. Local jurisdiction may prohibit that in some places. If you feel safer on the sidewalk, ride there—we always did. It is important to maintain a good image for bicyclists by being extremely courteous to pedestrians.

If you ride at night, you are required to have lights—a headlight is a must and a red taillight may be required. For safety, reflectors on the rear of your bike as well as reflective ankle bands make you more visible.

Some bicycling cautions: First, I have wiped out on loose gravel, and I warn of it wherever it was a problem, but keep in mind that loose gravel is not a constant. Second, you'll find lots of picturesque covered bridges in this book. They are great fun to see, but most are floored with wooden slats that can be tire-grabbers. I prefer to walk across. Know also that roads get slippery in rain and brakes are not as efficient when wet. Be especially cautious on wet painted lines, sewer grates, railroad tracks (wet or dry, always cross at a right angle), and fallen leaves. Dry fallen leaves can also trip you up, as can potholes and lots of other things; biking, like life, has hazards. Being a couch potato is not a healthy choice and it's no fun; so, to repeat myself, learn the rules, use common sense, and then, correctly and confidently, go ride a bike.

How to Use This Book

Rides are divided very generally into four categories, but cut me a little slack here; it's meant to be a guide and it's rather subjective. One cyclist's gentle elevation is another cyclist's hill, and a gentle elevation after 50 miles may seem more daunting than it did early in the ride. The Thornville route is short for a challenge, but its hills are relentless. On the other hand, the Little Miami Scenic Trail Challenge is 73 miles long but is an easy ride. Typically you don't ride it all at once.

- Rambles are the easiest and shortest rides. At 35 miles or less, they are pleasant outings on flat to rolling terrain. Don't rule out the possibility of a hill or two, but nothing daunting.
- Cruises are intermediate rides at 25 to 50 miles long and may have some moderate hills.
- Challenges are difficult and are for riders with some experience and in good condition. They are usually 40 to 60 miles in length.
- Classics are long and hard; they are over 60 miles. You might want to give yourself two days to cover the distance, or you might not.

But don't let those categories limit you—if you're in the neighborhood of a ride listed as a classic and feel like cycling, you can always ride a short distance as an out-and-back ride. Likewise, on a ramble you will surely come upon a road just begging to be explored to add more miles. You can do it without a map, but carrying a county map will give you more possibilities to lengthen or shorten a ride as you see fit.

I have included mileage marks and the names of crossroads where that seemed appropriate, for example, where road signs are few and far between or in places where the route gets confusing. I have not included them where they became tedious, as when you're riding through a little town on Main Street and you cross First, Second, Third, and Maple Streets each a block apart, or on a long straight stretch of road where you cross a road every mile or so, or on bike paths.

I once rode a bike route described in a book and came to a T intersection that was on the road but not in the book. I was miles from anything familiar and had no choice but to backtrack. I and the publishers have done our best to be precise and ensure that does not happen with this book. Having said that, I urge you to read the mileage marks as a general guide, not a rule. On many of our rides, Penny logged about a half mile farther than me although we rode the same route. Bicycle computers are not yet perfect and are definitely no more perfect than the people who measure the bike wheel and set the computer. Also, rounding up or down to the tenth can make a difference between my reading and yours, to say nothing of having to turn around and pick up a dropped water bottle or a map that blows out of your hand.

Passion Flower Quilt Barn

And finally, things are in a constant state of change. A subdivision might have been built along what was a quiet road when I rode. And a road that is quiet in the middle of the day might get busy during rush hour.

Ohio Bicycling Resources

Bicycle Museum of America, 7 West Monroe St. (SR 274), New Bremen; (419) 629-9249; www.bicyclemuseum.com.

Columbus Outdoor Pursuits, 1525 Bethel Rd., Suite 100, Columbus; (614) 442-7901; www.outdoor-pursuits.org. This group annually puts on the Great Ohio Bicycle Adventure (GOBA) and several other organized rides.

Ohio Bicycle Federation; www.ohiobike.org. Their Web site is a great resource for bike clubs, organized bike rides, the Ohio Bicycle Calendar, and more.

Ohio Department of Transportation Bicycle/Pedestrian Office, 1980 West Broad St., Columbus; (614) 752-4685; www.dot.state.oh.us; click on the bicycle link for bicycling information of every kind and ordering information for *Ohio Bicycling Street Smarts.* This manual teaches safe bicycling techniques on roads and streets. It is available in a printed version or online.

Map Legend

Transportation

Featured Route	————
Featured Trail	··············
Optional Route	———
Interstate Highway	═(70)═
U.S. Highway	═(27)═
State Road	—(101)—
County/Local Road	———
Dirt Road/Trail	---------

Hydrology

Lake/Reservoir/ Major River	⬭
River/Creek	∼∼

Land Use

Large Park/ Large Wildlife Area	▭
State Line	—·—·—·—

Symbols

Trailhead (Start)	❿
Mileage Marker	17.1◆—
Small Park	🌲
Visitor Center	❓
Wildlife Area	🐦
Historical Site	🏛
Point of Interest/ Structure	■
Lodge	🛏
Picnic Area	⊼
Capital	✪
City	◉
Town	○
Bridge	⋈
Church	†
Marina	⚓
Airport	✈
University/College	🎓
Direction Arrow	→
Option Arrow	→

1 Oxford Ramble

This is a great ride from Oxford, home of Miami University and a tidy, attractive college town. You can choose the route to Brookville Lake or the shorter option. It's a country ride with lots to see and enough hills to have an edge without making you beg.

Start: Oxford Community Park.
Length: 31.7 miles with a 21.2-mile option.
Terrain: Flat to rolling with a couple of small hills; more hills (one big one) around Brookville Lake.

Traffic and hazards: Mostly quiet rural roads; some traffic around Oxford. On the longer route there is fairly heavy traffic for 0.1 mile on SR 101.

Getting there: Take Oxford Millville Road/US 27 into Oxford. Coming from the north, turn right (south) onto Locust Street and then right (west) onto Spring Street, which becomes Fairfield Road out of town. Coming from the south, turn left (west) onto Spring Street. The park is on the right at 6801 Fairfield Road (the park also has an entrance from Brookville Road).

The Ride

The 113-acre Oxford Community Park, the staging area for both routes, is nicely designed and a popular place to be. It has athletic fields, hiking trails, play areas, and more. You can spend some time and add some miles just biking around it. Kay Rench Drive goes through the park and is accessible from Fairfield and Brookville Roads.

The longer ride and the shorter option both cross into Indiana and then back again. Road names change when you cross the border, but don't look for signs on these rural roads.

Exit the park and go left on Fairfield Road; pass the airport. It takes a couple of hills to get out of town. The traffic soon thins and you're in the country. A mile after you enter Indiana you will come to Harmony Road. To follow the shorter option, turn right onto Harmony Road. The longer ride keeps on going through New Bath, where they used to keep the bank locked because they had so many robberies—customers had to knock to get in. Next you'll come into Old Bath, but you'll hardly notice—it's just a cluster of homes.

I have tried to be precise with directions because many roads are not marked. In Old Bath cross unmarked CR 200 East. It is a mix of gravel and rough pavement. Keep going. At the second crossroad turn left onto Liberty Pike, just before the Franklin County water tower. In the middle of a pleasant downhill glide, turn right onto Whitcomb Road and go up that pleasant glide. Just past the buck deer standing on a rock on the right, the road bends a hard left. Take the next road to the right; this is narrow, unmarked Pea Ridge Road. Cross SR 101 and keep going. Enjoy that long swoop down to the lake. You'll see the entrance to the Scenic Trail before you come to the lake.

Cows chillin' in the pond along the Oxford Ramble

At 5,260 acres, Brookville Lake is well known for fishing, boating, swimming, and more. It is adjacent to both the Mounds and the Quakertown State Recreation Area. Both have beaches and camping, and Quakertown has a marina. The Mounds are so called because there is a prehistoric Native American mound there.

As you start out on the Scenic Trail, remember that big downhill on Garr Hill Road? Well, now it's time to pay the piper and go back up. However, there is enough pleasant scenery and wildlife to distract you.

Be cautious for the brief ride on SR 101. Turn right on the first road you see and then in a stone's throw turn left onto Oxford Pike. Follow this scenic route through a couple of little towns, past a pleasant farm pond that usually hosts a few ducks afloat, and all the way back to Mixerville. At the T turn right onto Hetrick Road, which becomes Brookville Road when you enter Ohio. Cross Indian Creek and be ready for a final hill and a little more traffic as you return to Oxford.

Miles and Directions

0.0 Exit the park on Kay Rench Drive, the road that goes through the park. Turn left onto Fairfield Road.

0.8 Cross Riggs Road.

2.2 Enter Indiana and Fairfield Road becomes Bath Road—but don't expect a sign.

3.2 Cross Harmony Road. **Option:** To follow the 21.2-mile option, see below.

Oxford Ramble

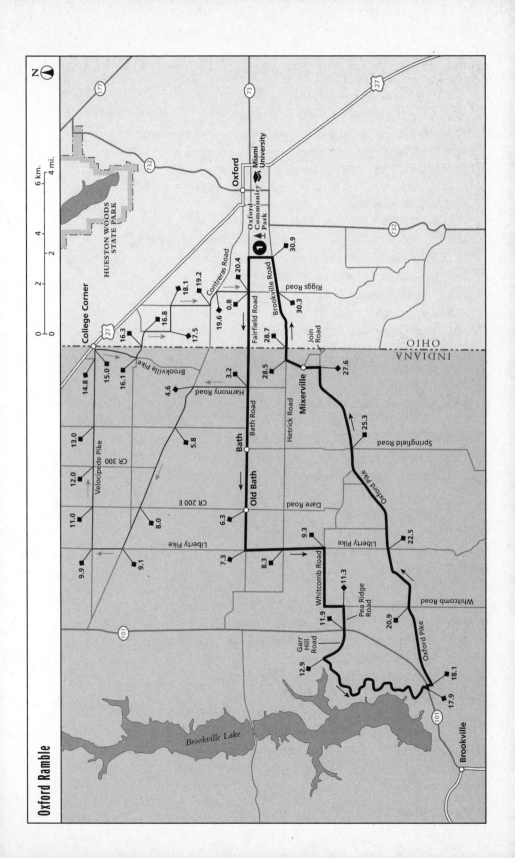

6.3 Cross Dare Road/CR 200 East.

7.3 Turn left onto Liberty Pike.

8.3 Cross Hetrick Road.

9.3 Turn right onto Whitcomb Road.

11.3 Turn right onto the first road you come to. This is unmarked Pea Ridge Road.

11.9 Cross SR 101 and continue straight on Garr Hill Road.

12.2 When Pea Ridge goes left, keep going straight on Garr Hill.

12.9 Follow the Scenic Trail to the left, but first go have a look at Brookville Lake. There are primitive restrooms.

17.9 The Scenic Trail T's into SR 101—turn left.

18.0 Go right onto Cooley Road, past the McCullough Hyde Medical Building.

18.1 At the stop sign turn left onto Oxford Pike; there's no road sign.

20.9 Cross Whitcomb Road.

22.5 Cross Liberty Pike.

25.3 Cross Springfield Road.

27.6 Bend to the left and stay on Oxford Pike when Join Road goes straight.

28.5 At the T turn right onto Hetrick Road.

28.7 Enter Ohio and the road becomes Brookville Road.

30.3 Cross Riggs Road.

30.9 Turn left onto Kay Rench Drive.

31.7 Return to the parking lot.

Option

3.2 Go right on Harmony Road.

4.6 At the T turn left onto Contreras Pike.

5.8 Cross Stone Road.

8.0 Cross CR 200 East.

9.1 At the four-way stop, go right on Liberty Pike.

9.9 Turn right onto Velocipede Pike.

11.0 Cross CR 200 East.

12.0 Cross CR 300 East.

13.0 Cross Stone Road.

14.8 In College Corner Velocipede becomes Church Street.

15.0 At the T turn right onto Brookville Pike and go past the cemetery.

16.1 Hang a left onto Sand Run Road.

16.3 Cross into Ohio and the road becomes Hayworth Road.

16.8 At the T turn right onto Stout Road.

17.5 At the hard bend to the left, the road becomes Shera Road.

18.1 At the T turn right onto Taylor Road.

19.2 You'll come to yet another T; turn left onto Contreras Road.

19.6 Turn right onto Riggs Road.

20.4 Take a left onto Fairfield Road.

21.2 Turn right onto Kay Rench Drive and return to the park.

Local Information

Oxford Convention and Visitors Bureau: 30 West Park Place, 2nd Floor, Oxford; (513) 523-8687; www.enjoyoxford.org.

Attractions

Hueston Woods State Park: College Corner; (513) 523-6347; www.hwresort.com. Located in Butler and Preble Counties, the park has nearly 3,000 acres of natural resources for outdoor recreation, such as hiking, fishing, canoeing, and, unique to this region—fossil hunting. You can spend the night at the lodge and eat at the Hueston Woods Trailblazer Dining Room, a full-service dining room with a spectacular view of Acton Lake. The Johnny Appleseed Lounge has a friendly ambience and the cocktails are generous.

Restaurants

Kona Bistro and Coffee Bar: 31 West High St., Oxford; (513) 523-0686. Upscale casual dining.

La Bodega Delicatessen: 11 West High St., Oxford; (513) 523-1338. Contemporary deli-box lunches.

Accommodations

Maplevale Farm Bed and Breakfast: 3891 Oxford Millville Rd./US 27, Oxford; (513) 523-8909; www.maplevale.com. A lovely park setting.

White Garden Inn: 6195 Brown Rd., Oxford; (513) 524-5827; www.whitegardeninn.com. Named the country's best inn near a college or university. "Arrive as a traveler, leave as a friend" is the motto.

Bike Shops

BikeWise Oxford: 9 North Beech St., Oxford; (513) 523-4880; www.bikewiseoxford.com.

Restrooms

Start/finish: Oxford Community Park.
Mile 12.9: Brookville Lake Marina; pit toilet.

Maps

DeLorme: Ohio Atlas & Gazetteer: Page 58.
DeLorme: Indiana Atlas & Gazetteer: Page 47.

2 Hueston Woods Ramble

This popular route takes you from Hueston Woods State Park over rural roads and through serene countryside to Harshman Covered Bridge and then back in time by means of an old Native American legend. The rolling hills around Four Mile Creek, which the covered bridge traverses, jazz up the route.

Start: Hueston Woods State Park Lodge near Oxford.
Length: 32.5 miles with an option for a shorter 21.4-mile ride.
Terrain: Flat to rolling with a couple of hills on the park road and by the bridge.

Traffic and hazards: Traffic is light, but this is the country—cars tend to speed. Camden College Corner Road is very winding. Watch the loose gravel when you go down the hill on Junction Road. The planks across covered bridges can snare bike tires; consider walking across.

Getting there: From US 27 between Oxford and College Corner, take Todd Road (it only goes one way) a couple of miles to Hueston Woods State Park. Turn left onto Main Loop Road and follow the signs to the lodge.

The Ride

They tell a folklore story about the Native Americans in the Four Mile Creek valley near the Harshman Covered Bridge. Indians remained in that creek valley longer than in any other part of Preble County. A few families of Delawares camped there as late as 1815, giving this part of the Four Mile Creek valley the setting for the legend of Talawanda, a beautiful Native American maiden (many things in the area are named after this maiden). As the story goes, Talawanda had her jealousy aroused when her suitor suggested that if she would go down near a certain large sycamore tree growing in the creek bank, she could see the most beautiful girl in the forest. Curiosity overcame her anger. She went to the place described but could see no one. Then she happened to look into the pool of still water below the tree, where she saw her reflection. A big wedding powwow soon followed.

As you start the ride, notice all the turkey vultures hanging around the Hueston Woods Lodge; it was built in the area where they roosted and they never left. Following Main Loop Road to exit via the service road requires a little effort: It's hilly. The service road signage indicates that no vehicles are allowed, but bicycles are permitted. Keep your head up going around the bends on Camden College Corner Road. Soon you'll come to the historic Hopewell Church, which still holds services during the summer. The cemetery is noted for the craftsmanship of its monuments.

Be cautious of the gravel on Junction Road at the start and at the junction with Simpson Road. As you bike along State Line Road, you are teetering on the brink of Ohio and Indiana. When you come to SR 725, you will see a WELCOME TO INDI-

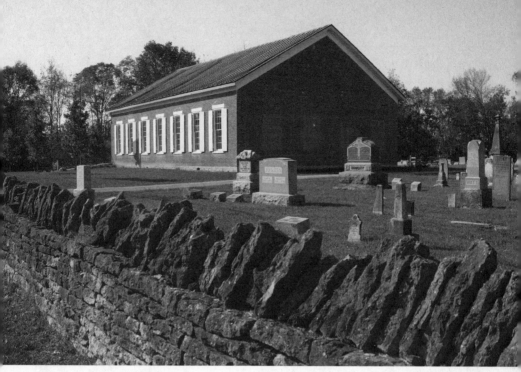

Hopewell Church and cemetery

ANA sign to the left and a WELCOME TO OHIO sign on the right. Continue straight on State Line Road when SR 725 goes into Ohio. You'll also cross a highway that is Indiana SR 227 on the left and Ohio SR 177 on the right. About this time you may be wondering if you missed a turn; you're on State Line for a long time. When you see Concord Road on the right, be ready to turn right onto Dixon Road in 1 mile.

If you have a thing for rocks, don't miss the red granite one in the Concord Churchyard. It is more than 1.5 billion years old and was carried south to Preble County at least 15,000 years ago by the Wisconsin Glacier.

In short order you will come to the Harshman Covered Bridge, built in 1894. Hear the *clop-clop* of the horses' hooves as they crossed it. Think of Talawanda peering into the pool of water. Think of life before computers.

You can contemplate all of these things as you pedal up the big hill just ahead. Bend to the left and then to the right when Allison Mill Road goes left. Go up the hill and then turn left onto Silver Hart Road, which is a picturesque, rolling (hilly) road in the beginning before it flattens out. Eaton Oxford Road is mostly flat. There's a jog on Paint Creek Four Mile Road. Once you're back in the park, it's a nice downhill coast to the lodge.

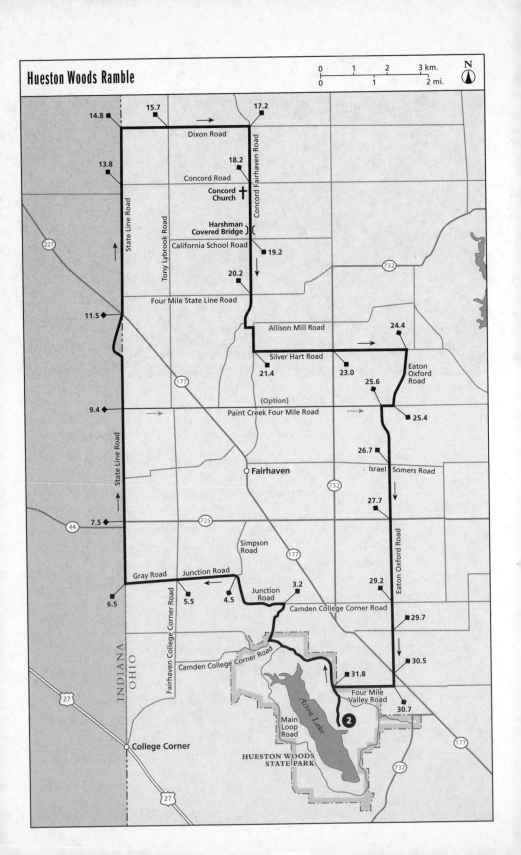

Hueston Woods Ramble

0 1 2 3 km.
0   1   2 mi.

N

14.8 ■   **15.7** ■   **17.2** ■

Dixon Road →

State Line Road

Tony Lybrook Road

Concord Fairhaven Road

13.8 ■

18.2 ■

Concord Road

Concord Church ✝

Harshman Covered Bridge)(

California School Road   ■ **19.2**

20.2 ■

Four Mile State Line Road

11.5 ◆

Allison Mill Road

24.4 ■

→

732

Silver Hart Road

21.4 ■   **23.0** ■

Eaton Oxford Road

25.6 ■

177

(Option)

9.4 ◆   →

Paint Creek Four Mile Road   →

■ **25.4**

26.7 ■

○ **Fairhaven**

732

Israel Somers Road

27.7 ■

↓

7.5 ◆

44   725

Simpson Road

177

Eaton Oxford Road

29.2 ■

Gray Road   Junction Road

←

6.5 ■   **5.5** ■   **4.5** ■   Junction Road

3.2 ■

Camden College Corner Road

■ **29.7**

Fairhaven College Corner Road

↓

30.5 ■

Camden College Corner Road

31.8 ■

Acton Lake

Four Mile Valley Road

30.7 ■

2

INDIANA   OHIO

27

Main Loop Road

College Corner ○

HUESTON WOODS STATE PARK

27   732   177

Miles and Directions

0.0 Exit the parking lot back toward Main Loop Road.

0.5 Turn left onto Main Loop Road.

2.2 Turn right onto the service road (look for it just past the MOUNTAIN BIKE CROSSING sign).

2.4 The road T's into Camden College Corner Road. Turn right.

3.1 Pass Hopewell Church and cemetery.

3.2 Turn left onto Junction Road—watch the gravel.

4.5 Continue left, staying on Junction when Simpson Road goes right.

5.5 Cross Fairhaven College Corner Road.

6.5 At the T turn right onto State Line Road.

7.5 Continue straight, still on State Line Road, when SR 725 goes right.

9.4 **Option:** To shorten the ride to a 21.4-mile loop, turn right here onto Paint Creek Four Mile Road and rejoin the route at mile 25.6 by going right onto Eaton Oxford Road.

11.5 Cross Indiana SR 227 to the left and Ohio SR 177 to the right.

13.8 Pass Concord Road on the right.

14.8 Turn right onto Dixon Road.

15.7 Cross Toney Lybrook Road.

17.2 Go right onto Concord Fairhaven Road.

18.2 Cross Concord Road.

18.3 Pass Concord Church, founded in November 1840.

19.1 Ride or walk through Harshman Covered Bridge.

19.2 Bear right across the next bridge, still on Concord Fairhaven Road, when California School Road crosses.

20.2 Cross Four Mile State Line Road.

21.4 Turn left onto Silver Hart Road.

23.0 Cross SR 732.

24.4 Turn right onto Eaton Oxford Road.

25.4 Jog right onto Paint Creek Four Mile Road.

25.6 Go left back onto Eaton Oxford Road.

26.7 Cross Israel Somers Road.

27.7 Cross SR 725.

29.2 Cross Camden College Corner Road.

29.7 Cross Morning Sun Road.

30.5 Cross SR 177.

30.7 At the T turn right onto Four Mile Valley Road.

31.8 Bend to the right, then turn left into the park and then left onto Main Loop Road.

32.0 Turn right, then bear left toward the lodge and coast 0.5 mile to the parking lot.

32.5 Return to the parking lot.

Local Information

Oxford Convention and Visitors Bureau: 30 West Park Place, 2nd Floor, Oxford; (513) 523-8687; www.enjoyoxford.org.

Attractions

Hueston Woods State Park: College Corner; (513) 523-6347; www.hwresort.com. Located in Butler and Preble Counties, the park has nearly 3,000 acres of natural resources for outdoor recreation, such as hiking, fishing, canoeing, and, unique to this region—fossil hunting. You can spend the night at the lodge and eat at the Hueston Woods Trailblazer Dining Room, a full-service dining room with a spectacular view of Acton Lake. The Johnny Appleseed Lounge has a friendly ambience and the cocktails are generous.

Restaurants

High Street Grill: 116 East High St., Oxford; (513) 523-3134. Upscale casual dining with full bar.

Kona Bistro and Coffee Bar: 31 West High St., Oxford; (513) 523-0686. Big-city dining with small-town prices.

La Bodega Delicatessen: 11 West High St., Oxford; (513) 523-1338. Contemporary deli-box lunches.

Oxford has a college-town assortment of fast-food restaurants.

Accommodations

Maplevale Farm Bed and Breakfast: 3891 Oxford Millville Rd./US 27, Oxford; (513) 523-8909; www.maplevale.com. A lovely park setting.

White Garden Inn: 6195 Brown Rd., Oxford; (513) 524-5827; www.whitegardeninn.com. Named the country's best inn near a college or university.

Bike Shops

BikeWise Oxford: 9 North Beech St., Oxford; (513) 523-4880; www.bikewiseoxford.com.

Restrooms

Start/finish: Hueston Woods Lodge.

Mile 18.3: Concord Church—there's a pit toilet on the back corner of the property.

Maps

DeLorme: Ohio Atlas & Gazetteer: Page 58.

3 Fort Saint Clair Cruise

Preble County is still farm country—Eaton is is only city. Expect to see plenty of corn and bean fields, big tractors, and picturesque farms.

Start: Fort Saint Clair State Park, Eaton.
Length: 40.8 miles.
Terrain: Flat to rolling.

Traffic and hazards: Lots of one-lane rural roads with very light traffic; moderate traffic around Eaton. There are several busy highway crossings.

Getting there: Take US 127 to Eaton, which is west of Dayton; in town, turn west onto SR 122. In less than a mile, turn left onto Camden Road/SR 355. The entrance to the park is less than a half mile down on the right.

The Ride

Generals Arthur St. Clair and Anthony Wayne built Fort Saint Clair here in 1792. It was one of a chain of forts built to protect the army supply line that supported U.S. troops in the struggle with the Indians for control of the Northwest Territory. A small garrison was stationed at the fort, and convoys traveling up and down the line spent the night there.

In the early dawn of November 6, 1792, while the soldiers slept, Indians attacked the fort. The battle went back and forth all day, but by nightfall Chief Little Turtle was the victor; six men from the garrison were killed. To the west of the fort site stands the old gnarly "Whispering Oak" tree, which witnessed the battle. Legend says that when the wind whistles through its leaves, you can hear the story of the events witnessed by the tree. The graves of the six fallen soldiers rest under its branches.

Eventually the Indians were defeated and left the territory. Settlers came, and they needed a way to get their goods across the many creeks that meander through the area. Preble County once had twenty-nine covered bridges; six remain. They were built between 1829 (the oldest covered bridge in the state) and 1895. This ride visits two of them: Christman Covered Bridge, which spans Seven Mile Creek, was named for Soloman Christman, who owned a farm south of the bridge. Geeting Covered Bridge, spanning Paint Creek, has had its share of damage. A windstorm tore the roof off in 1914. In 1969 a truck ripped some of the roofing out of the bridge. Heavy trucks crushed the floor several times. But with a little help from the county engineers, it has survived.

To see those bridges and the beautiful rural countryside of Preble County, find a place to park in Fort Saint Clair State Park—there are several options. The park is encircled by a one-way paved road. Cycle your way around to the exit and turn left onto Camden Road. SR 122 into Eaton is busy, but you can ride on the sidewalk. On

Christman Covered Bridge

Park Avenue you'll pass Water Works Park, an Eaton city park. You could also use this as a staging area, but you'd miss the history. Turn left onto Eaton New Hope Road and you immediately come upon Christman Covered Bridge. It seems an anomaly so close to town.

On Spacht Road you'll begin to see some of the flat, scenic farmland this county has to offer. Spacht Road has several S-curves. Turn onto Winnerline Road—notice the interesting boulders, which must be the result of glacial movement.

Prices Creek Road is a winding, rolling road going along and over Price Creek and other streamlets with a series of one-lane bridges. About a mile after turning onto Lewisburg Western Road, you will see Geeting Covered Bridge up ahead on Price Road; however, the route bears right, still on Lewisburg Western. Go up the rise and bear right on Yohe Road. About 5 miles later you will turn onto Kimmel Road and cross Price Creek for the last time. Several interesting little cemeteries are in this area, if exploring old headstones interests you. After the turn onto Maple Grove Road, the route gets a little more rolling.

Come into New Hope, cross US 35, and you're in the home stretch now. Traffic picks up a little as you approach Eaton. From Washington Jackson Road turn right, back onto Park Avenue by the community park. Then right and left your way back to Fort Saint Clair.

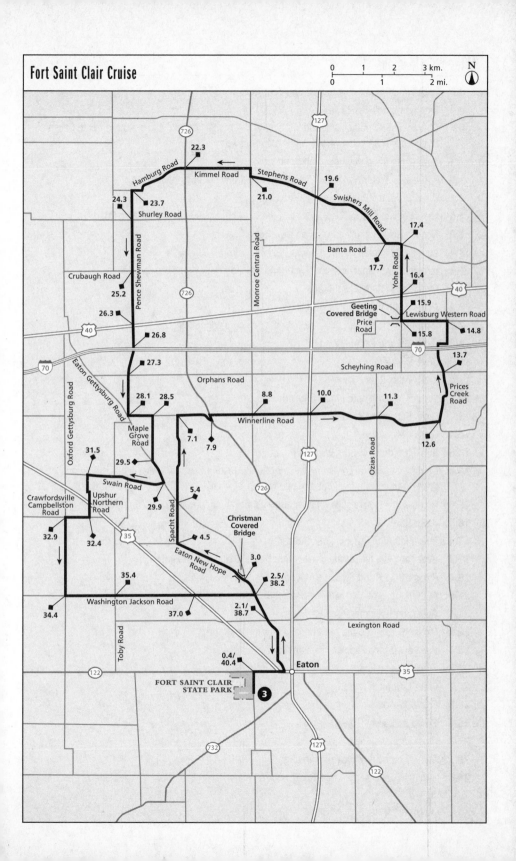

Fort Saint Clair Cruise

0 1 2 3 km.
0 1 2 mi.

N

127

726
22.3
Hamburg Road
Kimmel Road
Stephens Road
19.6
21.0
Swishers Mill Road
24.3
23.7
Shurley Road
17.4
Banta Road
Yohe Road
17.7
16.4
Pence Shewman Road
Monroe Central Road
Crubaugh Road
25.2
15.9
Geeting
Covered
Bridge
Lewisburg Western Road
40
26.3
Price
Road
26.8
15.8
14.8
40
70
27.3
Orphans Road
Scheyhing Road
13.7
70
Eaton Gettysburg Road
8.8
10.0
11.3
Prices
Creek
Road
28.1
28.5
Winnerline Road
Oxford Gettysburg Road
Maple
Grove
Road
7.1
7.9
12.6
31.5
Ozias Road
29.5
127
Swain Road
Upshur
Northern
Road
29.9
5.4
726
Crawfordsville
Campbellston
Road
Spacht Road
Christman
Covered
Bridge
32.9
32.4
35
4.5
3.0
Eaton New Hope
Road
2.5/
38.2
35.4
2.1/
38.7
Washington Jackson Road
37.0
Lexington Road
34.4
Toby Road
0.4/
40.4
122
Eaton
35
FORT SAINT CLAIR
STATE PARK
3
732
127
122

Miles and Directions

0.0 Exit the park and turn left onto Camden Road/SR 355.

0.4 Turn right onto SR 122.

0.8 Go through the traffic light, and just across the bridge carefully turn a hard left onto Seven Mile Road—not Walnut Street, which also goes left.

1.1 Seven Mile Road becomes Park Avenue.

1.5 Pass Eaton Water Works Park, which is an optional starting point.

2.1 Cross Lexington Road.

2.5 Cross Washington Jackson Road and the road becomes Eaton Gettysburg Road.

3.0 Turn left down the hill onto Eaton New Hope Road.

3.1 Traverse Christman Covered Bridge, built in 1895.

4.5 Turn right onto Spacht Road, a one-lane rural road with some rough patches.

5.4 Cross Eaton Gettysburg Road.

7.1 At the T turn right onto Winnerline Road.

7.9 Jog left on SR 726 and then turn right, back onto Winnerline.

8.8 Cross Monroe Central Road.

10.0 Cross US 127.

11.3 Cross Ozias Road.

12.6 At the T turn left onto Prices Creek Road.

13.7 Cross Scheyhing Road.

14.1 Cross I-70.

14.8 Turn left onto Lewisburg Western Road.

15.8 Go right, staying on Lewisburg Western Road. Geeting Covered Bridge is just ahead on Price Road. Have a look but don't go that way.

15.9 Go up a rise (you're still on Lewisburg Western), then bear right onto Yohe Road.

16.4 Cross US 40.

17.4 Take a left onto Swishers Mill Road.

17.7 Bear right, still on Swishers Mill, when Banta Road goes straight.

19.6 Cross US 127 and Swishers Mill becomes Stephens Road.

21.0 At the T jog right onto Monroe Central Road.

21.1 Go left onto Kimmel Road.

22.3 Cross SR 726 and the road becomes Hamburg Road.

23.7 Hang a left onto Pence Shewman Road.

24.3 Cross Shurley Road.

25.2 Cross Crubaugh Road.

26.3 Cross US 40.

26.8 Go up and over I-70.

27.3 Cross Orphans Road.

28.1 At the T turn left onto Winnerline Road.

28.5 Turn right onto Maple Grove Road.

29.5 At the T go left onto Eaton Gettysburg Road.

29.9 Go right onto Swain Road.

31.5 Turn left onto Upshur Northern Road and watch the loose gravel.

32.1 Cross US 35 by the church in New Hope.

32.4 At the T turn right onto Crawfordsville Campbellston Road.

32.9 Go left onto Oxford Gettysburg Road.

34.4 Turn left onto Washington Jackson Road.

35.4 Cross Toby Road.

37.0 Cross US 35.

38.2 Turn right onto Park Avenue.

38.7 Cross Lexington Road.

39.3 Pass Water Works Park. The road soon becomes Seven Mile Road.

40.0 Turn right onto SR 122.

40.4 Hang a left back onto Camden Road.

40.8 Turn right into the park.

Local Information

Preble County's online tourism information center: www.destinationpreble.com.

Events

Preble County Pork Festival: Preble County Fairgrounds, 722 South Franklin St., Eaton; (937) 456-7273; www.porkfestival.org. Always the third full weekend in September. Offers great food, crafts contests and demonstrations, and entertainment.

Restaurants

Tea on the Main: 207 East Main St., Eaton; (937) 456-6049. Open 11 a.m. to 3 p.m. Sandwiches, salads, and desserts. Step back to a time of elegance.

Eaton Place Restaurant: 125 Eaton Lewisburg Rd., Eaton; (937) 456-3045.

Sarah's Pizza and Subs: 125 East Main St., Eaton; (937) 456-6871.

Accommodations

Sugar Valley Farm Bed and Breakfast: 7611 Sugar Valley Rd., Camden; (937) 452-3983. This bed-and-breakfast is surrounded by 180 acres of farmland. Enjoy quiet walks in the woods overlooking stone cliffs and rock-bottom creeks filled with fossils.

The Golden Inn: 8868 US 40 West, New Paris; (937) 437-0072; www.thegoldeninn.com. The motel sits on just over 11 acres in a quiet country setting. There are numerous fruit trees, hummingbird feeders, a butterfly garden, and plenty of room for walking.

Bike Shops

BikeWise Oxford: 9 North Beech St., Oxford; (513) 523-4880; www.bikewiseoxford.com.

Restrooms

Start/finish: Fort Saint Clair State Memorial.

Maps

DeLorme: Ohio Atlas & Gazetteer: Page 58.

4 Ohio River Ramble

If you do much biking in Cincinnati, you'll hear about this ride along the Kentucky side of the Ohio River; it's a classic. You'll enjoy picture-perfect views of the river and the farmland that nudges up against it. The route is an out-and-back, mostly flat with a few rolling hills and light traffic.

Start: The Anderson Ferry parking lot in Ohio or Kentucky.

Length: 20-mile (more or less) out-and-back.

Terrain: Mostly flat with a few rolling hills.

Traffic and hazards: Light traffic.

Getting there: From I-75 in Kentucky, take the Fifth Street exit, exit 192 (just across the bridge from Cincinnati), toward Covington/Newport. Take the Kentucky SR 8 ramp toward Ludlow. Follow Kentucky SR 8 about 7.5 miles to the Anderson Ferry.

In Ohio you can take US 50 into Anderson Ferry, turn toward the river on Anderson Ferry Road, and in a stone's throw drive your car or ride your bike onto the ferry. The ride is on the Kentucky side of the river. Part of the adventure is a ferryboat crossing.

Whichever way you travel, you may want to take a detour to the Ameristop Food Mart for a restroom or snack—they have a nice deli—before you head out on your bike. From Kentucky SR 8 turn left on Amsterdam Road—it is 0.2 mile east of the Anderson Ferry. Wind up the hill for 1.5 miles to the market.

The Ride

The Anderson Ferry has been in continuous operation since 1817. It was originally known as the Kottmyer Ferry but was later sold to the Anderson family. The ferry has been in operation so long that a dirt road leading to it in the early 1800s grew into Anderson Ferry Road, a major west-side road since the 1900s.

The ferry is the lone survivor of dozens of ferries that once served the Cincinnati area. Horses on each side of the river were originally used to pull it across. One of the first of Mr. Anderson's innovations was to put the horses on the ferry on a treadmill that powered the boat's paddle wheel. The ferry is now owned by Paul Anderson, who is not related to the first Anderson family.

You can park your car on the Ohio or Kentucky side of the river. Let your inner kid out—take a ride on the ferry even if you just go over and back. The fee for cars is $4 one way; the fee for bicycles is $1 each. The bike route begins on the Kentucky side.

Turn right from the parking lot onto Kentucky SR 8 and enjoy. You will soon pass McGlasson Farms' roadside market on the right—fresh garden produce in season.

Giles Conrad Park is on the right. It has restrooms, picnic tables, and water. You can ride through the park for about a half mile and then exit back and continue right on Kentucky SR 8.

The Anderson Ferry

At 8.2 miles there is a NO OUTLET sign. Keep going. At 9.7 miles you will see Freedom Grove trees, part of Sand Run Nursery, which includes a barn, conference center, and fields of trees, flowers, and shrubs. Four million American slaves were documented by the end of the Civil War. Combining their passion for reforestation and for the National Underground Railroad Freedom Center, Mary and Paul Hemmer Jr. conceived of the Freedom Tree project to commemorate the lives of the slaves and freedom fighters. The Hemmers' goal is to plant four million Freedom Trees. Proceeds from the sale of Freedom Trees are donated to the National Underground Railroad Freedom Center. As the trees at the nursery mature, they are planted in Freedom Groves that consist of anywhere from 40 to 400 trees. Currently there are forty-one Freedom Groves planted throughout Greater Cincinnati, which include more than 8,000 trees.

At about 10 miles the road becomes narrow and unmaintained; turn around whenever you're ready and enjoy the river views from the other direction.

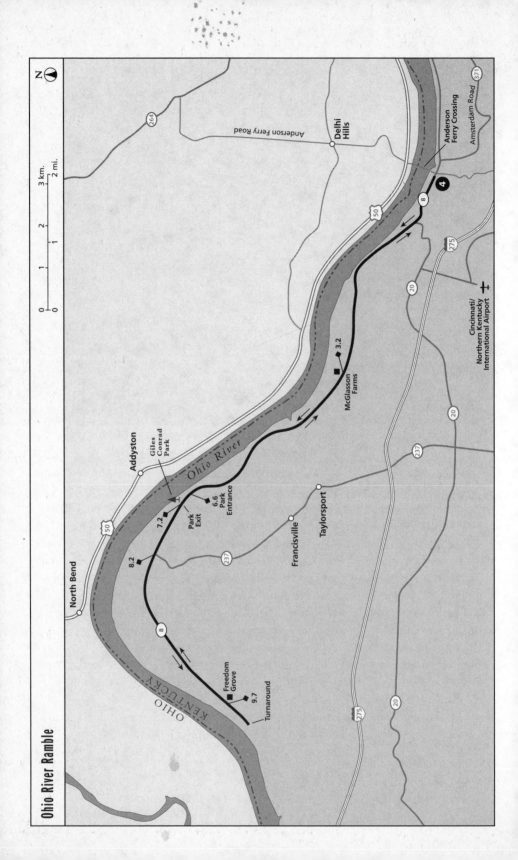

Ohio River Ramble

N

3 km.
2 mi.

264

Anderson Ferry Road

Delhi Hills

Anderson Ferry Crossing

Amsterdam Road

371

50

8

4

275

20

Cincinnati/
Northern Kentucky
International Airport

20

McGlasson Farms

3.2

237

Ohio River

Addyston

Giles Conrad Park

7.2

8.2

Park Exit

6.6 Park Entrance

Taylorsport

Francisville

237

North Bend

50

8

Freedom Grove

9.7

Turnaround

OHIO

KENTUCKY

275

20

Miles and Directions

0.0 From the Anderson Ferry parking lot in Kentucky, turn right onto Kentucky SR 8.

3.2 Pass McGlasson Farms' market stand, offering fresh produce.

6.6 Enter Giles Conrad Park, a Boone County park; restrooms can be found here.

7.2 Exit the park and continue right on SR 8.

8.2 Signage indicates NO OUTLET and NO TRUCK TURNAROUND. Keep going.

9.7 You'll come to Freedom Grove and the end of the maintained road.

10.0 Turn around when you're ready.

20.0 Arrive back at the beginning/end of the ride.

Local Information

Northern Kentucky Convention and Visitors Bureau: 50 East RiverCenter Blvd., Suite 200, Covington, KY 41011; (859) 261-4677; www .nkycvb.com.

Attractions

McGlasson Farms' roadside market: 5832 River Rd./SR 8, Hebron, KY 41048; (859) 689-5229. This market is on the route and has fresh garden produce in season.

Restaurants

Ameristop Food Mart: 2500 Amsterdam Rd., Villa Hills, KY 41017; (859) 331-9354. Okay, it's not a restaurant but it has a nice deli. It's near the start of the ride.

Accomodations

Gateway Bed-and-Breakfast: 326 East Sixth St., Newport; (859) 581-6447 or (888) 891-7500; www.gatewaybb.com. A beautifully restored Italianate townhouse five minutes from downtown Cincinnati. About 5 miles from the Kentucky start of the ride.

Restrooms

Start/finish: Nearby Ameristop Food Mart.
Mile 6.6: Giles Conrad Park.

Maps

DeLorme: Ohio Atlas & Gazetteer: Page 4, D3.

5 Butler County Ramble

A pleasant tour in Butler County, this ride meanders through a variety of terrain, passes a former governor's mansion, the site of a historic grist mill, and Chrisholm Historic Farm—all the while giving you some great bicycling miles.

Start: The Hughes Center, a YMCA facility, in Hamilton.
Length: 26.2 miles.
Terrain: Flat to rolling with a couple of easy hills.
Traffic and hazards: Mostly roads with light traffic, heavier near Overpeck; the Trenton Road crossing is busy. Traffic is also heavier for a couple of miles on SR 744 and SR 122 and in the village of Trenton; the State Street crossing is busy. Avoid rush hour if possible.

Getting there: From I-75 take exit 29 to SR 63 west for about 5 miles. Go left (west) on SR 4 toward Hamilton for about 4 miles, then turn right (north) on Liberty Fairfield Road. In 1.5 miles turn left onto Augspurger Road and in 1 mile right onto Gephart Road. The Hughes Center is less than 2 miles on the left at 1770 Gephart Road, Hamilton.

The Ride

The Cincinnati Cycle Club has had people spinning their wheels since the 1880s. The group promotes cycling for all the right reasons—recreation, health, and friendship. They also do a lot of bicycling advocacy. This route was their annual "Spring Opener" ride one year.

The ride starts out rolling on Gephart Road and picks up a little traffic near Overpeck, which very soon dissolves as you come into Butler County farmland. Cotton Run Road is a long, mostly gradual uphill (sometimes not so gradual). Biking here in April and being a wildflower junkie, I was delighted to see a nice assortment of trout lilies and other spring wildflowers blooming along Cotton Run.

After turning onto Oxford Middletown Road, you will soon pass on the right the beautiful estate that was the birthplace of James M. Cox, governor of Ohio, U.S. representative, and a Democratic candidate for president of the United States in the election of 1920.

Just past that mansion is the village of Jacksonburg. Established in 1835, it takes pride in being Ohio's smallest unincorporated village (in 2007 it had sixty-nine residents). Traffic picks up when SR 744 and then SR 122 join the route. The shoulder comes and goes.

Turn onto Mosiman Road and enter the suburbs—if it's rush hour, there will be some traffic. You'll come to a T that is not well marked—go left to stay on Mosiman; at the second T go right. Coming into Miltonville, which lies along the banks of Elk Creek, you'll see the stone grist mill wheel, which is a memorial to Bamboo Harris.

The Cox estate

Harris was a freed black slave who built and operated the first water-driven grist mill on the creek. For fifty years his mill ground wheat and corn. Also, a Native American burial ground was located near the east bank of the creek. And the creek was so named because of the number of elk in the area.

You won't see any elk on your way to Trenton. As you come into the village, the road becomes North Miami Street. You'll come to a busy intersection where Miami Street crosses State Street, aka SR 73. There are fast-food restaurants nearby on State Street. When you cross the road, you want to continue straight onto South Miami Avenue. There are more direct ways to get out of Trenton, but the route described avoids traffic as much as possible.

From there it's a smooth ride along Woodsdale Road as it curves along the Miami River (just out of sight to the left). The route passes two Butler County Metroparks. Chrisholm Historic Farmstead is the site of the restored 1874 Samuel Augspurger farmhouse. This farm was the home of the leading family of the Amish-Mennonite settlement that existed in this river valley area in the nineteenth century. The eighty-four-acre Woodsdale Regional Park has miles of hiking trails.

After the turn onto Augspurger Road, the route crosses Wayne Madison Road, passes Lake Lindsay, and after a short uphill ride on Gephart Road returns to the Hughes Center.

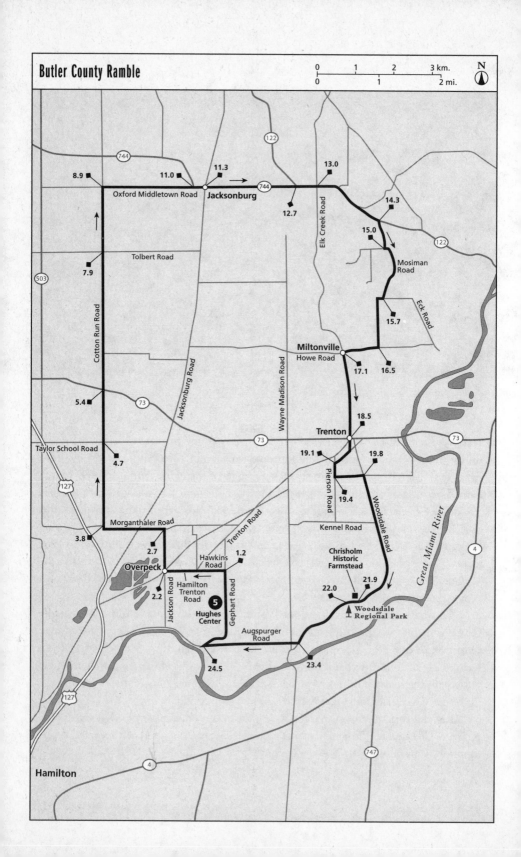

Butler County Ramble

0   1   2   3 km.
0   1   2 mi.

N

744

122

8.9   11.0   11.3   13.0

Oxford Middletown Road   Jacksonburg   744

12.7

14.3

Elk Creek Road   15.0

Tolbert Road   Mosiman Road

7.9

503   15.7   Eck Road

Cotton Run Road

Miltonville   Howe Road

5.4   73   17.1   16.5

Jacksonburg Road   Wayne Madison Road

Taylor School Road   18.5

4.7   73   Trenton   73

127   19.1   19.8

Pierson Road   19.4

Morganthaler Road   Kennel Road   Woodsdale Road

3.8

2.7   Hawkins   1.2   Chrisholm
Road   Historic
Farmstead

Overpeck   21.9   Great Miami River

Jackson Road   Hamilton   22.0   4
Trenton
Road   Woodsdale
Regional Park

2.2   5   Trenton Road

Hughes   Gephart Road
Center

Augspurger
Road

24.5   23.4

127

Hamilton   4   747

Miles and Directions

0.0 Exit the parking lot and turn left onto Gephart Road.

1.2 Turn left onto Hawkins Road.

1.4 At the three-way intersection, continue straight on what is now Hamilton Trenton Road.

2.2 Cross Trenton Road and continue right on Jackson Road past the Overpeck Post Office.

2.7 At the T go left onto Morganthaler Road.

3.8 Morganthaler bends a hard right; just after that continue straight onto Cotton Run Road when Morganthaler bears left.

4.7 Cross Taylor School Road.

5.4 Cross SR 73.

7.9 Cross Tolbert Road.

8.9 Turn right onto Oxford Middletown Road.

10.2 The Cox estate is on the right.

11.0 SR 744 comes in from the left.

11.3 Cross Jacksonburg Road.

12.7 SR 122 adjoins from the left at this intersection. There is a restroom in the gas station on the left.

13.0 Cross Elk Creek Road.

14.3 Turn right onto Mosiman Road.

15.0 Go left (still on Mosiman) when Marts Road goes right.

15.7 Go right (still on Mosiman) when Eck Road bears left.

16.5 Turn right onto Howe Road.

17.1 Turn left onto Elk Creek Road, which becomes North Miami Street in Trenton.

18.5 In Trenton carefully cross State Street, which is also SR 73 (look right and left—there are restaurants, including locally owned Richard's Pizza, and gas stations on State Street if you need refreshments or a restroom). The road kind of Y's here; take the smaller road, South Miami Avenue, which goes slightly left, not the busier road, which is Main Street and goes slightly right.

18.7 At the yield sign go right onto Riverside Drive.

19.1 Turn left onto Pierson Road.

19.4 Take a left onto Maple Avenue.

19.8 Go right onto South First Street.

19.9 Cross Oak Street and South First becomes Woodsdale Road.

21.9 Pass Chrisholm Historic Farmstead.

22.0 Pass Woodsdale Regional Park.

23.4 Turn right onto Augspurger Road.

23.5 Cross Wayne Madison Road.

24.5 Turn right onto Gephart Road.

26.2 Return to the Hughes Center.

Local Information

Greater Hamilton Convention and Visitors Bureau: One High St., Hamilton; (513) 844-8080 or (800) 311-5353.

Attractions

Jungle Jim's International Market: 5440 Dixie Hwy., Fairfield; (513) 674-6000; www.jungle jims.com. "Foodieland," they call it. It is a truly unique supermarket megastore.

Pyramid Hill Sculpture Park: 1763 Hamilton Cleves Rd./SR 128; (513) 887-9514. A 265-acre scuplture park and outdoor museum.

Restaurants

Richard's Pizza: 855 West State St., Trenton; (513) 988-2326. Locally owned Richard's has been in the pizza business since 1955. They offer a wide variety of menu items.

Accommodations

Gregory Creek Inn: 5110 Lesourdsville West Chester Rd., Hamilton; (513) 887-0725; www .gregorycreekinn.com. A bed-and-breakfast with two units (private baths) located on the Nieder-man family farm.

Bike Shops

Middletown Cycle Center: 206 South Verity Pkwy., Middletown; (513) 424-0211.

Restrooms

Mile 12.7: A gas station at the intersection of SR 744 with SR 122.

Mile 18.6: In Trenton.

Maps

DeLorme: Ohio Atlas & Gazetteer: Page 58.

6 Germantown Challenge

We're talking seriously good scenery here: This adventurous route leaves from the Germantown Nature Center, then goes over the Germantown Dam and through the historic village of—what else?—Germantown. If you feel like a longer ride, you can trek out to Sycamore State Park; if not, take a circuitous route back to the nature preserve. It's a great ride whatever the distance.

Start: Germantown Nature Center.
Length: 50.6 miles, or choose the shorter 30.4-mile option (mileage is shown for the longer route).
Terrain: Some of it is flat, more is rolling, and there are hills.

Traffic and hazards: Lots of light-traffic rural roads. Expect moderate traffic in the Germantown area. Diamond Mill Road on the longer route is busy.

Getting there: From SR 725 about 3 miles west of Germantown, turn north onto Boomershine Road. The Germantown Nature Center is less than a mile up on the right at 6910 Boomershine Road, Germantown.

The Ride

I usually like to ride this route in late summer when the prairie fields at the nature center are spectacular. However, the wildflowers are glorious in spring; redbud trees

Twin Creek winding through the valley

and spring beauties bloom along the roads, and there is a hillside of trillium on Preble County Line Road.

If you like natural history, visit the Germantown Nature Center, where the ride begins and ends. This ecologically friendly underground facility features a variety of changing displays. The 1,665-acre metropark surrounding it has spectacular ravines, towering trees, wildflowers, prairies, and excellent opportunities to observe wildlife— a bobcat has been sighted there. Twin Creek, which meanders along this route, runs through the park.

To give you an idea of the terrain, the ride starts out going down alongside the sledding hill of the metropark. Then it goes back up. Flat terrain takes you to an attention-grabbing view from the Germantown Dam. The view overlooks Twin Creek winding through the valley. This dam was one of five built after the 1913 flood to protect the region from flooding; completed in 1921, it is 110 feet high and 1,200 feet long.

Ride around and down Creek Road, where a park road off to the left takes you to the creek. You can search for Ordovician fossils there.

Cautiously turn left onto SR 725 and bike through a short section of downtown Germantown, a National Historic Site. Founded in 1804 by a community of German settlers, it became known for its mills, its tobacco-related industries, and later in the century for the nationally known Mudlick Whiskey Distillery.

You'll pass the Florentine Hotel, one of the oldest in the state, and other historic buildings. The village is small, and you may want to leave the route and explore. Notice the lions—they're resting in side yards, gardens, front yards, everywhere. Former resident Homer Kern made 300 of the 400-pound lawn ornaments while employed by Buckeye Concrete; he retired in 1995 at age 95. Those lions stand guard in ten states.

As you ride away from Germantown, Little Twin Creek twines along with its namesake road; I lost track of the number of times they cross. This section of the ride is lovely. Big farms, flat rural roads, little traffic. Chicken Bristle Road (you've got to love that name) is narrow, and while there are not a lot of cars, they tend to go fast. Turn right onto Fuls Road for the longer ride to Sycamore State Park; continue straight on Chicken Bristle for the shorter route.

Traffic picks up as you approach Diamond Mill Road; you're going toward Dayton. Diamond Mill is busy, and busier during rush hour. The road takes you into and through Sycamore State Park. The park takes its name from the huge sycamore trees that line the banks of Wolf Creek, which winds through the park. Once a heavily forested area, this fertile land attracted settlers; they cleared and plowed. At one point the land was scheduled to be subdivided. When that did not work out, it was given to the state and became a park in 1979. Second-growth forest is beginning to cover that farmland.

Heading west, bike along pleasant, rolling roads until you come to a T; then go left onto unmarked Preble County Line Road. This long straight road goes from flat to rolling and back again with a hill or two along the way. Come to Spitler Road, where the longer and shorter routes join together for a scenic ride through the Twin Creek valley in Preble County. Return to Preble County Line Road for the rolling to hilly but always picturesque return to the nature center.

Miles and Directions

0.0 Leave the nature center and turn right onto Boomershine Road.

1.3 At the T turn right onto Manning Road.

2.3 Go right onto Conservancy Road.

4.0 At the three-way stop sign, go left across the bridge.

4.1 Scenic overlook at the Germantown Dam.

4.4 Take a left onto Creek Road.

5.8 Turn left onto SR 725 (called Market Street in Germantown).

7.1 Go left onto Cherry Street.

7.2 Cross Center Street.

8.2 Bear left onto Little Twin Road.

9.4 At the T turn left onto Manning Road.

10.0 Take a right onto Venus Road.

11.0 Cross Farmersville West Carrollton Road.

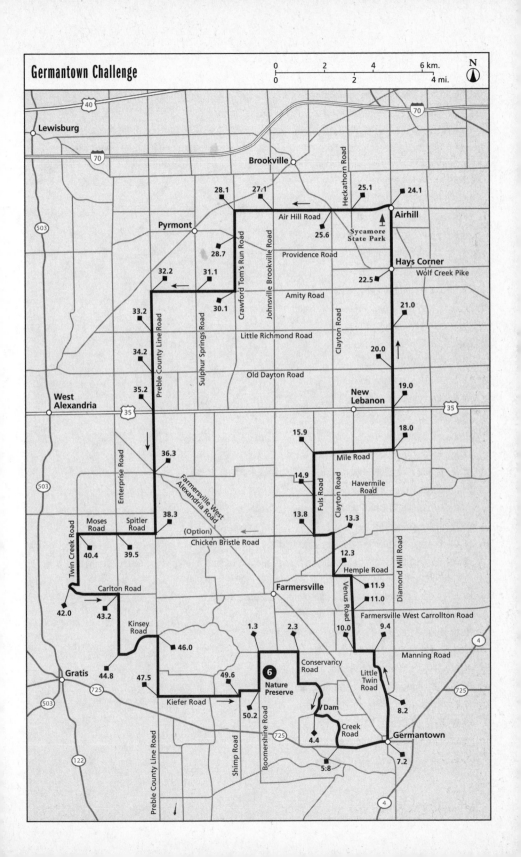

11.9 At the T turn left onto Hemple Road.

12.3 Go right onto Clayton Road.

12.9 Cross Dayton Farmersville Road.

13.3 Turn left by the cemetery onto Chicken Bristle Road.

13.8 Turn right onto Fuls Road. **Option:** For the shorter ride continue straight on Chicken Bristle Road. At 18 miles jog right on Preble County Line Road and then left onto Spitler Road. Rejoin the longer route there, at mile 38.3, where it turns right onto Spitler.

14.9 Cross Havermile Road.

15.9 Turn right onto Mile Road.

16.3 Cross Clayton Road.

18.0 Go left onto Diamond Mill Road.

19.0 At the traffic light carefully cross US 35.

20.0 Cross Old Dayton Road.

21.0 Cross Little Richmond Road.

22.5 Cross Wolf Creek Pike. Enter Sycamore State Park.

24.1 Turn left onto Air Hill Road.

25.1 Cross Heckathorn Road.

25.6 Cross Wolf Creek Pike.

27.1 Cross Johnsville Brookville Road.

28.1 Turn left onto Crawford Tom's Run Road.

28.7 Cross Providence Road.

30.1 Go right onto Amity Road.

31.1 Cross Sulphur Springs Road.

32.2 At the T turn left onto unmarked Preble County Line Road.

33.2 Cross Little Richmond Road.

34.2 Cross Old Dayton Road.

35.2 Cross US 35.

36.3 Cross Farmersville West Alexandria Road.

38.3 Turn right onto Spitler Road (it's a one-lane road and sometimes the sign is down) and enter Preble County.

39.5 Cross Enterprise Road; Spitler becomes Moses Road.

40.4 Turn left onto Twin Creek Road.

42.0 Twin Creek Road becomes Carlton Road.

43.2 Go right onto Enterprise Road.

44.8 Take a left onto Kinsey Road.

46.0 Turn right onto Preble County Line Road.

47.5 Go left onto Kiefer Road.

49.6 Take a left onto Shimp Road.

50.2 Turn right onto Boomershine Road.

50.6 Go left into the nature center.

Local Information

Dayton/Montgomery County Convention and Visitors Bureau: 1 Chamber Plaza, Suite A, Dayton; (937) 226-8211 or (800) 221-8235; www.daytoncvb.com.

Attractions

Cox Arboretum: 6733 Springboro Pike, Dayton; (937) 434-9005; www.coxarboretum.org. About 189 acres of gardens and natural areas, including a butterfly house.

Accommodations

Gunckel Heritage Bed-and-Breakfast: 325 West Market St., Germantown; (937) 672-5312; www.bbonline.com/oh/gunckel. A Victorian-Italianate built in 1826 by Philip Gunckel, the founder of Germantown. This bed-and-breakfast is on the route. The bikeway that winds around Twin Creek is just down the street.

The Guest House Inn: 21 South Main St., Germantown; (937) 855-7785; www.bbonline/oh/ guesthouse. Built in 1863, the frame house was renovated in 2007. Very near the bike route and just down the street from the bikeway that winds around Twin Creek.

Restaurants

The Florentine Restaurant: 21 West Market St., Germantown; (937) 855-7759.

The Cardinal Roost: 16 West Center St., Germantown; (937) 855-2473. Fifties-style diner with ice cream and fountain drinks.

Bike Shops

Kettering Bike Shop: 3120 Wilmington Pike, Kettering; (937) 293-3293; www.ketteringbikeshop.com.

Restrooms

Start/finish: Germantown Nature Center.
Mile 7.2: Germantown.

Maps

DeLorme: Ohio Atlas & Gazetteer: Page 59.

7 Caesar Creek Challenge

This is a ride of steep gorges, deep woods, prairie fields, and sparkling lakes and streams. You won't be bored. Allow some time to explore the Caesar Creek Visitor Center. Set among prairie grasses and native wildflowers, it is beautiful and has exhibits featuring local natural history.

Start: Caesar Creek Visitor Center, Waynesville.
Length: 32.0 miles.
Terrain: Rolling with hills.

Traffic and hazards: The route is mostly on quiet rural roads; some have moderate traffic and some are narrow and winding. SR 380 and SR 73 are busy, but the distance is short.

Getting there: From I-71 take exit 45 to SR 73. Go west on SR 73 for 8 miles to Corwin and turn left onto Clarksville Road. Drive just over 2 miles to the Caesar Creek Visitor Center on the left at 4020 Clarksville Road, Waynesville.

The Ride

I can't ride this route without remembering the Gurneyville Road pigs. Riding in the area of that road one summer day, I passed a field of pigs and piglets. The piglets

Caesar Creek Lake

were napping as I passed. One mama pig spied me and made a noise that I guessed to be a pig warning; it was not pretty. Those piglets leapt to their feet and, with their mamas, all headed off as one in the same direction and in a big hurry. They didn't get up and look around, they didn't take a minute to stretch; they just got up and ran, squealing all the way. I had to stop my bike I was laughing so hard. Those are the things you would miss if you didn't bike.

Caesar Creek takes its name from a member of the Shawnee. Caesar was a black slave captured by the Shawnee as he was coming down the Ohio River. He was later adopted by them and became one of the earliest settlers in the valley.

Many of the scenic features of this area were formed by glaciers. You'll see rocky gorges and deep valleys; it is a hilly route, yet there are extensive sections of flat bottomland. The sedimentary limestones and shales in the region indicate a sea that covered the state ancient ages ago. The excellent fossil finds in the park reinforce that. Fossil hunting is a major attraction at Caesar Creek, drawing people from all over the Midwest. This is one of the few areas where visitors are permitted to collect the unique fossils formed during the Ordovician Period. Whether you like fossils or whether you don't even know (or care) that Ohio's state fossil is a trilobite, it is still a scenic area in which to bike.

When you leave the visitor center and ride out of the park, you'll see more areas of native prairie wildflowers. Cross SR 73, go down the hill past the cemeteries, and cross the Little Miami Scenic Trail; this is Corwin, a staging area for the bike trail—there are restrooms and vending machines. If you take the side-trip into Waynesville, expect great shops and unique restaurants.

Leaving Corwin, the route parallels the bike trail on New Burlington Road, which has a river view. You could ride on the trail for about a mile and a half. Exit the trail when it crosses New Burlington Road, which would be mile 4.6 on the route. Crossroads are identified on the Little Miami Scenic Trail.

You will leave Warren County, go briefly into Greene, and then drop down into Clinton before returning to Warren. You will pass the boat ramp and go right onto unmarked Roxanna New Burlington Road (Cornstalk Road continues straight ahead) in Greene County. As you cross into Clinton County, Roxanna New Burlington stops at SR 380, then in just under a mile you go right onto New Burlington Road again. Soon the route crosses over Caesar Creek—it's quite a view and quite a long way down—and comes into the Caesar Creek Wildlife Area. The restored wetlands and prairies attract all manner of wildlife—this is a great birding area. Cross another bridge, swoop down a hill, and keep going past Gurneyville Road, and look out for pigs.

On Oregonia Road you will pass the Caesar Creek Pioneer Village; on Clarksville enjoy a breathtaking ride over the dam before returning to the visitor center.

Miles and Directions

0.0 Exit the Caesar Creek Visitor Center and turn right onto Clarksville Road.

1.0 Cross Middletown Road.

2.3 Cross SR 73.

2.7 Cross the Little Miami Scenic Trail. Clarksville Road becomes Corwin Avenue. **Side-trip:** Continue straight for 0.5 mile to visit Waynesville, known as the Antiques Capital of the Midwest—shops and unique restaurants.

3.0 Turn right onto New Burlington Road.

4.6 Cross the bike trail again.

8.5 At the Y bear left onto Compton Road—New Burlington goes off to the right and ends.

10.4 Turn right onto unmarked Roxanna New Burlington Road; Cornstalk Road is marked—it continues straight.

11.6 Go right onto SR 380.

12.4 Take a left onto New Burlington Road.

16.8 Turn right onto Hackney Road.

18.0 Cross Stingley Road.

18.5 Cross Gurneyville Road.

20.5 At the T go right onto Center Road.

21.2 Turn left onto Lewis Road.

22.0 Cross SR 380—Lewis becomes Brimstone Road.

23.3 Turn left, staying on Brimstone, when Ward Road continues straight.

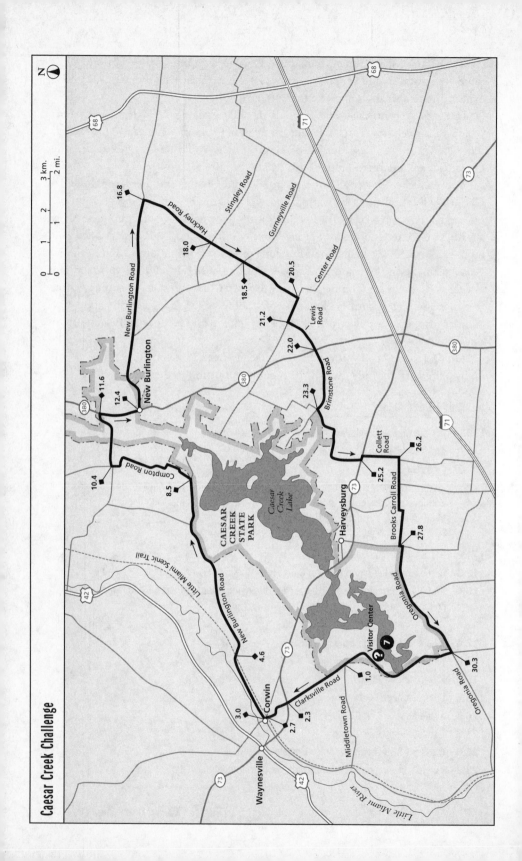

Caesar Creek Challenge

25.2 Jog left onto SR 73 and then right onto Collett Road.

26.2 Collett bends right and becomes Brooks Carroll Road when you enter Warren County.

27.8 Turn left onto Oregonia Road.

30.3 Go right onto Clarksville Road.

32.0 Finish at the visitor center.

Local Information

Warren County Convention and Visitors Bureau: (513) 204-1900 or (800) 791-4386; www.ohioslargestplayground.com.

Attractions

Caesar Creek State Park: 8570 East SR 73, Waynesville; (513) 897-3055; www.caesar creekstatepark.com. Offers some of the finest outdoor recreation in southwest Ohio including boating, hiking, fishing, camping, and fossil hunting.

Restaurants

Der Dutchman Restaurant: 230 US 42 North, Waynesville; (513) 897-4716; www.derdutch man.com. Authentic Amish Kitchen Cooking, a gift shop, and an inn.

Accommodations

River Walker Bed and Breakfast: 156 Corwin Rd., Oregonia; (513) 934-3921; www.river walkerbed.com. Located on the Little Miami Scenic Trail and a short walk from the Little Miami River.

Cranberry Cottage Bed and Breakfast: 102 North Main St., Waynesville; (513) 897-5419 or (937) 307-7022. A beautiful restored home on the main street of Waynesville and near the bike trail.

Bike Shops

Wheeliefun Multi-Sport and Bike Shop: 706 Deerfield Rd., Lebanon; (513) 934-0600; www .wheeliefun.com.

Restrooms

Start/finish: Caesar Creek Visitor Center.
Mile 2.7: At the bike trail in Corwin.

Maps

DeLorme: Ohio Atlas & Gazetteer: Pages 59, 60.

8 Ripley Ramble

This ride travels the hills and hollows between Ripley, nestled alongside the Ohio River, and Georgetown, two small towns brimming with history. The area is called Freedom Landing because it saw some of the Underground Railroad's most intense activity.

Start: In the Ohio River town of Ripley.
Length: A 25.7-mile lariat-shaped ride—out and back the same way with a loop on the end.
Terrain: Long gradual ascents and descents.

Traffic and hazards: Avoid rush hour if possible. Overall, traffic is light. There are a few more cars near Georgetown. Old US 68 is narrow with no shoulder.

Getting there: Take US 52 into Ripley, which becomes Second Street in town. Turn southwest, toward the Ohio River, onto Main Street. You can park at the Ripley Public Library, 27 Main Street—it has a restroom—or anywhere on Main or Front Street on the Ripley River Walk.

The Ride

The Underground Railroad was a clandestine network of routes and safe houses that helped enslaved Americans find freedom. The Ohio River was a dividing line between slavery and freedom. Ripley, an important stop on the Underground Railroad, had some of the most active stations in Ohio. During the Civil War leading Confederate raiders had sworn to burn "this damned abolitionist hellhole to the ground." As you look out over the river, remember that before the locks were put in, the river was narrower and shallower than it is now. It was a good place for slaves who were seeking freedom to cross. Red Oak and Eagle Creeks both drain into the river at Ripley; those creek beds threw off tracking dogs, while the hills and valleys provided hiding places and escape routes—think about that as you bike along Free Soil Road. Also, Rosa Washington Riles, known for her portrayal as "Aunt Jemima" of Aunt Jemima Pancake Mix fame, is buried nearby.

The Ripley River Walk, dotted with benches and plantings and scenic views, is so pleasant you may have to convince yourself to leave. But do. Biking along the river walk on your way out of Ripley, you'll pass by several Underground Railroad stations including Parker House, home of the ex-slave John Parker. Parker purchased his freedom and then went on to obtain several patents on things that helped eliminate the need for slaves. At night he crossed back into Kentucky to help slaves escape. The Signal House, according to legend, displayed a light in the attic when the waterfront was safe for slave transport. Not actually on the route, the Rankin House sits high over the river, and it was to it that many slaves climbed on their way to freedom.

But that's not all: The area around Eagle Creek is known as Logan's Gap, named after the general who used it as a disembarkment point after destroying the Indians in the state during the late eighteenth century. Frontiersman Simon Kenton also used the creek as a landing point during his many travels in Ohio.

The Rankin House, a major Underground Railroad stop

Along the route—depending on the time of year—you may notice tobacco growing in the fields or in float beds waiting to go into the field. Tobacco was an important part of the farm scene in southern Ohio. Since the government "buyout" in 2004, the tobacco crop is taken to receiving stations rather than sold at auction. Most of Ripley's crop is now sold across the river in Kentucky, and many tobacco acres, as you will notice along the route, are now producing grapes, green peppers, and goats.

Georgetown is the boyhood home of former U.S. President Ulysses S. Grant, and his home is open to the public. Mycle's Cycles is also in Georgetown; owner Michael Hart mapped this and other routes in the area.

Start the ride by traveling north along the Ripley River Walk. Turn right onto Sycamore Street and then bear left onto US 52 very briefly before going right onto Old US 68. Begin the long gradual climb out of town. Be patient—you're going to be on this road for about 5 miles.

After you bend to the right and cross a bridge, turn left onto unmarked Centerpoint Road, where you'll be riding along Straight Creek. Bald eagles have a nest not too far from here.

Continue straight onto Old A and P Road. This is a little confusing because Old

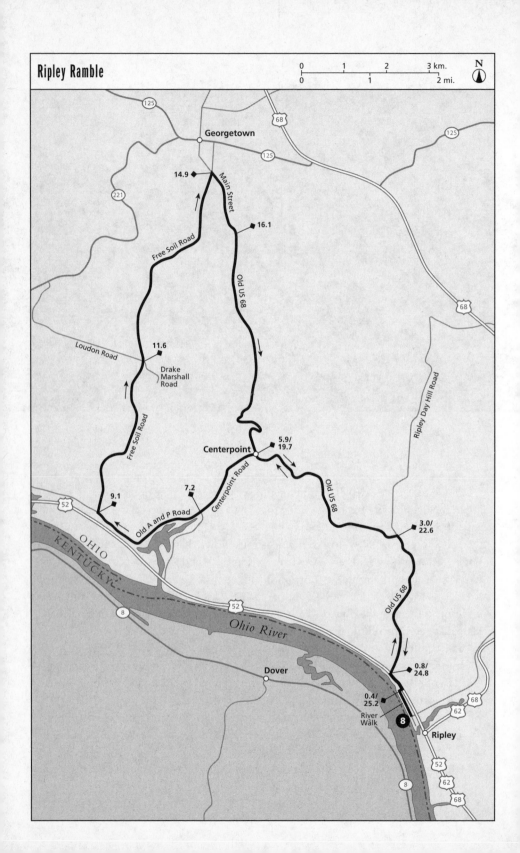

Ripley Ramble

0   1   2   3 km.

0   1   2 mi.

N

125

Georgetown

68

125

14.9

221

Main Street

16.1

Old US 68

Free Soil Road

Loudon Road

11.6

Drake
Marshall
Road

Ripley Day Hill Road

Free Soil Road

Centerpoint

5.9/
19.7

9.1

7.2

Centerpoint Road

Old US 68

52

Old A and P Road

3.0/
22.6

OHIO

KENTUCKY

Old US 68

8

52

Ohio River

0.8/
24.8

Dover

0.4/
25.2

River
Walk

8

68

62

8

Ripley

52

62

8

68

A and P also goes left and across a bridge—don't go that way. In a few more miles, turn right onto Free Soil Road and begin the long trek to Georgetown, pondering who might have gone before on this aptly named road.

At the top of the hill, you can take a short side-trip into Georgetown, where you will find restaurants and shops. Stop in to see to Michael Hart at Mycle's Cycles and his dog Roxanne.

The ride back to Ripley on Old US 68 is mostly—but not all—downhill.

This route is one of the day trips on the Adventure Cycling Association's Underground Railroad route, which traverses 2,007.5 miles from Mobile, Alabama, to Owen Sound, Canada. Adventure Cycling Association is a national, member-supported, nonprofit bicycling organization dedicated to inspiring people of all ages to travel by bicycle for fitness, fun, and self-discovery. . . . Who could argue with that? For more information visit www.adventurecycling.org.

Miles and Directions

0.0 Turn right from Main Street onto Front Street and ride along the river walk.

0.4 Turn right onto Sycamore Street.

0.56 Go left onto Second Street.

0.57 Bear left onto US 52.

0.8 Turn right onto Old US 68 across from the Old Sunset Bar and Grill.

3.0 Bear left, still on Old 68, when Ripley Day Hill Road goes right.

5.9 Turn left onto Centerpoint Road, which is unmarked. This is just after Old US 68 bends right and crosses a bridge.

7.2 Continue straight on Old A and P Road (the road that goes left across the bridge is also Old A and P—ignore that and keep going straight).

9.1 Turn right onto Free Soil Road.

11.6 Cross Loudon Road to the left and Drake Marshall Road to the right.

14.0 Enter Georgetown.

14.9 Turn right onto Main Street for a long, mostly downhill ride back to Ripley. **Side-trip:** Turn left and ride for 0.6 mile to visit Georgetown, a pleasing small town. You can find restaurants, restrooms, and Mycle's Cycles bike shop.

16.1 Main Street becomes Old US 68.

19.7 Go left onto Old US 68.

22.6 Continue right on Old US 68 when Ripley Day Hill Road goes left.

24.8 Turn left onto US 52.

25.1 Turn right onto Sycamore Street.

25.2 Turn left onto Front Street.

25.6 Stop at Rockin' Robin's Soda Shoppe for an ice cream.

25.7 Go check out a book at the library.

Local Information

Brown County Ohio Tourism: 325 West State St., Georgetown; (937) 378-1970; www.brown countytourism.com.

Events/Attractions

Ripley Farmers Market: Takes place every Saturday morning from 9 a.m. until noon, May 26 through September 22, on Main Street across from the library.

Ohio Tobacco Festival: Showcases the heritage of tobacco farming and takes place on the fourth weekend in August. For information contact Ohio Tobacco Festival, Inc., (937) 392-1590 or (937) 373-3651.

Restaurants

Cohearts Riverhouse: 18 North Front St., Ripley; (937) 392-4819. Just a short walk from the ride start; fresh, great cooking, award-winning local wines; overlooking the Ohio River.

Rockin' Robin's Soda Shoppe: On the Ripley River Walk, 8 North Front St., Ripley; (937) 392-1300. This shop is on the route near the start/end. Old-fashioned soda fountain and hand-dipped ice creams and shakes. Homemade soups and sandwiches daily.

Accommodations

The Signal House Bed and Breakfast: 234 North Front St., Ripley; (937) 392-1640; www .thesignalhouse.com.

Bike Shops

Mycle's Cycles: 106 East Cherry St., Georgetown; (937) 378-5700; www.myclescycles.com.

Restrooms

Start/finish: Ripley Public Library.
Mile 14.9: On the side-trip into Georgetown.

Maps

DeLorme: Ohio Atlas & Gazetteer: Page 76.

9 Little Miami Scenic Trail Challenge

The Little Miami Scenic Trail is a treasure trove of beauty and history. The trail is also an entirely pleasant ride. Winding along the meanders of the Little Miami River, it is among the longest paved trails in the United States, stretching 73 miles from Springfield to Newtown.

Start: Xenia Station is the trail hub. There are several staging areas (parking, restrooms, water) on the trail, and other parking options are available.
Length: 73.0 miles.
Terrain: Mostly flat, although there is a slight ascent going northward. The trail is generally smooth, but hey, it's 73 miles long, so expect occasional unevenness and for a sporadic tree root to bulge the surface.
Traffic and hazards: Beware of children and dogs near the popular stops, especially on weekends. There are some busy road crossings.

Getting there: Xenia Station, 150 Miami Avenue, Xenia, is 1 mile south of the intersection of US 35 and US 68. Xenia Station is not at either end of the trail but rather 16.7 miles from the northern end of the trail and 56.3 miles from the southern end.

Heading out toward Loveland

The Ride

The Little Miami Scenic Trail runs through five counties, several jurisdictions, and a variety of names. From Xenia to Yellow Springs, the trail is called locally the Yellow Springs Bikeway. From Xenia to Milford it's called the Little Miami Scenic Trail, and in Loveland it's the Loveland Trail. From Spring Valley north the trail is managed by Greene County and for the last 9 northern miles by Clark County's National Trail Parks and Recreation District. South of Spring Valley it becomes the Little Miami State Park and is managed by the Ohio Department of Natural Resources. A trail corridor as a state park is a unique new concept to the state park system. The newest section south of Terrace Park is managed by the Hamilton County Park District.

This trail is a work in progress, with spurs and extensions planned in many areas. Stringing alongside the Little Miami River for many miles, the trail goes under and over many interesting bridges. A nice feature is that the names of the bridges and crossroads are marked.

While on the bike trail, for heaven's sakes mind your trail manners: Bicyclists yield to everyone; don't litter—ever—anywhere; announce to other users when you're passing; respect private property; pull off the paved trail to stop.

The trail section going north from Xenia to Yellow Springs is the most popular. That ride goes through Xenia on sidewalks marked with yellow paint. It takes a few road crossings to get to the trail proper near Shawnee Park, a city park (an optional trail route to Shawnee Park that does not go through Xenia is described at the Xenia Station). From the park the trail wends through wooded sections, farm fields, and past a riding stable to Yellow Springs. Full of interesting shops and unique restaurants, this is a funky little town and fun to explore. Young's Jersey Dairy, famous for its superb ice cream, is nearby. On the trail, about 1.7 miles north of Yellow Springs, turn right onto Jackson Road and in 0.5 mile go left onto US 68. This is a busy road, but in a very short distance you'll come to Young's. It is an incredibly well-known spot to bicyclists and ice-cream eaters in general.

Continuing north to Springfield, the trail officially ends at I-70. You can pedal into Springfield on a combination of marked roads and bike paths to where the Buck Creek and Simon Kenton Trails begin.

Riding south from Xenia toward Spring Valley, you'll come to a swampy area along-side the trail, which is Spring Valley Wildlife Area—look for the signs. An access trail leads to the wildlife area (a well-known birding hot spot), but bikes are not permitted.

Continuing south, the Little Miami River begins to come into view. Expect tall cliffs, towering sycamores, and a profusion of birds, wildlife, and wildflowers. Several canoe access points and canoe liveries are situated along the river. You'll probably hear and see canoeists and kayakers.

Just past Corwin, from the trail you can see the Corwin-Nixon Covered Bridge on Middletown Road.

South of Oregonia listen for the timbre of tires as you approach the Jeremiah Morrow Bridge. This bridge carries I-71 traffic across the Little Miami River gorge. At 239 feet above the river, it is the tallest bridge in the state.

Next the trail passes Fort Ancient. This site features 18,000 feet of earthen walls built 2,000 years ago by people using primitive tools. Portions of the walls were used in conjunction with the sun and moon to provide a calendar system. A short, unpaved path leads to Fort Ancient. There is an admittance fee.

The next staging area is Morrow—the Loveland-to-Morrow section of the trail was the first completed. It was near my home and was the first bike trail in the area. I rode it often with family and friends. Parking is limited and spaces may fill on weekends.

South of Morrow you will pass the abandoned Peters Cartridge Factory; it's a landmark. According to the Little Miami Trail Web site, the company made cartridges for the United States and its allies during World War I. Coming into Loveland, you'll find a wonderful trail ambience with restaurants featuring outdoor dining and ice-cream shops.

Cycling south toward Milford, the trail goes past Camp Dennison. During the Civil War, Camp Dennison was used as a training center, recruiting depot, and hospital post. It was named in honor of Governor William Dennison, the twenty-fourth governor of Ohio.

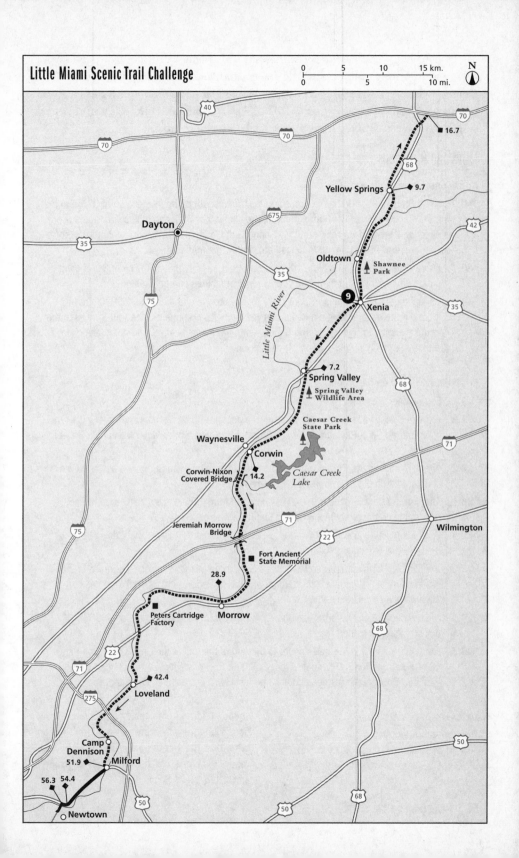

Little Miami Scenic Trail Challenge

0   5   10   15 km.
0   5   10 mi.

N

■ 16.7

70

68

40

70

Yellow Springs ◆ 9.7

Dayton

675

35

Little Miami River

35

Oldtown ⚲ ↑ Shawnee Park

9 Xenia

75

68

◆ 7.2
Spring Valley
↑ Spring Valley Wildlife Area

Caesar Creek State Park ↑

71

Waynesville

Corwin

Corwin-Nixon Covered Bridge ■ 14.2

Caesar Creek Lake

Jeremiah Morrow Bridge

71

Wilmington

22

75

■ Fort Ancient State Memorial

28.9

Peters Cartridge Factory ■   Morrow

68

22

71

■ 42.4

275

Loveland

Camp Dennison ⚲
51.9 ◆   Milford

56.3 ■   ◆ 54.4

50

50

68

◯ Newtown

50

The newest section of trail winds south from Milford. It goes through Avoca Park, across Wooster Pike, past Little Bass Island, and on to the Little Miami Golf Center. This part of the trail is maintained by the Hamilton County Park District and requires a $2 parking fee. Eventually the trail will continue south to Lunken Airport and then connect with the Ohio River Trail. Life will be good.

Miles and Directions

Northbound from Xenia Station:

0.0 Xenia Station, at 150 Miami Avenue, Xenia, 1 mile south of the intersection of US 35 and US 68, is considered the hub of the trail. The Little Miami Trail and others spur out in five directions: east (to Dayton), north (to Springfield), southeast (to Jamestown), northeast (to London), and south (almost to Cincinnati). Follow the trail north.

9.7 Arrive at Yellow Springs Station, 100 Dayton Street, Yellow Springs. The chamber of commerce office is in the station, and you can find brochures and trail information.

16.7 Continuing north from Yellow Springs, it is 7 miles to the end of the trail at I-70. From there a route travels along marked roads with some trail segments for about 3 miles to the Heritage Center in Springfield. The Simon Kenton Trail begins there, and the intersection with the Buck Creek Trail is about 2 miles north.

Southbound from Xenia Station:

0.0 Leave Xenia Station.

7.2 Arrive in Spring Valley. Street parking is available, and two restaurants allow parking for trail use: Spartan Spirit Restaurant, 13 West Main Street, and Spring Valley Mercantile Co., 17 West Main Street.

14.2 After a 7-mile ride to Corwin, you'll find a staging area on Main Street and at the Corwin Peddler Restaurant, 69 Maple Street, Waynesville.

28.9 After leaving Corwin, pedal 14.7 miles south to Morrow. There is a staging area at Phegley Park at the corner of Main and Center Streets in Morrow.

42.4 Continuing south, journey 13.5 miles to Loveland, where C. Roger Nisbet Park, 211 Railroad Avenue, is a staging area.

51.9 The distance from Loveland to Milford is 9.5 miles. In Milford the closest address to the staging area is 5 Glendale Milford Road, which is the address for Milford Monument, near the entrance to the bike trail.

54.4 The newest section of the trail is south from Milford 2.5 miles to Avoca Park, 8063 Wooster Pike, Cincinnati.

56.3 From Avoca Park it is 1.8 miles south to the end of the trail at the Little Miami Golf Center, 3811 Newtown Road, Cincinnati. Avoca Park and the golf center are maintained by the Hamilton County Park District, and a $2 park sticker is necessary to park there.

Local Information

The trail has a great Web site with a complete section-by-section description of the trail with photos. It lists restaurants, bike stores, ice-cream shops, bed-and-breakfasts, and area attractions along the way. There's also information on other bike trails in the area. Go to www.miami valleytrails.org, then click on "Trails by Name" and "Little Miami Scenic Trail."

10 Clifton Ramble

Enjoy this terrific low-traffic, high-scenery ride. The route journeys through John Bryan State Park, passes Grinnell Mill, travels out to Cedarville and a little beyond, and then meanders back. All this is in gorgeous big-farm country with lots of farm critters, beautiful farmhouses and barns, and few cars.

Start: Clifton Gorge State Nature Preserve.
Length: 31.1 miles.
Terrain: Mostly flat, some rolling, and one easy hill.

Traffic and hazards: Mostly light traffic; some traffic in Cedarville, where there is a sidewalk, and for a very short distance on the return to Clifton.

Getting there: Take US 68 into Yellow Springs. Go east on SR 343 for not quite 3 miles; turn right onto Jackson Street. The Clifton Gorge State Nature Preserve parking lot is right there on the right.

The Ride

Imagine a river's rush of water 40 feet down, walled in by limestone cliffs adorned with graceful ferns, hemlock trees, and other foliage. That's Clifton Gorge. It encompasses 2 miles of the Little Miami State Scenic River, and *National Geographic* called it one of the nation's fifty most beautiful places. The river enters the area at Clifton and drops 130 feet through layers of bedrock, creating quite a surge. Take time to follow the short path right behind the parking lot, which leads to an amazing overlook of the gorge. The Rim Trail continues on for maybe a half mile along the gorge. There's a point where a pioneer jumped across the gorge to escape from the Indians. Signage there tells the story.

When you're ready to bike, exit the parking lot and go left on Jackson Street. This route was originally mapped out by the Ohio Department of Transportation, and an occasional green sign along the way indicates that. You'll see the first one after you cross SR 343 and then go left. This first area is mostly flat. Traffic is light once you get away from Clifton. The Yellow Springs Country Bed and Breakfast is on Hilt Road.

Soon you'll come to the entrance to John Bryan State Park, the most scenic park in western Ohio. The Little Miami runs through it. Besides fishing, hiking, and mountain bike trails, the park has an area set aside for rock climbing and rappelling.

Continuing on Bryan Park Road, use caution as you swoop down the winding hill into the gorge. Pass the Grinnell Mill, now also a bed-and-breakfast. Cars travel a little faster on Clifton Road, but they are few; watch for the left turn onto Clark Run Road. I saw lots of bluebird houses on Tarbox Cemetery Road; it looked like someone maintained a bluebird trail. Be careful of gravel on the turn onto Conley Road—I wiped out there once; also, Conley is rolling.

Traffic picks up a little closer to Cedarville. This route skirts around the edge of the town (there are several restaurants on Main Street). The road becomes Bridge

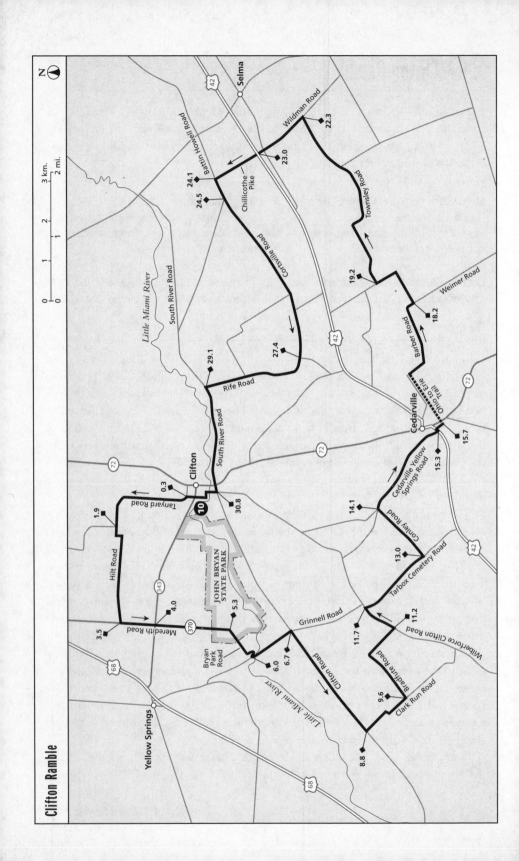

Clifton Ramble

N

3 km.
2 mi.
0 1 2 3

Selma
42

Battin Howell Road
Wildman Road
22.3
23.0
24.1
24.5
Chillicothe Pike
Cotsville Road
Townsley Road
Little Miami River
South River Road
19.2
Weimer Road
18.2
Barber Road
Ohio to Erie Trail
Cedarville
15.7
15.3
Cedarville Yellow Springs Road
29.1
Rife Road
27.4
South River Road
42
72
14.1
Conley Road
13.0
Tarbox Cemetery Road
42
Clifton
72
0.3
Tanyard Road
30.8
10
1.9
Hilt Road
343
5.3
Bryan Park Road
JOHN BRYAN STATE PARK
Meredith Road
4.0
3.5
370
Grinnell Road
11.7
11.2
Wilberforce Clifton Road
Bradfute Road
Clifton Road
6.0
6.7
Little Miami River
9.6
Clark Run Road
8.8
68
Yellow Springs
68
72

Burros watching bikers on Clifton Road

Street at the incorporated limit, and it T's into Xenia Avenue. From there you can see the right turn onto Miller Street, and from Miller you can see the bike path (part of the Ohio to Erie Trail). Pass the library and the Hearthstone Inn. You can use the restroom in the library, or there are public restrooms a little farther down. Go on the bike lane for a block, then the path opens again. Barber Road runs parallel to the bike path. Keep going until Barber crosses the bike path, just past the 8.5-mile marker. Exit the trail by going right onto Barber.

On Wildman Road you'll come to a stop sign. Look ahead and you can see Chillicothe Pike; that is where you want to be. To get there, jog right then left onto Chillicothe, go down a hill, cross the bike path and US 42, and continue up the hill on Chillicothe. Here the route becomes gently rolling. Less than a half mile after going left on Battin Howell Road, you will come to a Y. Signage is confusing—here's what happens: Battin Howell stops, and Cortsville Road goes straight ahead and to the right. Continue straight on Cortsville.

On South River Road the Little Miami is on the right. Sometimes you can see it; mostly you can't. When you return to Clifton, ignore the bike route sign that tells you to turn right. Carefully cross SR 72 and be careful on Wilberforce Clifton Road. You'll see the mill—it is just to the right on Water Street.

If you're looking for a few more miles to ride, the Little Miami Scenic Trail has a staging area in Yellow Springs; in fact, the 10 miles from Yellow Springs to Xenia is the most popular section of this 73-mile trail. In Yellow Springs the staging area is a rebuilt train depot at 100 Dayton Street at the intersection with US 68.

Miles and Directions

0.0   Exit the parking lot and turn left onto Jackson Street.

0.1   Cross North Street/SR 343.

0.3   Go left on Tanyard Road.

1.9   Continue straight on Hilt Road—Tanyard goes right.

3.5   At the T turn left onto Meredith Road/SR 370.

4.0   Cross SR 343.

5.1   Pass the entrance to John Bryan State Park.

5.3   Go around a bend and SR 370 ends; you're now on Bryan Park Road.

6.0   Turn left onto Grinnell Road.

6.2   Keep straight when Grinnell Drive goes right.

6.7   Turn right onto Clifton Road.

8.8   Go left onto Clark Run Road.

9.6   Take a left onto Bradfute Road.

11.2   Turn left onto Wilberforce Clifton Road.

11.7   Go right onto Tarbox Cemetery Road.

13.0   Take a left onto Conley Road—gravel alert!

14.1   At the T turn right on Cedarville Yellow Springs Road.

15.3   At the Cedarville incorporated limit, the road becomes Bridge Street.

15.7   At the T turn left onto Xenia Avenue.

15.8   Turn right on Miller Street.

15.9   Go left onto the Ohio to Erie Trail by the library.

16.0   Cross Main Street by the Hearthstone Inn and Suites. The bike path becomes a bike lane for 1 block.

16.8   Turn right onto Barber Road (past the 8.5-mile marker when Barber crosses the trail).

18.2   Bend left on Barber when Weimer Road continues straight.

19.2   Turn right onto Townsley Road.

22.3   At the T turn left onto Wildman Road (there's no sign; you're under the power lines).

23.0   Jog right and then left onto Chillicothe Pike, crossing the bike path and US 42.

24.1   Turn left onto Battin Howell Road.

24.5   Continue straight on Cortsville Road (Battin Howell ends; Cortsville continues straight and to the right).

27.4   At the Y go right onto Rife Road.

29.1   Turn left onto South River Road.

30.7   Carefully cross SR 72.

30.8 Turn right onto Wilberforce Clifton Road.

31.0 Take a left onto Water Street (the Clifton Mill is to the right). Water Street bends to the right and becomes Jackson Street.

31.1 Finish. Walk the short path to the Clifton Gorge overlook.

Local Information

Greene County Convention and Visitors Bureau: 1221 Meadowbridge Dr., Beavercreek; (937) 429-9100 or (800) 733-9109; www .greenecountyohio.org.

Attractions

Clifton Mill: 75 Water St., Clifton; (937) 767-5501; www.cliftonmill.com. Just a short walk from the Clifton Gorge parking lot. You can tour the mill, plus there's a restaurant and gift shop. The mill is known for its amazing Christmas display.

Young's Jersey Dairy: 6880 Springfield Xenia Rd., Yellow Springs; (937) 325-0629; www .youngsdairy.com. Famous for delicious home-made ice cream; also has a full menu plus family fun and seasonal events.

Restaurants

Main Street Station Restaurant: 19 South Main St., Cedarville; (937) 766-4874. Near the bike route.

Winds Cafe: 215 Xenia Ave., Yellow Springs; (937) 767-1144.

Accommodations

Grinnell Mill Bed and Breakfast: 3536 Bryan Park Rd., Yellow Springs; (937) 767-9108; www .grinnellmill.com. Beautiful accommodations in a restored mill on the banks of the scenic Little Miami River.

Hearthstone Inn and Suites: 10 South Main St., Cedarville; (877) OHIO-INN (toll free); www.hearthstone-inn.com. Recommended by Fodor's. Blends Ohio themes and ambience with the warmth and charm that only a small town can provide.

Yellow Springs Country Bed and Breakfast: 1570 Hilt Rd., Yellow Springs; (937) 405-8174; www.yscountrybedandbreakfast.com. Relax in a restored Federalist home with a spacious yard on a quiet country road.

Bike Shops

Village Cyclery: 110 Dayton St., Yellow Springs; (937) 767-9330.

Restrooms

Mile 15.9: On the bike path in Cedarville.

Maps

DeLorme: Ohio Atlas & Gazetteer: Page 60.

11 Buck Creek Cruise

This Clark County ride travels through a mix of farmland and suburbia. Part of the route travels along the Ohio to Erie bike path. On that path, which is edged with native prairie plantings, you will visit the South Charleston staging area, featuring an old train depot museum.

Start: Buck Creek State Park.
Length: 41.0-mile loop.
Terrain: Flat to rolling.

Traffic and hazards: Traffic is moderate to heavy near the park, especially during rush hour. Otherwise the route follows mostly quiet rural roads.

Getting there: From I-70 near Springfield, take exit 62 to US 40 and go west about 2 miles toward Springfield. Turn right onto North Bird Road. In about a mile it crosses Old Columbus Road, and Bird Road becomes Buck Creek Lane. Follow it a short distance to the Buck Creek State Park office, across from the beach at C.J. Brown Reservoir, at 1901 Buck Creek Lane, Springfield.

The Ride

To appreciate some of the features of the route, you need to travel 12,000 years back in time. The glaciers had receded, leaving low hills called moraines—places where the glacier had halted; those are the bumps and hillocks, which are deposits of gravel and sand. Old river valleys were filled by those deposits. Numerous springs now well up through that sand and gravel. The nearby city of Springfield is named for the springs seeping up from the meadows. The springs also account for the many bogs and fens in Clark and Champaign Counties.

To begin the ride, exit the park office parking lot, just across from the beach, and turn left on Buck Creek Lane. At the first traffic light, cross Old Columbus Road, and the road becomes North Bird Road. Pass the Springfield Composting Facility. When North Bird bends slightly right and becomes Leffel Lane, take East Possum Road to the left. Now the route becomes more rural. Look for chimney swifts circling over Rei Fishing Lakes. Just past the lakes where Crabill Road T's into Pitchin Road—there is no road sign, but you'll see a house straight ahead—bear right onto Pitchin.

When you come to a T on Dolly Varden Road, the signage is confusing; turn left, staying on Dolly Varden, while South Charleston Clifton Road goes right. Cross US 42 and turn left onto the bike path. The sign indicates BIKE PATH #4.

The trail travels through farmland and is edged with prairie plantings. There is a pleasant staging area in South Charleston with restrooms, water, shops, and a bike shop. Follow the decorative lampposts to the train depot museum and log cabin on Mound Street (the Country Kitchen Restaurant is on Columbus Street/US 42). Follow the Ohio to Erie Trail signs along Mound Street for a few blocks. Turn right onto Church Street and it's a short distance to the bike path. Continue to the left on the bike path. The big feed mills and resident flocks of starlings give evidence of

South Charleston train depot museum

Springfield's agriculture heritage. In a few miles take Neil Road to the left and exit the bike path.

Traffic picks up when you turn left onto Old Columbus Road again. When you come to Buck Creek Lane, turn right and ride back to the park.

Miles and Directions

0.0 Turn left from the park office parking lot onto Buck Creek Lane.

0.7 Cross Old Columbus Road and continue straight, now on North Bird Road.

1.8 Cross US 40.

2.6 Cross SR 41.

4.2 Turn left onto East Possum Road.

5.5 Turn left onto Crabill Road.

6.0 Turn right, still on Crabill, when Mitchell Road goes straight.

7.2 Bear right onto Pitchin Road just past the Rei Fishing Lakes.

8.0 Turn left onto Old Springfield Road.

9.7 Cross River Road.

11.6 Turn right onto Dolly Varden Road.

13.0 Continue straight, still on Dolly Varden, when Clifton Road goes left.

14.1 At the T turn left, remaining on Dolly Varden; South Charleston Clifton Road goes right.

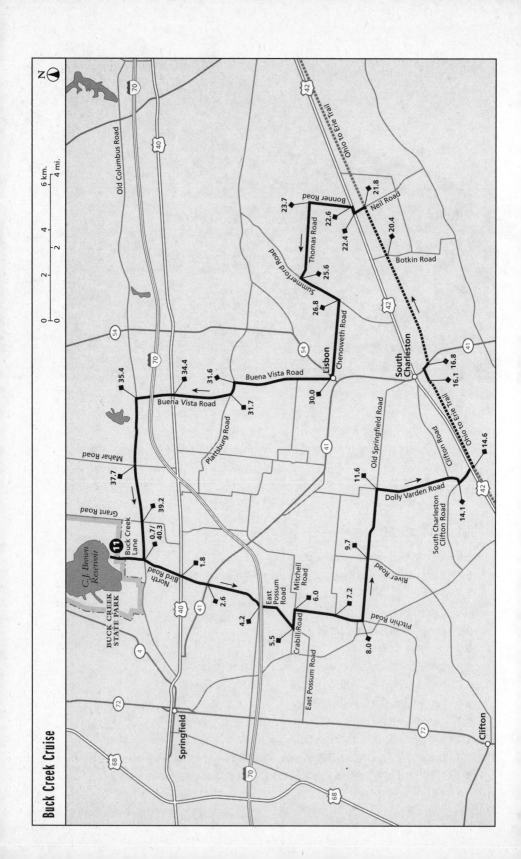

Buck Creek Cruise

14.6 Cross US 42 and turn left onto the Ohio to Erie Trail.

16.0 Follow the gaslights to the staging area by the train depot museum. You'll find restrooms and an ice-cream shop.

16.1 Turn right onto Mound Street.

16.6 Take a right onto Church Street.

16.8 Return to the Ohio to Erie Trail and go left.

20.4 Cross Botkin Road.

21.8 Exit the trail by turning left onto Neil Road.

22.4 Turn right onto US 42.

22.6 Go left onto Bonner Road.

23.7 Bonner bends a hard left, reenters Clark County, and becomes Thomas Road.

25.6 Just past a hard bend to the right, turn left onto Summerford Road.

26.8 Turn right onto Chenoweth Road.

29.9 Turn left onto SR 54. Springfield Baptist Church is just ahead on the right.

30.0 Take a right onto Buena Vista Road.

31.6 Jog left onto Plattsburg Road.

31.7 Go right, back onto Buena Vista Road.

34.4 Cross US 40 by the Lamp Shop.

35.0 Cross I-70.

35.4 At the T turn left onto Old Columbus Road.

37.7 Cross Bowman/Mahar Roads.

39.2 Cross Grant/Redmon Roads.

40.3 Turn right onto Buck Creek Lane.

41.0 Arrive back at the beach and parking lot.

Local Information

Greater Springfield Convention and Visitors Bureau: 20 South Limestone St., Springfield; (937) 325-7621 or (800) 803-1553; www .springfield-clarkcountyohio.info.

Attractions

Buck Creek State Park: 1901 Buck Creek Lane, Springfield; (937) 322-5284. The park offers cottages for rent and camping. C.J. Brown Reservoir has been designated an Important Bird Area by Audubon Ohio (a birding guide is available at the park). A paved bicycle trail at the beach connects to the Little Miami Scenic Trail.

Restaurants

The Country Kitchen Restaurant: 122 East Columbus St., South Charlestown; (937) 462-9088.

The Hickory Restaurant: 652 North Limestone St., Springfield; (937) 323-1779. An award-winning, down-home restaurant with all kinds of entrees. If you like pizza, this is the place.

Accommodations

The Houstonia: 25 East Mound St., South Charleston; (937) 462-8855 or (888) 462-8855. This historic bed-and-breakfast, one of America's top twenty-five, is right on the bike route. Foster Houston was a friend to any sort of politician or monied gentry of the early twentieth century. Therefore, stories of intrigue, glamour, and downfall abound at the inn.

Bike Shops

The Bicycle Stop: 1355 West First St., Springfield; (937) 342-4780; www.bicyclestop.com. **Springfield Cyclery:** 1300 Mitchell Blvd., Springfield; (937) 399-1304.

Restrooms

Start/finish: Buck Creek State Park beach. **Mile 16.0:** South Charleston staging area.

Maps

DeLorme: Ohio Atlas & Gazetteer: Pages 50, 60.

12 Clark Lake Ramble

This is a pleasant meander out to nowhere in particular and back. A couple of not-too-bad hills jazz up the picturesque, mostly rolling route.

Start: Clark Lake Wildlife Area near Springfield.
Length: 28.5-mile loop.
Terrain: Some rolling, some flat, a couple of hills.

Traffic and hazards: Mostly light traffic that picks up a bit on Mechanicsburg Catawba Road.

Getting there: From I-70 take exit 62 to US 40/National Highway. In about a quarter mile, turn left onto Bowman Road; then in a mile turn right onto Old Columbus Road and in just over another mile left onto Vernon Asbury Road. The wildlife area is on the right at 1750 Vernon Asbury Road, South Vienna.

The Ride

You may not see any red fox or white-tailed deer at Clark Lake Wildlife Area, the staging area for this ride, but they are there—we saw both not too far away. The area looks so tranquil, but wildlife abounds. You probably will see Canada geese and maybe a couple of fishermen in pursuit of the bass, bluegill, crappie, and channel cats that swim there. The 180-acre lake was formed in 1957 when Sinking Creek was dammed. The wildlife area is owned by the Ohio Department of Natural Resources, Division of Wildlife.

This ride is rolling, thanks to a receding glacier that was moving southward even as warmer temperatures were beginning to melt it. A glacier moves somewhat like an upside-down conveyor belt—the top moves faster than the bottom. So you can imagine it morphing slowly south, spitting out bits of sand, silt, clay, and cobbles, forming linear ridges of elevated terrain. As you ride, you will see those ridges. It is the kind of terrain where most (but not all) of the downhills give you enough momentum to get back to the top.

You will ride through lots of farmland, with fields of wheat, corn, and beans. Sweet corn, tomatoes, green beans, and other vegetables are produced there. The annual South Vienna Corn Festival has crafts and lots of good food. You will also pass

Rounding the bend toward Clark Lake

a big dairy farm—there are several in the area, and they have created typical big-farm controversy. Many fields along the way once grew corn but are now growing new homes. Urban sprawl is eating up the farms. It comes from Columbus, Dayton, and Springfield, all directions.

Turn right as you leave the wildlife area. You will curve around the lake and get several scenic views. Bear left and remain on Vernon Asbury when Jones Road continues straight. This area is woods, farmland, and new homes. Stay on Vernon Asbury until it dead-ends onto Neer Road. When you ride into Champaign County, Neer Road becomes Brigner Road. Stay on Brigner when Neer goes left. You'll see more houses, and traffic will pick up a little as you approach Mechanicsburg. Before you get there, however, turn right onto Mechanicsburg Catawba Road—this road has moderate traffic. Swoop down a hill and past a cemetery before turning left onto Wren Road. Wren meanders around and up and down through beautiful farm vistas. We saw a private home offering a drive-through confessional but did not take advantage. You'll pass an old Methodist church before turning left onto Lundy Lane. This section of the route is flatter and is a mix of urban homes and rural farmyards. Jones Road gets a little rolling. When you come to Vernon Asbury Road, continue straight and follow it back to Clark Lake.

Miles and Directions

0.0 Exit the wildlife area and turn right onto Vernon Asbury Road.

1.9 Bear left, still on Vernon Asbury, when Jones Road continues straight.

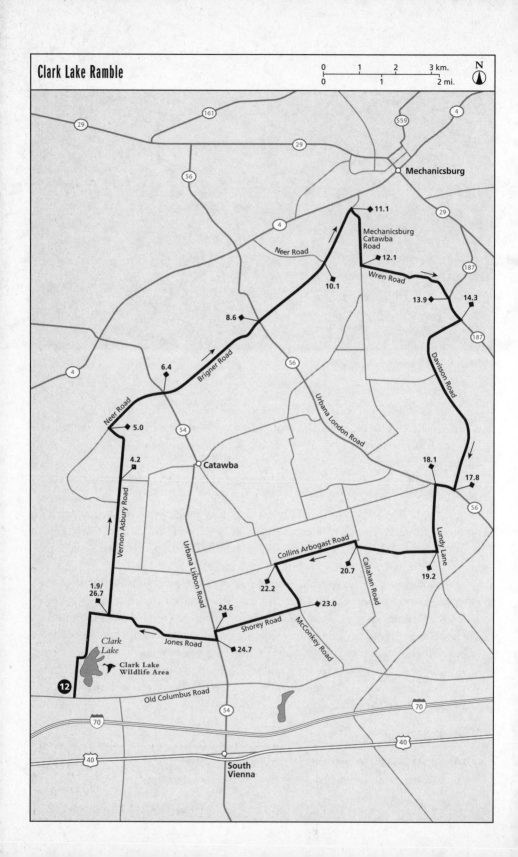

Clark Lake Ramble

0   1   2   3 km.
0   1   2 mi.

N

Mechanicsburg

161

29

29

559

4

56

4

29

◆ 11.1

Mechanicsburg
Catawba
Road

◆ 12.1

Neer Road

187

Wren Road

10.1

13.9 ◆   ■ 14.3

187

8.6 ◆

56

Brigner Road

Davisson Road

6.4 ■

Neer Road

54

Catawba

Urbana London Road

18.1 ◆   ■ 17.8

56

◆ 5.0

■ 4.2

Vernon Asbury Road

Lundy Lane

Collins Arbogast Road

Callahan Road

20.7 ◆   ■ 19.2

1.9/
26.7 ■

22.2 ■

Urbana Lisbon Road

24.6 ■   ◆ 23.0

Shorey Road

McConkey Road

Jones Road   ■ 24.7

Clark
Lake

Clark Lake
Wildlife Area

12

Old Columbus Road

54

70

70

40

40

South
Vienna

4.2	Continue straight on Vernon Asbury when Vernon Catawba Road turns right.
5.0	Turn right onto Neer Road.
6.4	Cross SR 54; Neer Road becomes Brigner Road.
8.6	Cross SR 56.
10.1	Stay on Brigner when Neer goes left.
11.1	Turn right onto Mechanicsburg Catawba Road.
12.1	Take a left onto Wren Road.
13.9	Turn right onto SR 187.
14.3	Go right on Davisson Road.
17.8	Turn right onto SR 56/Urbana London Road.
18.1	Go left on Lundy Lane.
19.2	Turn right onto Collins Arbogast Road.
20.7	Jog right on Callahan Road.
20.8	Bend left back to Collins Arbogast.
22.2	Turn left onto McConkey Road.
23.0	Go right on Shorey Road.
24.6	Jog left onto SR 54/Urbana Lisbon Road.
24.7	Go right on Jones Road.
26.7	Continue straight, now on Vernon Asbury Road.
28.5	Reach the finish.

Local Information

Greater Springfield Convention and Visitors Bureau: 20 South Limestone St., Springfield; (937) 325-7621 or (800) 803-1553; www.springfield-clarkcountyohio.info.

Events/Attractions

Cedar Bog Nature Preserve: 980 Woodburn Rd., Urbana; (800) 860-0147.
South Vienna Corn Festival: (937) 568-8065; www.southvienna.org. Held the first weekend after Labor Day.

Restaurants

The Hickory Restaurant: 652 North Limestone St., Springfield; (937) 323-1779. An award-winning, down-home restaurant with all kinds of entrees. If you like pizza, this is the place.

Accommodations

The Houstonia: 25 East Mound St., South Charleston; (937) 462-8855 or (888) 462-8855. This historic bed-and-breakfast is one of America's top twenty-five. Foster Houston was a friend to any sort of politician or monied gentry of the early twentieth century, and stories of intrigue, glamour, and downfall abound at the inn.

Bike Shops

The Bicycle Stop: 1355 West First St., Springfield; (937) 342-4780; www.bicyclestop.com.
Springfield Cyclery: 1300 Mitchell Blvd., Springfield; (937) 399-1304.

Restrooms

Start/finish: There is a Port-O-Let at Clark Lake.

Maps

DeLorme: Ohio Atlas & Gazetteer: Page 50.

13 Fort Jefferson Ramble

Listen for the voices of history here: It's the land of Indian wars and the Treaty of Greenville, the homeland of Annie Oakley, and the meeting place of Lewis and Clark. All this on an idyllic cruise through flat to gently rolling Ohio farmland with light traffic. It's a pleasing ride whether you choose the full 40 miles or the shorter 21-mile route.

Start: Fort Jefferson State Memorial, Greenville.
Length: 40.4 miles with an option for a shorter 20.5-mile route.

Terrain: Mostly flat, some rolling.
Traffic and hazards: Mostly light.

Getting there: From US 127 go west onto Weavers Fort Jefferson Road. Continue for 1.3 miles—you will cross SR 121. The park is on the left at 3981 Weavers Fort Jefferson Road, Greenville.

The Ride

"Oats and beans and barley grow," the old song goes. On this ride it would be corn and beans and wheat and the rhythm would be lost, but you won't lose your rhythm on this farmland tour. Fort Jefferson Park and Monument marks the site of an advance outpost of General Arthur St. Clair, built in October 1791. It was the first settlement in Darke County. The general named the fort in honor of Thomas Jefferson, then secretary of state. During the Indian Wars of 1790–1795, the United States felt it necessary to build forts in contested territory. Fort Jefferson was one of a chain of forts, with a hard day's march in between, stretching from Fort Washington, Cincinnati, to Fort Deposit, Waterville. There's a stone monument, but nothing of the fort remains today.

On November 4, 1791, in the "Battle of the Wabash," forces under Chief Little Turtle inflicted the worst defeat ever by Indians upon the U.S. Army. Over 600 soldiers were killed and 300 wounded. During the next twenty-four hours, survivors made their way back to Fort Jefferson. Within two years General "Mad" Anthony Wayne established the second official settlement in the county, Green Ville (now Greenville). In October 1793 Wayne used Fort Jefferson as a supply base during the campaign that resulted in the American victory of Fallen Timbers in August 1794. The subsequent August 1795 Treaty of Greenville ensured peace in Ohio for the next decade.

William Clark and Meriwether Lewis were both in the area when the treaty was signed. They met here and began their lifelong friendship. Darke County—and this is the only county in the United States with that name—was also home to Annie Oakley. She supported her family by shooting and selling game to grocery stores and restaurants around Greenville. They liked the game she sold; it had little damage because her aim was so precise. If you're interested in Annie, visit the Garst Museum in Greenville.

Reminder of what happened at Fort Jefferson

Glaciers have left their footprint, too. Sections of the ride to the east of the fort tend to be flat, while the route to the southwest tends to be rolling. As you start the ride, traveling east from the monument, the road is winding and rolling. After you cross US 127, the roads flatten. You'll find light traffic on Jaysville St. Johns Road, but after a left onto Delisle Fourmans Road all is quiet.

The shorter route turns right from Delisle Fourmans onto Myers Tillman Road (for whatever reason, most of the roads have double names here). The longer ride continues on Delisle Fourmans to a right onto Gordon Landis Road.

Follow Dull Road as it doglegs to the right and then to the left. Ride through the village of Ithaca, a little gathering of houses. Continuing to travel south, the route becomes rolling.

You'll cross into Preble County, and Fraziers Road becomes Davis Road. Ride along Holtzmuller Road, then head north again on Monroe Central Road, which becomes Emrick Road when you reenter Darke County.

On Arcanum Hollansburg Road bear right when first Harter, then Stephens, and finally Royer Road turn off to the left. Then bear left, still on Arcanum Hollansburg Road, when Hollansburg Sampson Road goes right.

Turn right onto Weavers Fort Jefferson Road, then turn left onto Weavers Station Road, which is also Weavers Fort Jefferson Road, although signage did not indicate that the last time I rode there.

Fort Jefferson Ramble

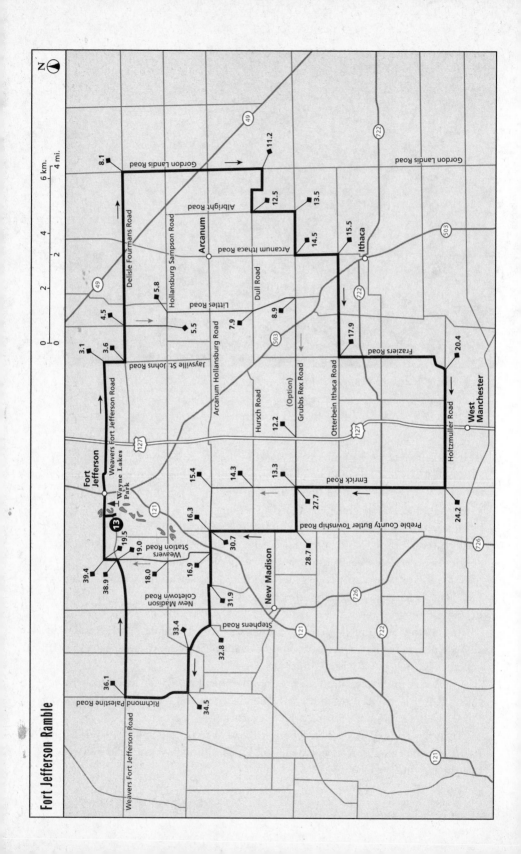

The 20.5-mile optional route rejoins here. Turn right, still on Weavers Fort Jefferson Road, when Weavers Station continues straight. Enjoy the scenic return through Wayne Lakes Park.

There are two interesting sites on the shorter route: As you cross SR 503, notice the golf course. It has a tunnel under the road for players to cross the highway. At the corner of Preble County Butler Township and Weavers Station Roads, look for the window full of Ohio license plates in the shape of the state—I hope it is still there.

Miles and Directions

0.0 Turn right from the park onto Weavers Fort Jefferson Road and ride back toward US 127.

1.3 Cross US 127.

3.1 Turn right onto Jaysville St. Johns Road.

3.6 Go left onto Delisle Fourmans Road.

4.5 Pass Myers Tillman Road. **Option:** To follow the 20.5-mile route, see below.

8.1 Turn right onto Gordon Landis Road.

11.2 Take a right onto Dull Road.

12.5 Turn left onto Albright Road.

13.5 Go right onto Grubbs Rex Road.

14.5 Turn left onto Arcanum Ithaca Road.

15.5 Go right onto Otterbein Ithaca Road.

17.9 Turn left onto Fraziers Road. Cross into Preble County and the road becomes Davis Road.

20.4 Make a right onto Holtzmuller Road.

24.2 Go right onto Monroe Central Road, which becomes Emrick Road when you return to Darke County.

27.7 Turn left onto Grubbs Rex Road.

28.7 Grubbs Rex T's into Preble County Butler Township Road. Turn right.

30.7 Turn left onto Arcanum Hollansburg Road.

31.9 Continue right on Arcanum Hollansburg when Harter Road goes left.

32.4 Cross New Madison Coletown Road.

32.8 Stay on Arcanum Hollansburg when Stephens Road goes left.

33.3 Bear right when Royer Road goes left.

33.4 Bear left, still on Arcanum Hollansburg, when Hollansburg Sampson Road goes right.

34.5 Turn right onto Richmond Palestine Road.

36.1 Go right onto Weavers Fort Jefferson Road.

38.9 Take a left onto Weavers Station Road.

39.4 Turn right onto Weavers Fort Jefferson Road.

40.4 Arrive back at Fort Jefferson Monument.

Option

4.5 Turn right onto Myers Tillman Road.

5.5 Go left onto Hollansburg Sampson Road.

5.8 Take a right onto Littles Road.

7.0 Cross Arcanum Hollansburg Road.

7.9 Cross Dull Road.

8.9 Turn right onto Grubbs Rex Road.

9.6 Cross SR 503.

12.2 Cross US 127.

13.3 Go right onto Emrick Road.

14.3 Cross Hursch Road.

15.4 Turn left onto Arcanum Hollansburg Road.

16.3 Cross Preble County Butler Township Road.

16.7 Cross SR 121.

16.9 Turn right onto Weavers Station Road.

18.0 Cross Hollansburg Sampson Road.

19.0 Cross Weavers Fort Jefferson Road to the left and Hi-Wind Road to the right. Rejoin the longer route here at mile 38.9, continuing straight on Weavers Station Road.

19.5 Take a right onto Weavers Fort Jefferson Road.

20.5 Arrive back at Fort Jefferson Monument.

Local Information

Darke County Visitors Bureau: 537 South Broadway, Greenville; (800) 504-2995; www.visitdarkecounty.org.

Attractions

The Annie Oakley Center at Garst Museum: 205 North Broadway, Greenville; (937) 548-5250.
Bear's Mill: 6450 Arcanum Bear's Mill Road, Greenville; (937) 548-5112; www.bearsmill.com.

Restaurants

Maid-Rite Sandwich Shop: 125 North Broadway, Greenville; (937) 548-9340. This is one of the most unique eateries around. It features legendary sandwiches.

Accommodations

Wayman's Corner Bed and Breakfast: 633 Central Ave., Greenville; (937) 316-6074; www.waymanscorner.com. A unique retreat in the heart of Ohio.

Bike Shops

Weaver's Bikes: 701 Wayne St., Greenville; (937) 548-1035.

Restrooms

There is no restroom at the monument. Greenville is about 4 miles north on US 127, then west on SR 571 for just over a mile. You'll find fast-food restaurants and restrooms there.

Maps

DeLorme: Ohio Atlas & Gazetteer: Page 48.

14 Bear's Mill Ramble

The peaceful setting of Bear's Mill will put you in a good frame of mind for this ride. The flat roads traverse big-farm country.

Start: Bear's Mill near Greenville.
Length: 24.5 miles.
Terrain: A bit rolling near the start and finish but mostly flat.

Traffic and hazards: Light traffic, although the cars go fast.

Getting there: From US 36, head 5 miles east of Greenville and turn south onto Arcanum Bear's Mill Road. The mill is 0.25 mile up on the right at 6450 Arcanum Bear's Mill, Greenville.

The Ride

You can't miss the old, tall building that is Bear's Mill resting in a park-like setting. Plants of interesting shape and texture grow under tall trees. Greenville Creek meanders through the property. The creek provides the power that turns the mill's underwater turbines, which power the milling machinery. Two dams create a 2-mile lake area from which water is channeled to the millrace. Water gates enable the stream water to be diverted into the race to power the turbines. Bear's Mill, built by Gabriel Baer in 1849, is one of the few operating water-powered mills in Ohio today.

You hate to leave the mill. But do. Start out going south on this easy, pastoral route; it wanders through some gorgeous newer homes spliced with old farmsteads. Farming has made progress, however, and you will see lots of big grain farms and big new farm equipment.

Several turns gradually take you south in the first miles, but the roads are well marked and the turns are easy to see. The route turns east on Hogpath Road (makes you wonder what hogs trod that path before). It is a bit more heavily traveled than the other roads. Then the route drops south before again going east for a long lazy stretch on Arcanum Painters Creek Road. You will pass through a little cluster of homes that is Painter Creek when you cross SR 571. The route heads north again on Red River West Grove Road.

If you're getting bored of flat, the route gets a little rolling again with a couple of interesting creek crossings as you near the mill. Several turns moving generally west keep you on the most rural roads for the ride back.

Allow enough time for a visit to the mill. In the gift shop, you can buy the flours and meals ground there.

Bear's Mill Ramble

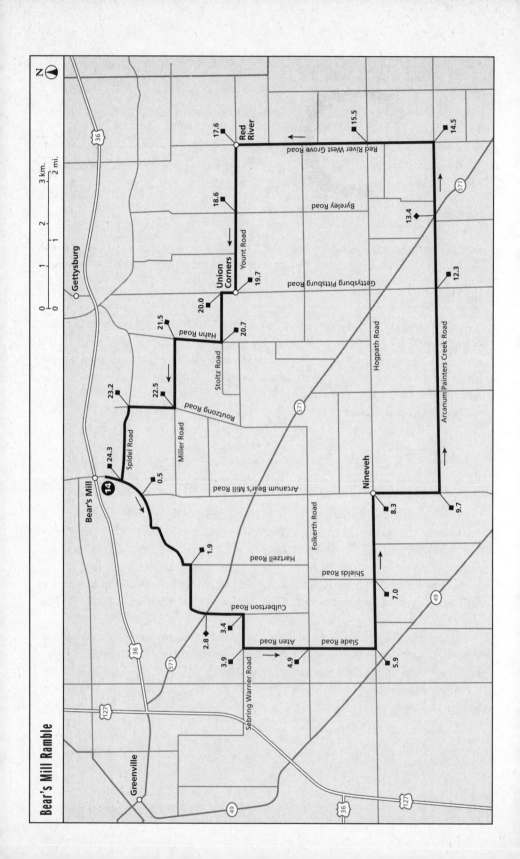

Bear's Mill

Miles and Directions

0.0 From the parking lot across the street from Bear's Mill, turn left and ride south up the hill away from US 36.

0.5 Bear right onto Hartzell Road.

1.9 Turn right onto Culbertson Road.

2.8 Cross SR 571.

3.4 Go right onto Sebring Warner Road.

3.9 Take a left onto Aten Road.

4.9 Cross Folkerth Road; Aten becomes Slade Road.

5.9 At the T turn left onto Hogpath Road.

7.0 Cross Shields Road.

8.3 Turn right onto Arcanum Bear's Mill Road.

9.7 Go left onto Arcanum Painters Creek Road.

12.3 Cross Gettysburg Pittsburgh Road.

13.4 Cross SR 571.

14.5 Turn left onto Red River West Grove Road.

15.5 Cross Hogpath Road.

17.6 Take a left onto Yount Road.

18.6 Cross Byreley Road.

19.7 Turn right onto Gettysburg Pittsburgh Road.

20.0 Go left onto Stoltz Road.

20.7 Take a right onto Hahn Road.

21.5 Turn left onto Miller Road.

22.5 Go right onto Routzong Road.

23.2 Take a left onto Spidel Road.

24.3 Turn right onto Arcanum Bear's Mill Road.

24.5 Finish at the mill.

Local Information

Darke County Visitors Bureau: 537 South Broadway, Greenville; (800) 504-2995; www .visitdarkecounty.org.

Attractions

Bear's Mill: 6450 Arcanum Bear's Mill Road, Greenville; (937) 548-5112; www.bearsmill .com. This 1849 mill is on the National Register of Historic Places. The grist mill is still in use. Tours are available; the Mill Store offers freshly ground flours and meals plus other home, gift (pottery is a specialty), and gourmet items.

The Annie Oakley Center at Garst Museum: 205 North Broadway, Greenville; (937) 548-5250.

Restaurants

Maid-Rite Sandwich Shop: 125 North Broadway, Greenville; (937) 548-9340. This is one of the most unique eateries around. It features legendary sandwiches.

Accommodations

Wayman's Corner Bed and Breakfast: 633 Central Ave., Greenville; (937) 316-6074; www .waymanscorner.com. A unique retreat in the heart of Ohio.

Bike Shops

Weaver's Bikes: 701 Wayne St., Greenville; (937) 548-1035.

Restrooms

There are no restrooms available on the route.

Maps

DeLorme: Ohio Atlas & Gazetteer: Page 48.

15 New Bremen Cruise

From the village of New Bremen, just a block from the Bicycle Museum of America, this ride meanders south to Lake Loramie State Park and then north to Grand Lake St. Marys State Park. The route travels through the land of the cross-tipped churches, past scenic farms, and through pleasant villages. It is mostly flat with little traffic. In other words, this ride is not to be missed.

Start: New Bremen, in the parking lot by the chamber of commerce.
Length: 42.4 miles.
Terrain: Mostly flat.

Traffic and hazards: For most of the ride, traffic is light. There is slow-moving traffic in New Bremen and Minster. There's moderate traffic for 0.1 mile on SR 364 before entering the bike path at Grand Lake St. Marys.

Getting there: From I-75 take exit 102 and go west on SR 274 for about 11 miles into New Bremen, where 274 becomes Monroe Street. Or from US 127 go east on SR 274 for 9 miles into New Bremen. The chamber of commerce is at 107 West Monroe Street (if you're looking for information about the area, stop in). The parking lot is adjacent to the chamber of commerce.

The Ride

The village of New Bremen was established in 1832 in the wilderness of west-central Ohio by a group of thirty-three German immigrants. They soon converted the wilderness into the scenic and tidy farmland the route traverses. In 1845 the completion of the Miami and Erie Canal between Cincinnati and Toledo brought people and trade to the region, and you will bike past remnants of the canal. While the businesses have changed, the town remains prosperous and unique.

The German Catholics who settled this region built beautiful churches, schools, rectories, and convents. This area is known as "the Land of the Cross-Tipped Churches," and spires reaching into the heavens are scattered along the route.

Enjoy the crossing over Lake Loramie at the Luthman Road Launch Ramp. Built in 1844–45, this lake was one of the original canal feeder lakes. Turn right onto SR 362—traffic is light—by the park office. Continue on SR 362 or ride through the park parallel to the highway and then exit onto SR 362 and go right. You'll begin to see the historic structures that are remnants of the Erie Canal.

Follow SR 362 into Minster. Notice the two steeples of St. Augustine. As you're leaving the downtown area, turn left onto Canal Road, cross briefly from Auglaize County into Shelby County, and then cross back again to head toward Grand Lake St. Marys on Tri-Township Road. Penny and I rode this way on a late summer day and abundant monarch butterflies graced the roadsides with color.

On your way envision the forest wilderness, prairies, and wetlands that were once here where you now see fields of corn and soybeans. In fact, the land beneath St.

One of many scenic, tidy farms

Marys was once a great area of wet prairie. Hand-dug in the 1830s, this lake was built as a reservoir for the Miami and Erie Canal to maintain the canal's 5-foot water depth. You'll pass part of the 3-mile feeder that connected the lake to the canal.

There is moderate traffic on SR 364, which you cross and then stay on for one-tenth of a mile before entering the East Bank bike trail (there is no signage but you'll see the trail), which goes into the park and along the lake. The lake is on a major migration route, and water birds use it as a resting stop. Bald eagles, long absent from the area, nest again at the wildlife refuge on the southwest corner of the lake.

Exit the park and go straight across SR 364 onto Feeder Road past the fish hatchery. You'll pass beautiful farms on the way back to New Bremen. When you see the water towers, you'll know you're almost back.

Miles and Directions

0.0 The parking lot is on the corner of Main and Monroe Streets. From the parking lot turn left onto Main Street.

0.2 Turn right onto West Plum Street.

0.3 Go left onto Herman Street.

0.6 Hang a right onto Erie Road.

0.9 Go left, staying on Erie.

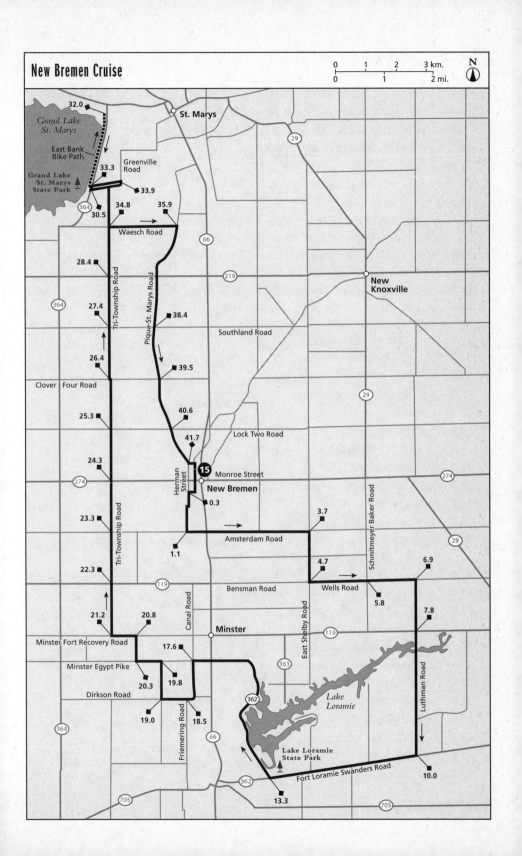

New Bremen Cruise

0 1 2 3 km.
0 1 2 mi.

N

St. Marys

Grand Lake St. Marys

32.0

East Bank Bike Path

Grand Lake St. Marys State Park

33.3

Greenville Road

33.9

364

30.5 34.8 35.9

Waesch Road

66

28.4

219

New Knoxville

29

Tri-Township Road

Piqua-St. Marys Road

364

27.4

38.4

Southland Road

26.4

39.5

Clover Four Road

25.3

40.6

41.7

Lock Two Road

29

24.3

15 Monroe Street

New Bremen

274

Herman Street

0.3

274

29

23.3

1.1

Amsterdam Road

3.7

Schmitmeyer Baker Road

22.3

Tri-Township Road

4.7

6.9

119

Canal Road

Bensman Road

Wells Road

21.2 20.8

5.8

7.8

Minster

Minster Fort Recovery Road

17.6

East Shelby Road

119

Minster Egypt Pike

363

Luthman Road

20.3 19.8

362

Dirkson Road

Lake Loramie

19.0 18.5

Friemering Road

66

Lake Loramie State Park

364

362

Fort Loramie Swanders Road

10.0

13.3

705

705

1.1   Turn left onto Amsterdam Road.

1.6   Cross SR 66.

3.7   Take a right onto East Shelby Road.

4.7   Turn left onto Wells Road, which is Bensman Road to the right.

5.8   Cross Schmitmeyer Baker Road.

6.9   Turn right onto Luthman Road.

7.8   Cross SR 119.

10.0   Go right onto Fort Loramie Swanders Road.

13.3   Turn right onto SR 362.

13.4   Pass the Lake Loramie State Park office. There are restrooms and water in the park. You can continue straight on 362 or explore the park. Several exits return to 362.

17.6   Go through Minster, then turn left onto Canal Road, which becomes Friemering Road when you cross into Shelby County.

18.5   Continue straight on Dirkson Road when Friemering Road goes left.

19.0   Turn right onto Bruns Road, which becomes Eiting Road when you return to Auglaize County.

19.8   Turn left onto Minster Egypt Pike.

20.3   Turn right onto Enneking Road.

20.8   Go left onto Minster Fort Recovery Road.

21.2   Take a right onto Tri-Township Road.

22.3   Cross SR 119.

23.3   Cross Amsterdam Road.

24.3   Cross SR 274. **Bailout:** Turn right and ride 2.5 miles back to New Bremen.

25.3   Cross Lock Two Road.

26.4   Jog left onto Clover Four Road then right, back to Tri-Township Road.

30.2   Go left onto Greenville Road.

30.5   Turn right onto SR 364.

30.6   Go left into Grand Lake St. Marys State Park and enter the out-and-back East Bank bike path. You'll find restrooms and water in the park.

32.0   Turn around at the end of the path and return to where you entered the park.

33.3   Exit the park, cross SR 364, and continue straight on Feeder Road.

33.9   Turn right onto Greenville Road.

34.0   Go left onto Tri-Township Road.

34.8   Take a left onto Waesch Road.

35.9   Turn right onto Piqua-St. Marys Road.

38.4   Cross Southland Road.

39.5   Cross Clover Four Road.

40.6   Cross Lock Two Road.

41.7   Go left onto Pearl Street.

41.8   Turn right onto Main Street.

42.4   Arrive at the parking lot.

Local Information

Southwestern Auglaize County Chamber of Commerce: 107 West Monroe St., New Bremen; (419) 629-0313; www.auglaize.org. Stop in at the chamber right next to the start of the ride for information about the region. There is a map of a walking tour of the town.

Auglaize and Mercer Counties Convention and Visitors Bureau: 900 Edgewater Dr., St. Marys; (419) 394-1294 or (800) 860-4726; www.seemore.org.

Attractions

Grand Lake St. Marys State Park: 834 Edgewater Dr., St. Marys; (419) 394-3611.

Lake Loramie State Park: 4401 Fort Loramie Swanders Rd., Minster; (937) 295-2011.

Bicycle Museum of America: 7 West Monroe St., New Bremen; (419) 629-9249. Within walking distance of the start of the ride. The Bicycle Museum of America is home to the one of the leading collections of antique and classic bicycles in the United States. The exhibits are always changing.

New Bremen Historic Association Museum: 120 North Main St., New Bremen; (419) 629-3495.

Restaurants

The Grille: 17 West Monroe St., New Bremen; (419) 629-2389. Premier eatery featuring steaks, seafood, and pasta. Enjoy the unique bicycles that are part of the decor.

Coffee Co. & Books, Inc.: 107 West Monroe St., New Bremen; (419) 629-8009. A big-city coffeehouse with small-town charm.

Accommodations

Edgewater Cottage: Nichelson Dr., Celina; (419) 733-8105 or (419) 629-3396. A lakefront oasis on Grand Lake St. Marys.

Bike Shops

Bushman's Bike Shop: 10498 East Shelby Rd., New Knoxville; (419) 629-2170.

Restrooms

Start/finish: New Bremen.

Mile 13.4: Lake Loramie State Park.

Mile 30.6: Grand Lake St. Marys State Park.

Maps

DeLorme: Ohio Atlas & Gazetteer: Page 39.

16 Ohio City Ramble

This is an easy ride from Ohio City, south of Van Wert; through pleasing farmland with fields full of corn, beans, and wheat; to Moser Memorial Park with its historic log cabin in Wren; and back. When the wind is at your back, you'll feel as if you're flying. When it's not, you won't.

Start: Ohio City Community Center Park in Van Wert County.
Length: 26.2 miles.
Terrain: Mostly flat.

Traffic and hazards: You'll find light traffic near Ohio City and Wren, with quiet roads in between.

Getting there: From Van Wert take US 127 for 7 miles south to SR 709. Go right (west) about 2 miles to SR 118 in Ohio City. Turn left and the park, also called Fireman's Park, is on the left.

The Ride

Pity poor Isaac Van Wart. Van Wert County was named after him, but his name appeared erroneously as Van Wert on a document and the new spelling stuck. On the other hand, would you rather be known as Van Wart or Van Wert? Maybe he would have been pleased.

Van Wert is part of the territory lying along the southern edge of what was known as the Great Black Swamp. Because it was swampland for probably several centuries, the land is very fertile. And flat—although the southern part of the county begins to roll a little. The present Lincoln Highway and Main Street in Van Wert is built on a visible ridge that is thought in centuries past to have been the bank of what is now Lake Erie.

On this ride in Van Wert County, you will find roads intersecting roads called by the same name: On Harrison Willshire you will cross Harrison Willshire Line Road ("Line" is not on the road sign). From Glenmore Road you will turn right onto Glenmore Road. I asked the county engineer about that, and he said it raises some issues; they have tried to change it, "but the local residents just have a fit. It's crazy but the people have spoken and that's just the way it is." You have to appreciate the humor in the situation.

The route starts off with three turns in short order. Then it settles down and becomes relaxing, moving from little subdivisions to farmland and back again.

The side-trip into Wren is interesting, providing a bit of history. Moser Memorial Park is pleasant, a good place for a quiet respite.

Enjoy the slight uphill ride on Clayton Road—hills are in short supply in this part of the state. Then you'll turn onto Ainsworth Road, which is smooth and enjoyable. You'll come into Glenmore, which is just a cluster of houses and a railroad track.

Log cabin in Wren

Then you're onto the second Glenmore Road for most of the ride back to Ohio City. The road is pleasant and smooth.

Miles and Directions

0.0 Exit the parking lot and turn right onto SR 118, also called North Shane Street.

0.3 Turn right onto 58-A (Ohio City-Venedocia Road).

0.9 Turn left onto Burris Road when SR 709 continues straight.

1.4 Go left onto Glenmore Road.

1.8 Cross SR 118.

2.4 Turn right onto Liberty Union Road/CR 77.

3.4 Cross Wren Landeck Road.

4.9 Cross Emerson Road.

5.4 Turn left onto Van Wert Willshire Road/CR 6.

6.4 Cross Richey Road.

7.4 Hang a right onto Dull Robinson Road.

7.9 Turn left onto Kreischer Road.

9.0 Cross Bergner Road.

10.0 Cross Convoy Heller Road.

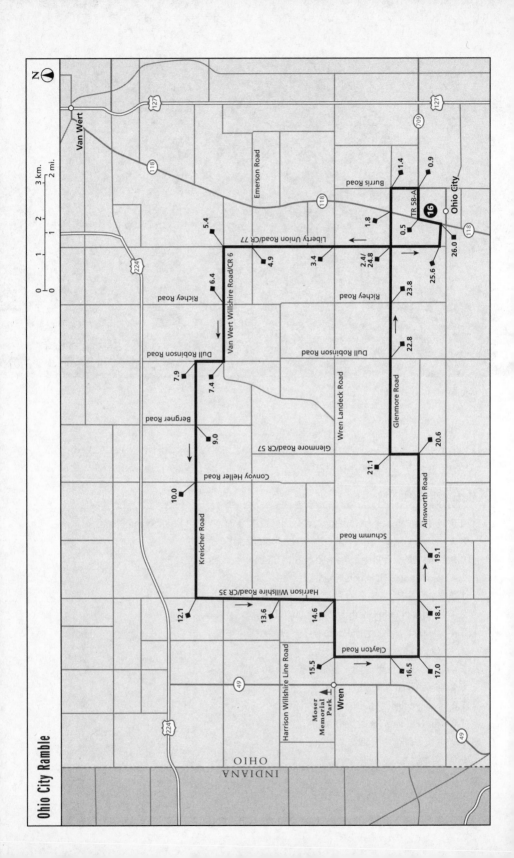

Ohio City Ramble

12.1 At the T turn left onto Harrison Willshire Road/CR 35.

13.6 Continue straight on Harrison Willshire Road when Harrison Willshire Line Road goes right.

14.6 Turn right onto Wren Landeck Road.

15.5 Go left onto Clayton Road. Side-trip: Continue straight on Wren Landeck (which becomes Jackson Road) 0.4 mile into Wren to the Moser Memorial Park and historic log cabin. You'll find a pleasant picnic area but no restrooms.

16.5 Cross Glenmore Road.

17.0 Turn left onto Ainsworth Road.

18.1 Cross Harrison Willshire Road.

19.1 Cross Schumm Road.

20.6 Go left onto Glenmore Road/CR 57 and come into Glenmore.

21.1 Turn right onto Glenmore Road.

22.8 Cross Dull Robinson Road.

23.8 Cross Richey Road.

24.8 Turn right onto Liberty Union Road/CR 77.

25.6 Turn left onto Woodlawn Street.

26.0 Turn left onto North Shane Street/SR 118.

26.2 Turn right, back into the park.

Local Information

Van Wert Convention and Visitors Bureau: 118 West Main St., Van Wert; (419) 238-WERT (9378) or (877) 989-2282; www.visitvanwert .org. You can find maps for four county bike routes on its Web site, or stop in for a free copy of its map of bike tours and a historic driving tour.

Restaurants

Ohio City Express: 511 West Carmean St., Ohio City; (419) 965-9292. Pizza, sandwiches, salads. The Express is near the Ohio City Community Park, where the ride begins.

Balyeat's Coffee Shop: 133 East Main St., Van Wert; (419) 238-1580. A Van Wert tradition since 1924. Offers daily specials.

The Main Street Ice Cream Parlor: 111 West Main St., Van Wert; (419) 238-2722.

Accommodations

Hughes Inn Bed and Breakfast: 704 South Washington St., Van Wert; (419) 238-9888; www.hughesinn.com.

Bike Shops

Fast Eddie's Van Wert Bicycle: 105 East Main St., Van Wert; (419) 238-0661.

Restrooms

Start/finish: There are no restrooms at the park. From the park you can see the nearby Ohio City Express at the intersection of SR 118 and West Carmean Street. It has restrooms.

Maps

DeLorme: Ohio Atlas & Gazetteer: Page 38.

17 Defiance Ramble

Look for lots of scenic farmland as you travel through the land that was once the Great Black Swamp. The route follows part of the Northwest Ohio Rivers Council Memorial Bicycle Trail. Flat? Think of a lumpy pancake.

Start: Oxbow Lake State Wildlife Area near Defiance.

Length: 25.4 miles.

Terrain: Mostly flat.

Traffic and hazards: Light, but the roads are narrow and some of the cars go fast.

Getting there: From SR 15 turn east (it only goes one way) onto Schick Road. In 0.8 mile turn right onto Trinity Road and enter the wildlife area. At the T turn right and then left into the first parking area.

The Ride

Upon the completion of Fort Defiance in 1794, General "Mad" Anthony Wayne is said to have lifted a fist and stated that he "defied" the English and the Indians to take his fort. And the name Defiance stuck. Situated at the impressive confluence of the Maumee and Auglaize Rivers, Defiance has an amazing historical legacy; while Fort Defiance is gone, many historical markers tell the tale. If canals fascinate you, visit Canal Park to see a restored Miami and Erie Canal lock. An old apple tree in Pontiac Park pays tribute to Johnny Appleseed's influence in this part of the state. That park also offers a spectacular view of the confluence of the Auglaize and Maumee Rivers. And if you just like to bike, people in northwest Ohio say you don't need a map to ride in this area and that all of the roads are flat and low-traffic, and that's pretty much true.

This ride is a pleasant jaunt leaving from the forty-five-acre Oxbow Lake. It follows the Northwest Ohio Rivers Council Memorial Trail, a 6-mile route, for a while. Your curiosity may be piqued by the signs of a top-hatted man on a high-wheeled bicycle that mark the trail: Three members of the river council died in one year. Instead of planting a tree, the council decided to mark out a bike route in their memory. Nice idea, don't you think? One of the men, Clinton "Doc" Erman, had ridden a high-wheeled bicycle in Defiance-area parades for fifty years. The signs honor him.

You can add a couple of miles to this route by exploring the wildlife area where the ride begins and ends. The roads are paved; it is quiet and scenic. After you leave the wildlife area, the route meanders along the Tiffin River, a tributary of the Maumee, for a while. Although you don't see more than a glimpse of the Tiffin, you'll see the tree line that follows it.

The first part of the ride follows roads lined with homes; for some reason, maybe it's the river influence, there's an abundance of small lighthouse replicas in the yards,

Oxbow Lake

sort of like Defiance's answer to the concrete goose. Some of the land along Russell and Evansport Roads is wetlands. Look for great blue herons and other interesting birds, if that is your thing. There is a carryout restaurant on the left if you're hungry. In Evansport turn right onto First Street, which becomes Williams-Defiance County Line Road.

Christy Road is pleasantly rolling—hills are scarce in this neighborhood. This section of the route goes from farm fields to subdivision areas and back again. Kammeyer Road is a pleasant one-lane country road. From there, enjoy the easy ride back to the wildlife area.

Miles and Directions

0.0 Turn right out of the parking lot.

0.3 Go left onto Trinity Road/CR 147.

1.0 Cross Schick Road/CR 67; a sign indicates the Northwest Ohio Rivers Council Memorial Trail.

3.4 Cross Beerbower Road.

4.4 Turn right onto Scott Road/CR 100.

5.5 Take a right onto Wieland Road/CR 151.

7.1 Go left onto Russell Road/CR 89.

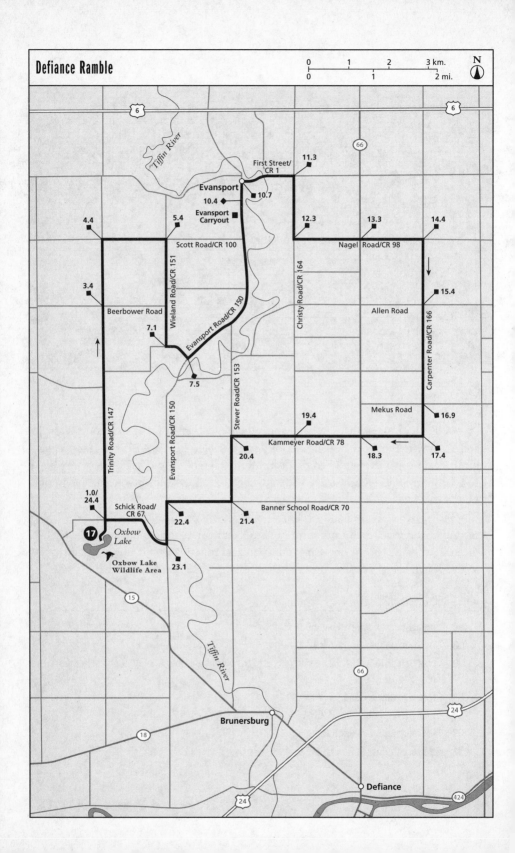

Defiance Ramble

0 1 2 3 km.
0 1 2 mi.

N

US 6

Tiffin River

First Street/CR 1 ■ 11.3

66

Evansport
■ 10.7
10.4 ◆
Evansport Carryout ■

Scott Road/CR 100

4.4 ■   5.4 ■   12.3 ■   13.3 ■   14.4 ■

Nagel Road/CR 98

3.4 ■

Beerbower Road

Wieland Road/CR 151

Christy Road/CR 164

Allen Road   ■ 15.4

Carpenter Road/CR 166

7.1 ■

Evansport Road/CR 150

7.5 ■

Stever Road/CR 153

Mekus Road   ■ 16.9

19.4 ■

Kammeyer Road/CR 78

20.4 ■   18.3 ■   17.4 ■

Trinity Road/CR 147

Evansport Road/CR 150

1.0/
24.4 ■

Schick Road/
CR 67

Banner School Road/CR 70

22.4 ■   21.4 ■

17 Oxbow Lake

23.1 ■

Oxbow Lake Wildlife Area

15

Tiffin River

66

24

Brunersburg

18

24

Defiance

424

7.5	Turn left onto Evansport Road/CR 150.
10.2	The Evansport Carryout on the left has pizzas, subs, etc. and restrooms.
10.4	Enter Evansport and the road becomes Main Street.
10.7	Turn right onto First Street/CR 1.
11.3	Turn right onto Christy Road/CR 164.
12.3	Turn left onto Nagel Road/CR 98.
13.3	Cross SR 66.
14.4	Turn right onto Carpenter Road/CR 166.
15.4	Cross Allen Road.
16.9	Cross Mekus Road.
17.4	Turn right onto Kammeyer Road/CR 78.
18.3	Cross SR 66.
19.4	Cross Christy Road.
20.4	Go left onto Stever Road/CR 153.
21.4	Turn right onto Banner School Road/CR 70.
22.4	Turn left onto Evansport Road/CR 150.
23.1	Turn right onto Schick Road/CR 67.
24.4	Turn left onto Trinity Road.
24.6	Turn right at the wildlife area sign.
25.4	Return to the parking lot.

Local Information

Defiance Development and Visitors Bureau: 301 Clinton St., Defiance; (419) 782-0739; www.visitdefianceohio.com.

Restaurants

Kissner's Restaurant: 524 Clinton St., Defiance; (419) 782-1116. Kissner's is included in the tour of historical landmarks in Defiance. The interior has changed very little since the restaurant opened in 1929. The gleaming mahogany-and-cherry bar is complemented by a high tin ceiling. Casual, good food.

Evansport Carryout: 1582 Evansport Rd., Defiance; (419) 428-4100. Pizzas, sandwiches, salads. It's on the route.

Eric's All American Ice Cream Factory: 1830 East Second St., Defiance; (419) 770-2422.

Accommodations

The Inn on Third Street: 325 West Third St., Defiance; (419) 438-8053.

Bike Shops

"R" Bike Shop: 520 Clinton Street, Defiance; (419) 782-6756.

Restrooms

Start/finish: Port-O-Let at Oxbow Lake State Wildlife Area.
Mile 10.2: Evansport Carryout.

Maps

DeLorme: Ohio Atlas & Gazetteer: Pages 28, 29.

18 Harrison Lake Cruise

In this part of Ohio in mid- to late summer, you can get dizzy watching the fields of corn or beans sway in the breeze; the fields are endless. The route journeys past farmland to Goll Woods State Nature Preserve, one of the finest examples remaining of the Great Black Swamp forest, and traverses Lockport Covered Bridge.

Start: Harrison Lake State Park beach near Archbold.
Length: 39.6 miles, or 47.9 miles with the optional side-trip ride to Wauseon.

Terrain: Mostly flat.
Traffic and hazards: Mostly light traffic, but the cars go fast. There's heavier traffic in and around Wauseon.

Getting there: The park office address is 26246 Harrison Lake Road, Fayette. The ride begins at the beach. From I-80/I-90/Ohio Turnpike, take exit 25 to SR 66 and go north for just over 3 miles. Turn left onto CR M and in about 2 miles turn right onto CR 26. The beach entrance is a short distance on the left. Or from US 127 go south on CR 26 for about 2 miles and turn right to the beach.

The Ride

As you bike along these northwestern roads, you begin to wonder, where are all the people? Northwestern Ohio is one of the most sparsely populated regions of the state mostly because it was all underwater at one time. Lake Erie was much bigger than it is today and covered much of the land. As it receded, the area that was once underwater reverted to swamplands. Because of the color of the soil and the dark shade beneath the giant trees, the area, 120 miles long and 30 to 40 miles wide, was known as the Great Black Swamp. Travel was difficult and the mosquitoes were horrendous. Settlers avoided the area.

Fulton County was also the site of the 1835 "Toledo War." The old state line of Michigan runs through the central part of the county near Seward. Ohio and Michigan battled for years over ownership rights; sometimes, because the area was so heavily forested, the two militias could not even find each other to do battle. After the war, which Ohio won, the state line was moved north 7 miles.

Harrison Lake State Park, the staging area for this ride, is popular for swimming, fishing, camping, and canoeing. The route leaves from the beach parking lot. From there ride back out to CR 26 and turn left. There is some traffic on CR N, which simmers down after crossing SR 66. Traveling along CR N, you'll notice Fulton Soil and Water Conservation District signs indicating a wetlands and flash flood warnings. Wetlands have been built in low-lying areas for flood control.

In Tedrow turn left onto Walters Avenue by the granary. Cross Spring Street and turn right onto Main Street. Cross CR J and the one-lane bridge before turning left onto CR HJ.

Lockport Covered Bridge

Enjoy the great view when you cross over the Ohio Turnpike. When you come to CR F, you can go right to continue the main route or go left for the Wauseon side-trip option. One reason to go into Wauseon is that it is the only place to find food (there are restaurants on Shoop Avenue) and restrooms, but there may be another reason: You'll be riding on the Northwestern Ohio Rails-to-Trails Bikeway in Wauseon. That bikeway is slated to eventually continue west and cross CR F about midway between Wauseon and Goll Woods. You could ride into Wauseon and have a pleasant jaunt on the bike route to CR F, then turn left and continue the route. Whether you take the option or not, you will eventually be riding west on CR F. The Homestead Ice Cream Shop is on the right just before SR 66.

The shady ride through Goll Woods offers a pleasant respite on a hot day. Some of the ancient oak trees in the preserve are more than 4 feet in diameter. In spring the wildflowers are magnificent.

Enter Williams County and go across the award-winning Lockport Covered Bridge. It was built in 1999 and replaced an old steel truss bridge. That steel truss bridge had replaced a covered bridge built in 1860. The more things change, the more they stay the same.

Follow CR 21N for several miles, passing the 1850 Quaker Meeting House. Come back into Fulton County, make a couple of turns, and return to the beach.

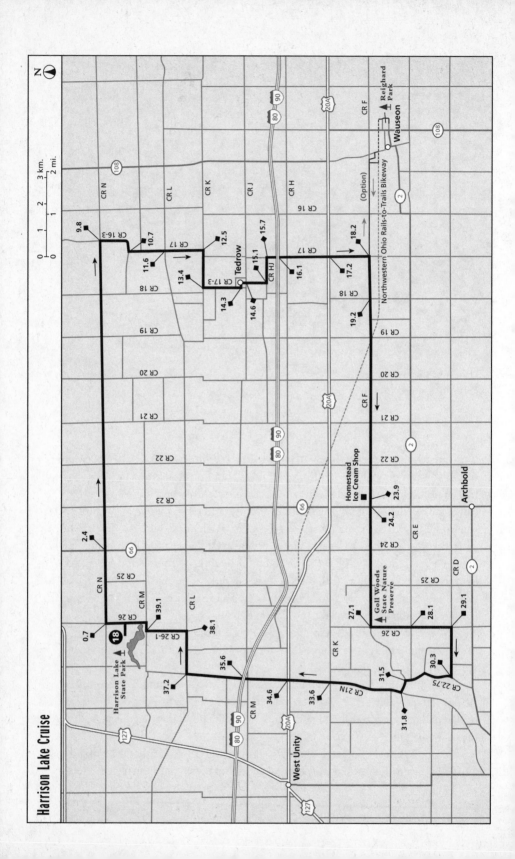

Harrison Lake Cruise

Miles and Directions

0.0 Exit the parking lot and turn left onto CR 26.

0.7 Turn right onto CR N.

2.4 Cross SR 66. At close to 1-mile intervals, cross CR 23, CR 22, CR 21, CR 20, CR 19, and CR 18.

9.8 Go right onto CR 16-3.

10.7 Take a left onto CR 17 when CR MN continues straight.

11.6 Cross CR L.

12.5 At the T turn right onto CR K.

12.7 Continue straight when CR 17 turns left.

13.4 Turn left onto CR 17-3.

14.2 Take a tour through Tedrow.

14.3 Turn left onto Walters Avenue.

14.4 Cross Spring Street.

14.5 Turn right onto Main Street.

14.6 Cross CR J and the one-lane bridge.

15.1 At the T turn left onto CR HJ.

15.7 Go right onto CR 17.

16.1 Cross I-80/I-90 and then CR H.

17.2 Cross US 20A.

18.2 Turn right onto CR F. **Side-trip:** Take a ride into Wauseon. Follow the Northwestern Ohio Rails-to-Trails Bikeway to a restroom and refreshments, and then return to the route. Follow the directions below.

19.2 Cross CR 18. At close to 1-mile intervals, also cross CR 19, CR 20, CR 21, and CR 22.

23.9 Pass the Homestead Ice Cream Shop, which has seasonal hours.

24.2 Cross SR 66/CR 23 and in 1-mile intervals CR 24 and CR 25.

27.1 Turn left onto CR 26 and enter Goll Woods State Nature Preserve.

28.1 Cross CR E.

29.1 Turn right onto CR D. In a mile enter Williams County and the road becomes CR H.

30.3 The road T's into CR 22.75; turn right.

31.3 Bear left on CR 22.75 when CR H-75 goes right.

31.5 At the T go left onto CR I-25. You can see Lockport Covered Bridge up ahead.

31.7 Cross the covered bridge.

31.8 Turn right onto CR 21N.

33.6 Cross CR K.

34.6 Cross US 20A.

35.6 Cross CR M and I-80/I-90.

36.7 Enter Fulton County and the road becomes CR 27-1.

37.2 Turn right onto CR L.

38.1 Take a left onto CR 26-1.

39.1 Go right onto CR M by the maintenance building.

39.3 Turn left onto CR 26, heading toward the beach.

39.6 Hang a left into the parking lot.

Side-trip

0.0 Turn left onto CR F.

1.0 Cross CR 16.

1.8 At the Wauseon city limits, the road becomes Linfoot Street.

2.3 Turn right onto Zenobia Street.

2.5 At the dead end turn left onto Willow Street.

2.6 Turn right onto Ottokee Street.

2.7 Cross Hickory Street and turn left onto the bike path.

3.4 Carefully cross Shoop Avenue—it is busy. You'll find markets, fast-food restaurants, and pizza places to the left.

3.6 At the stop sign exit the trail and go right onto Glenwood Street. Wauseon High School is just ahead on the left.

3.8 Curve to the left around Reighard Park (the high school stadium will be to your left).

3.9 Turn right onto Oak Street. The restroom is in the park, in the block building by the swings. Retrace your route to the bike trail and follow it to Krieger Street.

5.5 Exit the bike trail and turn right onto Krieger Street.

6.0 Turn left onto Linfoot Street.

8.3 Resume the route at mile 18.2 by turning left onto CR F.

Local Information

Archbold Chamber of Commerce: 300 North Defiance St., Archbold; (419) 445-2222; www.archbold.com.

Attractions

Sauder Village: 22611 SR 2, Archbold; (800) 590-9755; www.saudervillage.org. The Sauder Village, Farm and Craft Village is a colorful reminder of life in early Ohio. Visit an 1860s home and barnyard, the Craft Village where artisans display their skills, and a museum displaying antique tools and equipment. There are also retail shops where handcrafted items can be purchased.

Restaurants

The Barn Restaurant: Sauder Village, 22611 SR 2, Archbold; (800) 590-9755. Delicious home-style food. They have a generous salad bar but don't miss the broasted chicken. Buffet, family style, and full menu.

Stella Blue Restaurant: 301 North Defiance St., Archbold; (419) 445-2022. A casual restaurant with mouth-watering entrees, great desserts, and locally roasted coffees. It has a full bar.

Accommodations

Sauder Heritage Inn: 22611 SR 2, Archbold; (800) 590-9755; www.saudervillage.org.

Bike Shops

Wheel Shop: 140 North Main St., Bryan; (419) 633-1177.

Restrooms

Start/finish: Harrison Lake State Park at the beach.

Mile 3.9: On the optional ride, at Reighard Park in Wauseon.

Maps

DeLorme: Ohio Atlas & Gazetteer: Page 19.

19 Wabash Cannonball Ramble

This ride goes west on the North Fork of the Wabash Cannonball Trail and returns east on the South Fork, with a short road ride in between. Beginning at the Fallen Timbers Memorial, the route travels through the Oak Openings region, which The Nature Conservancy lists as one of the 200 "Last Great Places on Earth" because of its great diversity.

Start: Fallen Timbers Memorial near Maumee.
Length: 27.2 miles.
Terrain: Flat and flatter.

Traffic and hazards: Most of the ride is on the bike path. Fulton Lucas Road has very light traffic.

Getting there: Take exit 4 from US 23/I-475 to US 24 West. Exit US 24 at Jerome Road and follow the signs to Fallen Timbers State Memorial on Fallen Timbers Lane (on the opposite side of the highway from Fallen Timbers Mall). Park at the Fallen Timbers Memorial.

The Ride

The Wabash Cannonball rails-to-trails project, at 64 miles, is one of the longest in the state, although it is not all paved. The trail comprises two rail lines that converge at North Jerome Road. This ride goes west on the North Fork to where the pavement ends, then travels south on Fulton Lucas Road—eventually there will be a connector between the two trails here—and returns on the South Fork of the bike path. The North Fork travels through a section of the Oak Openings Preserve, named from the surrounding Oak Openings region, which is twenty-three times larger than the preserve. Oak Openings is home to Ohio's only moving sand dunes and more rare species than any other area in Ohio. Butterflies, birds, spring wildflowers, and prairie flowers are magnificent.

The ride begins near the site of the 1794 Battle of Fallen Timbers. This small park, overlooking the Maumee River floodplain, contains a monument honoring the combatants in the battle that decided the future of the Old Northwest Territory: Major General "Mad" Anthony Wayne, the Native Americans, and the Kentucky Militia. The monument was located there because at the time conventional wisdom said the battle was fought in the floodplain. In 1995 a local archaeologist, who did not accept conventional wisdom, began excavating in another area. He found artifacts clearly showing the area he was exploring to be the actual site of the battle. You'll ride past that site, the Fairfield Timbers Battlefield Project Center, a National Historic Site, on Jerome Road.

Start out by crossing the bicycle/pedestrian bridge over US 24. This trail leads to Jerome Road. From there turn left onto the rail-trail going west.

You may meet uniformed members of Volunteer Trail Patrol. This is a group of about 150 people who volunteer in all of the Toledo Metroparks. They must volunteer

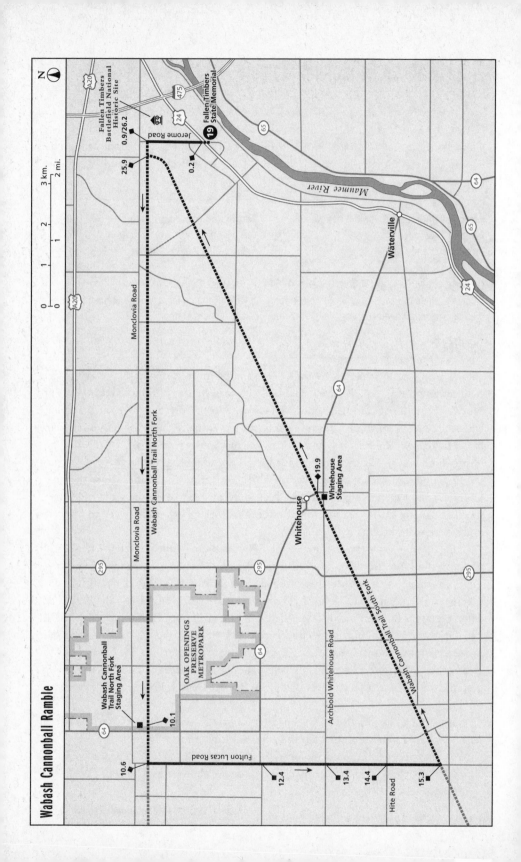

Wabash Cannonball Ramble

Battle of Fallen Timbers Monument

fifty hours a year; they are trained and certified in CPR and how to handle problems on the trail. The volunteers travel in pairs, carry cell phones, and provide maps and other park information.

The trail starts out in the 'burbs but shortly comes into picturesque scenery. You will pass through farm fields, forests, and prairie. We biked in late summer and enjoyed the blooms of joe-pye weed, jewelweed, and other prairie plants.

The North Fork staging area is at mile 10.1 on the route by the Waterville Swanton Road crossing. In 0.5 mile the paved section of trail ends. Exit the trail onto Fulton Lucas Road. In just under 5 miles turn left onto the South Fork section and ride east. The Whitehouse staging area is in Whitehouse at mile 19.9 by the Providence Street crossing. Go left on Providence and in less than 0.5 mile you'll come to Mikey P's and several other restaurants. The Generals Ice Cream shop is on the other side of Providence.

From there, except for a few bends in the road, it's a straight shot back to Jerome Street, across the bridge, and to the memorial. A path in Fallen Timbers Memorial goes down to the floodplain.

Miles and Directions

0.0   Exit the parking lot at the Fallen Timbers Memorial and take the bike/pedestrian bridge across Jerome Street.

0.2   When the bike route ends, continue on North Jerome Road.

0.9   Turn left onto the Wabash Cannonball Trail North Fork.

10.1   Reach the Wabash Cannonball Trail North Fork staging area. There are restrooms here.

10.6   Exit the trail and turn left onto Fulton Lucas Road.

12.4   Cross Sherman White Road (CR D in Fulton County).

13.4   Cross Archbold Whitehouse Road (CR C in Fulton County).

14.4   Cross Hite Road.

15.3   Turn left onto the Wabash Cannonball Trail South Fork.

19.9   Reach the Whitehouse staging area. Cross Providence Street/SR 64; you can turn left here and ride a couple of blocks to Mikey P's Restaurant.

20.0   Pass Generals Ice Cream.

25.9   Turn right back onto the North Fork.

26.2   Turn right onto North Jerome Road.

27.2   Arrive back at the start.

Local Information

Perrysburg Convention and Visitors Bureau: 105 West Indiana Ave., Perrysburg; (419) 874-9147; www.visitperrysburg.com.

Attractions

The Butterfly House: 11455 Obee Rd., Whitehouse; (419) 877-2733; www.butterfly-house .com. Live butterflies flutter from flower to flower.
National Center for Nature Photography: Secor Metropark, 10001 West Central Ave., Berkey; (419) 407-9757; www.naturephotocenter.com.
Metroparks Toledo: In Wildwood Preserve, 5100 West Central Rd., Toledo; (419) 407-9700; www .metroparkstoledo.com.

Restaurants

Mikey P's: 6670 Providence St., Whitehouse; (419) 877-0101. This is a family restaurant with good food just a short distance off the bike path. Breakfast, lunch, and dinner are served.

Accommodations

The Guest House: 122 West Indiana Ave., Perrysburg; (419) 874-9223; www.sydanddianes.com. An 1860s townhouse with beautiful gardens.

Bike Shops

Bike Works: 5631 Alexis Rd., Sylvania; (419) 882-0800; www.thebikeworks.com.
Cycle Werks: 116 East William St., Maumee; (419) 893-9375; www.shopcyclewerks.com.
The Bike Route: 5201 Monroe St., Toledo; (419) 885-3030; www.bikeroute.biz.

Restrooms

Start/finish: At the park.
Mile 10.1: North Fork staging area.
Mile 19.9: Town of Whitehouse.

Maps

DeLorme: Ohio Atlas & Gazetteer: Page 20.

20 Maumee River Challenge

Experience historic sites and enjoy great views of the Maumee River on this ride. See the reconstructed Fort Meigs, have a rural ride along Tontogany Creek, pay a quick visit to Bowling Green, enjoy Waterville with its canal history, and return along the riverside.

Start: Side Cut Metropark, Maumee.
Length: 40.2 miles with an option for a shorter 30.5-mile route.
Terrain: Flat to rolling.

Traffic and hazards: Heavy traffic for a short distance in Perrysburg and on SR 65. Waterville and Bowling Green have residential traffic. Many roads are quiet, one-lane roads with few cars.

Getting there: Take SR 23 to the Maumee/Waterville exit. Follow the Maumee exit ramp to US 24 East. Take US 24 east to Ford Street (look for the baseball diamond on the corner), turn right onto Ford, then turn right onto Broadway, which becomes River Road. Follow it into Side Cut Park's Silver Lake parking area. The address is 1025 River Road, Maumee.

The Ride

Side Cut Metropark is named for the former "side cut" extension of the Miami and Erie Canal that connected the main line of the canal with the city of Maumee. Three of the original limestone locks are preserved in the park.

This ride starts out in the city of Perrysburg—this is city riding, so you can ride on the sidewalk. From Conant Street stay right and get on the bike path to cross the Fort Meigs Memorial Bridge for the first of many great views of the Maumee. Turn right on SR 25/SR 65. Take a shortcut through the peaceful Fort Meigs Union Cemetery to avoid some traffic.

On SR 65 the route passes reconstructed Fort Meigs, a War of 1812 battlefield, where William Henry Harrison and his 1,200 men trumped the British and Indian siege of Fort Meigs, a supply outpost. It was a major victory for the Americans.

Traffic is fairly heavy on SR 65, but drivers are accustomed to and mostly respectful of bicyclists. Enjoy the gorgeous homes and occasional glimpses of the river along SR 65. You can see the remains of the Lima and Toledo Traction Company's bridge, built in 1907. At the time it was the longest steel-reinforced concrete bridge in the world. Look for the Roche de Boeuf (buffalo rock), also called Roche de Bout (rock of the river), an outcropping of rock with many stories surrounding it. It is said that Chiefs Little Turtle, Blue Jacket, and Tarhe the Crane met at the rock to plot strategy against the U.S. armies. Many people were outraged when the rock was partially destroyed to make room for one of the bridge piers. Although the bridge is crumbling now, the rock remains. Waterville celebrates a Roche de Boeuf Festival every year, while Toledo Metroparks named a shelter house Roche de Bout in its honor. A rock by any other name . . .

Roche de Bout: just visible at the bridge pier

Turn off the highway and into the country for a peaceful ride—part of it along the creek—to Tontogany. Take a break at the Tontogany Village/Custer Homestead Centennial Park. A historical marker there notes that it is near the site of the former Custer homestead of Emanuel and Maria Custer and was the boyhood home of Captain Tom Custer, two-time recipient of the Congressional Medal of Honor and brother of General George Armstrong Custer. They both died at the 1876 Battle of the Little Bighorn.

Continue on through more rural countryside. Cross Hull Prairie Road and ride into the industrial edge of Bowling Green. There are plenty of places to stop for refreshments. Return to farm country for the ride north on Hull Prairie.

Cross over the Maumee and into Waterville. That town's history is linked to the canal—the first boat passed through in 1843 on its way to Fort Wayne. In 1845 the U.S. government transported soldiers from Toledo to Cincinnati for the Mexican War, a trip that took fifty-six hours.

On the way back along the river, you'll see the flat rocks that extend into the river, which are known as the Maumee River Ledges. They are a rare form of habitat called an alvar, a limestone plain with little or no soil and scant vegetation.

Come into Side Cut Park by Jerome Road. Stay on River Road and return to the parking lot.

Miles and Directions

0.0 Exit the Side Cut Metropark going east on Broadway Street.

0.5 Cross Ford Street and, in short order, Duane, Rosamund, Cass, and Allen Streets.

1.0 Turn right onto Conant Street just past Saint Joseph's Church.

1.1 Cross Harrison Avenue and stay right to get on the bike path to cross the Fort Meigs Memorial Bridge.

1.8 Turn right onto West Boundary Street/SR 25 (some maps show this as part of SR 65) and follow the bike path.

2.0 Turn right into the Fort Meigs Union Cemetery at the last gate before SR 65 (aka West River Road).

2.3 Turn left toward SR 65. After 0.02 mile, exit the cemetery and go right on SR 65.

2.8 Arrive at Fort Meigs State Memorial Park.

4.3 Cross I-475.

7.8 Continue straight on SR 64/SR 65.

8.4 Stay right on SR 65 when SR 64 goes left.

11.3 Turn left onto SR 582.

11.6 Continue straight on Tontogany Creek Road when SR 582 goes left.

12.2 Jog across Robinson Road.

13.2 Cross over Cross Creek Road.

14.3 Go left onto North Street in Tontogany.

14.5 Come to Custer Homestead Centennial Park, where there is a restroom.

14.6 Turn left onto Tontogany Road and cross the bridge.

14.7 Turn right onto Hannah Road.

17.0 Cross Haskins Road/SR 64.

18.0 Cross Hull Prairie Road. **Option:** For a shorter 30.5-mile loop, turn left onto Hull Prairie and follow the route below from mile 27.7.

18.5 Turn right onto Brim Road.

20.0 Turn left onto West Newton Road.

20.7 Cross North Main Street/SR 25; there are restaurants and restrooms here in Bowling Green.

22.3 Take a left onto Barr Road.

23.1 Turn left at the T onto Nims Road.

23.6 Hang a right onto Mercer Road.

24.3 Go left onto Simonds Road.

24.6 Turn right onto Hilt Road.

25.1 The road T's into Sugar Ridge Road; go left.

26.0 Turn left onto North Dixie Highway/SR 25.

26.3 Turn right onto Union Hill Road.

26.9 The road bends left and becomes Brim Road.

27.2 Continue straight on Hannah Road when Brim goes left.

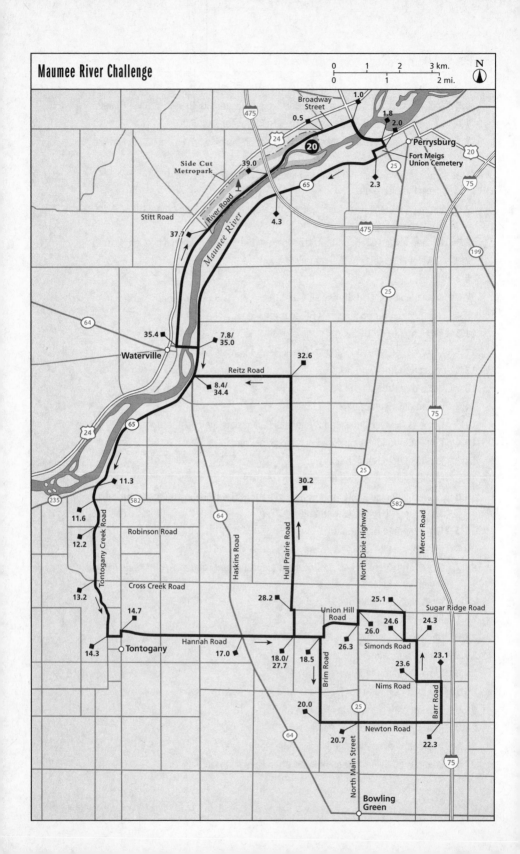

Maumee River Challenge

0   1   2   3 km.
0   1   2 mi.

N

Broadway Street
1.0
0.5
1.8
2.0
20
Perrysburg
Fort Meigs
Union Cemetery
2.3
39.0
Side Cut Metropark
65
4.3
Stitt Road
37.7
River Road
Maumee River
475
199
35.4
64
Waterville
7.8/ 35.0
32.6
Reitz Road
8.4/ 34.4
25
75
30.2
11.3
582
235
11.6
Robinson Road
64
12.2
Tontogany Creek Road
Haskins Road
Hull Prairie Road
North Dixie Highway
582
Mercer Road
28.2
25.1
Sugar Ridge Road
Cross Creek Road
13.2
Union Hill Road
24.6
24.3
14.7
26.0
Simonds Road
23.6
23.1
14.3
Tontogany
Hannah Road
17.0
26.3
Brim Road
Nims Road
Barr Road
18.0/ 27.7
18.5
20.0
25
20.7
Newton Road
22.3
64
North Main Street
75
Bowling Green

27.7	Turn right onto Hull Prairie Road.
28.2	Bear left, still on Hull Prairie, when Self Road goes right.
30.2	Cross Middleton Pike/SR 582.
32.6	Turn left onto Reitz Road.
34.4	At the T turn right onto River Road/SR 64/SR 65.
35.0	Turn left onto SR 64 north toward Waterville.
35.2	Cross the Maumee State Scenic River.
35.4	Turn right onto North River Road.
37.7	Stay right on River Road when Stitt Road goes left.
38.3	Enter Side Cut Metropark and pass Jerome Road—continue straight on River Road.
39.0	Go under I-475.
40.2	Turn left into the parking lot.

Local Information

Perrysburg Convention and Visitors Bureau: 105 West Indiana Ave., Perrysburg; (419) 874-9147; www.visitperrysburg.com.

Attractions

National Center for Nature Photography: Secor Metropark, 10001 West Central Ave., Berkey; (419) 407-9757; www.naturephotocenter.com.

Metroparks Toledo: In Wildwood Preserve, 5100 West Central Rd., Toledo; (419) 407-9700; www.metroparkstoledo.com.

Restaurants

Stella's Restaurant and Bar: 104 Louisiana Ave., Perrysburg; (419) 873-8360; www.stellas restaurantandbar.com.

Accommodations

The Guest House: 122 West Indiana Ave., Perrysburg; (419) 874-9223; www.sydanddianes.com. An 1860s townhouse with beautiful gardens.

Bike Shops

Bike Works: 5631 Alexis Rd., Sylvania; (419) 882-0800; www.thebikeworks.com.

Cycle Werks: 116 East William St., Maumee; (419) 893-9375. Also at 2485 South Main St., Bowling Green; (419) 352-9375; www.shopcycle werks.com.

The Bike Route: 5201 Monroe St., Toledo; (419) 885-3030; www.bikeroute.biz.

Restrooms

Start/finish: At the park.

Mile 14.5: Custer Homestead Centennial Park in Tontogany.

Mile 20.7: Fast-food restaurants and shops in Bowling Green (this is a breakfast ride for the Toledo Area Bicyclists, and they always eat at Burger King).

Maps

DeLorme: Ohio Atlas & Gazetteer: Page 20.

21 Rawson Ramble

What's not to like about this ride to Rawson? It's a relaxing route through picturesque Ohio land. Findlay is flat and rural—biking country. There's corn, beans, and wheat as far as the eye can see, and that's almost to Kansas, Dorothy.

Start: Liberty-Benton Middle School near Findlay.
Length: 25.0 miles.

Terrain: Flat.
Traffic and hazards: Traffic is light, although it may be fast-moving.

Getting there: Take exit 157 from I-75. Travel west on SR 12 for 1.8 miles. The school is on the right at 9050 SR 12.

The Ride

This bike ride travels from Liberty-Benton Middle School out to the village of Rawson through typical northwest Ohio farmland; Hancock County (named after John Hancock, first signer of the Declaration of Independence) has 1,150 farms—300,000 acres of farmland. The farms are mostly typical Ohio—corn, beans, and wheat. Two ethanol plants recently opened in the region.

You have to notice the way the roads in this part of the state are laid out in a sections. Early surveyors experimented with several survey systems. This northwest section of Ohio was about the last of the experiment, and by then the surveyors had pretty much settled on the sectionalized or grid system on their way west. It also helps that the land is flat; surveyors didn't have to go through low areas to avoid hills as they would have to do in southeastern Ohio. You'll notice that most of the roads that do any meandering are going alongside a creek.

To get out on the grid and start this ride, exit the parking lot on the west side of the school; if you're facing the building, that's to your left. In just over a half mile, you will turn onto TR 89. How's this for great biking? Smooth roads, no hills, few cars (although they may go fast on these country roads).

You'll be on TR 130 for a while, crossing several roads. After a couple of T turns, you're on CR 54. Most northwestern Ohio roads travel a square-mile grid; CR 54 will get your attention as it snakes around alongside Ottawa Creek.

You will turn onto CR 12, and it continues curving, then takes the plunge right across the creek and gets back to the grid. Follow CR 12 into Rawson, home of the 1968 state champion football team. Rawson is a pleasant little village with a church, a post office, a railroad crossing (Doctor LaQuinta Rawson was the first president of that railroad, and the town is named in his honor), and a very pleasant park.

The route crosses up and over I-75. CR 26 goes right on the way up—don't go that way. On the way down take CR 26 to the left. You will ride through the Hancock County Habitat Restoration area, which is mostly hunting ground.

Holding up the rain

Turn left onto CR 9 and then CR 84, then turn right onto TR 139. After bending to the right and then left (for no apparent reason, because it goes right across the streamlet called Aurand Run), you'll see the school up ahead. Easy enough, wasn't it?

Miles and Directions

0.0 Exit the school parking lot and turn right (north) onto CR 139.

0.8 Turn left onto TR 89.

2.4 Go left onto TR 130.

3.7 Cross CR 86.

4.1 Cross SR 12.

5.2 Cross CR 84.

6.2 Turn right at the T onto TR 79.

7.9 Turn left onto CR 54.

9.3 Turn left onto CR 12.

9.5 Bear left, staying on CR 12 when CR 54 goes right.

10.6 Enter Rawson. CR 12 becomes Main Street. Continue straight through Rawson, crossing Church, Vance, Henderson, and High Streets (not shown on map).

11.4 There are restrooms at the Rawson Community Park.

11.6 Cross CR 37.

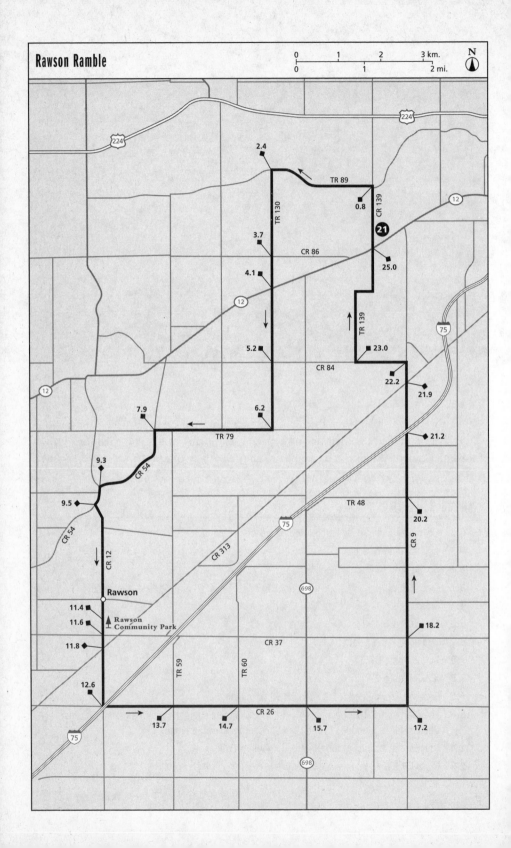

Rawson Ramble

11.8 Cross CR 313.

12.5 Continue straight when CR 26 goes to the right.

12.6 Ride up the rise and over I-75. Just past I-75 turn left onto CR 26.

13.7 Cross TR 59.

14.7 Cross TR 60.

15.7 Cross SR 698.

17.2 Turn left onto CR 9.

18.2 Cross CR 37.

20.2 Cross TR 48.

21.2 Ride over I-75.

21.9 Cross CR 313.

22.2 Turn left onto CR 84.

23.0 Turn right onto TR 139.

25.0 Cross SR 12 and return to the school.

Local Information

Findlay Hancock County Convention and Visitors Bureau: 123 East Main Cross St., Findlay; (419) 422-3315 or (800) 424-3315; www.visit findlay.com.

Local Events

Hancock Horizontal Hundred: Held in the Findlay area, this is one of the flattest rides in Ohio. It's a century ride, albeit with shorter options, put on by the Hancock Handlebars Bicycle Club. It happens in September. For information: (419) 422-0427; e-mail hancockhandlebars@woh.rr .com; www.hancockhandlebars.org.

Restaurants

The Tavern at the Inn: 200 East Main Cross St., Findlay; (419) 422-5682 or (800) 825-1455. Casual dining—great food, pleasing ambience.

Flag City Pizza: 2401 North Main St., Findlay; (419) 422-5949; www.flagcitypizza.com. Great local pizza.

Fort Findlay Coffee and Doughnut Shoppe: 1016 Tiffin Ave., Findlay; (419) 425-5550; www .fortfindlaycoffee.com. Founded in 2001, the shop has an in-house roasterie. It offers fifty-plus varieties of doughnuts, bagels, bagel sandwiches, muffins, and soups.

Dietsch Brothers Fine Chocolate and Ice Cream: 400 West Main Cross St., Findlay; (419) 422-4474; www.dietschs.com. Established in 1937, this is one of Findlay's landmark businesses.

Accommodations

The Findlay Inn: 200 East Main Cross St., Findlay; (419) 422-5682 or (800) 825-1455.

Bike Shops

Bicycle Shop: 125 West Sandusky St., Findlay; (419) 423-2729.

Restrooms

Mile 11.4: Rawson Community Park.

Maps

DeLorme: Ohio Atlas & Gazetteer: Page 30.

22 Findlay-to-Fostoria Cruise

This route travels between Flag City (Findlay) and Train City (Fostoria). But don't let that "city" word worry you. The excursion meanders mostly along quiet, scenic country roads. And forget your granny gear—flat is the word.

Start: Riverbend Park in Findlay.
Length: 31.3 miles.
Terrain: Flat.
Traffic and hazards: The area in and around Fostoria is busy, especially at the intersection of Independence Avenue and Findlay Street. Expect 0.5 mile of heavy traffic on SR 568 with no shoulder.

Getting there: From SR 568 just east of Findlay, go south onto TR 241 and across the bridge. In a stone's throw, when TR 241 T's into TR 208, turn left into Riverbend Park, 16618 TR 208, Findlay. In 0.3 mile turn left into the Oxbow Bend parking lot.

The Ride

On Flag Day, June 14, 1968, every house in the entire city of Findlay is said to have flown an American flag, earning the city the title of Flag City. John B. Cooke moved to Findlay in the mid-1960s and decided to make that happen. The Hancock County Chapter of the Sons of the American Revolution helped to buy 14,000 flags, and they were distributed by Boy Scouts, Girl Scouts, and Campfire Girls. This bit of trivia is included because you will see many signs alluding to this title and lots of flags flying along the route.

More trivia: The ride leaves from Riverbend Park along the Blanchard River, which was the Old Mill Stream in the song written in 1908 by Hancock County resident Tell Taylor.

Leave the parking lot and turn left onto TR 208, which soon becomes TR 207. Continue straight on TR 207, which also goes off to the right. Follow TR 207 when it bends a hard left. The route wends its way through some of Hancock County's 300,000 acres of farmland—agriculture is one of the leading growth industries in the county.

Traffic picks up on CR 23, which becomes Independence Avenue as you approach Fostoria. Pass Lake Mosier. The intersection of Independence and Findlay Street is a busy one. Just head toward the grain silos on Findlay unless you want to take a hard right onto Lytle Street for ice cream.

Fostoria is known for glassware and trains. Once the home of thirteen different glass plants, from 1887 through 1920 it was the heart of the glassware industry in the United States. Two local excavation companies harvested the rich limestone quarries in the area.

Turning left onto South Vine Street, go slowly over the crisscrossing railroad tracks. Two railroads service the city with three high-volume main lines. A hundred

Flag City

or more trains may pass through the city on any given day. Rail fans from all over come to watch the activity. From South Vine Street the route goes left onto West Tiffin Street. You could continue straight on South Vine for about 4 blocks to City Park on the left—it has restrooms. From there you can ride to the bike path that encircles the two reservoirs. Exit the city on the Tiffin Street Overpass, and you'll have a great view of the tracks and an opportunity for train photos—the overpass was constructed with that in mind. You will also overlook the reservoirs.

Soon you're back in the country for the return to the park. Turn right onto SR 568 for a brief ride in the traffic before going left onto TR 241 to return to the park over the scenic old bridge. Go left onto TR 208 and left back into the parking lot.

Before leaving, it is worth climbing the steps for a look at the Findlay Reservoirs, the city's water source; Reservoirs 1 and 2 are adjacent to one another. Reservoir 2 is the largest aboveground reservoir in the state, with a capacity of six billion gallons—enough to supply the city for two years in case of a drought.

Miles and Directions

0.0   From the parking lot turn left onto TR 208.

0.1   TR 208 runs into TR 207, which turns right and continues straight. Ride straight ahead on TR 207.

2.6   Cross SR 568.

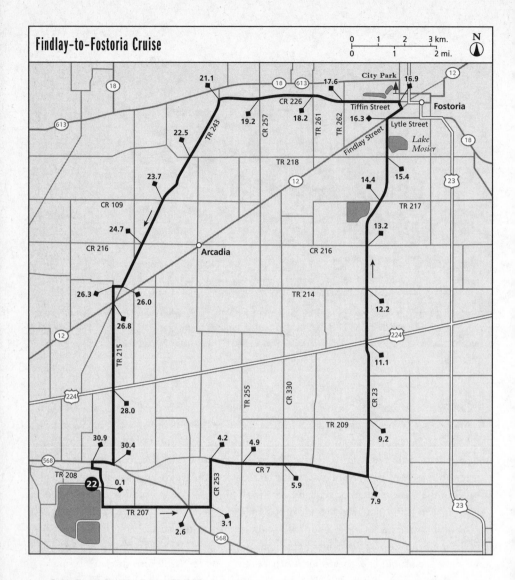

Findlay-to-Fostoria Cruise

3.1 Turn left at the T onto CR 253.

4.2 Turn right onto CR 7.

4.9 Continue by bearing slightly to the right on CR 7 when TR 255 goes left.

5.9 Cross CR 330.

7.9 Turn left onto CR 23.

9.2 Cross TR 209.

11.1 Cross US 224.

12.2 Cross TR 214.

13.2 Cross CR 216.

14.4 Cross TR 217.

15.4 When you cross TR 218, CR 23 becomes Independence Avenue. Lake Mosier is ahead on the right.

16.3 Take a slight right onto Findlay Street, toward the grain bins. **Side-trip:** Make a hard right onto Lytle Street and follow less than a half mile to JB Twisters Ice Cream & Things (no restrooms). Return to Findlay Street to continue the route.

16.5 Turn left onto South Vine Street. Ride slowly over the crisscrossed railroad tracks; this is Train City.

16.9 Turn left onto West Tiffin Street. Follow it out of town and up and over the Tiffin Street Overpass. **Side-trip:** Don't turn onto Tiffin Street—continue 4 blocks past Tiffin straight ahead on South Vine Street. City Park, on the left, has restrooms. You can also find access to the bike path loops around the reservoirs. Return to Tiffin Street and turn right to continue the route.

17.2 West Tiffin Street becomes CR 226.

17.6 Cross TR 262.

18.2 Cross TR 261.

19.2 Cross CR 257.

21.1 Turn left at the T onto TR 243.

22.5 Cross TR 218.

23.7 Cross CR 109.

24.7 Cross CR 216.

26.0 Go right onto TR 143.

26.3 Turn left onto TR 215.

26.8 Cross SR 12.

28.0 Cross US 224.

30.4 Hang a right onto SR 568—if you hit it at rush hour, you might want to walk your bike on the grass.

30.9 Turn left onto TR 241, reenter Riverbend Park, and cross the 1895 bridge.

31.0 Turn left at the T onto TR 208.

31.3 Turn left into the Oxbow Bend parking lot.

Local Information

Findlay Hancock County Convention and Visitors Bureau: 123 East Main Cross St., Findlay; (419) 422-3315 or (800) 424-3315; www.visit findlay.com.

Events/Attractions

Hancock Horizontal Hundred: Held in the Findlay area, this is one of the flattest rides in Ohio. It's a century ride, albeit with shorter options, put on by the Hancock Handlebars Bicycle Club. It happens in September. For information: (419) 422-0427; e-mail hancockhandlebars@woh.rr .com; www.hancockhandlebars.org.

Fostoria Glass Heritage Museum: 109 North Main St.,Fostoria;(419)453-5077;www.fostoria glass.com.

LE & W Historic Train Depot: 128 West North St., Fostoria; (419) 435-1781; www.fostoriairon triangle.com.

Restaurants

The Tavern at the Inn: 200 East Main Cross St., Findlay; (419) 422-5682 or (800) 825-1455. Casual dining—great food, pleasing ambience.

Accommodations

The Findlay Inn: 200 East Main Cross St., Findlay; (419) 422-5682 or (800) 825-1455.

Triple T Bed and Breakfast: 6717 TR 515, Findlay; (419) 424-1417 or (877) 424-1418; www.tripletbnb.com. A uniquely quiet lodging experience with horseback trail riding. It's on the bike route.

Bike Shops

Bicycle Shop: 125 West Sandusky St., Findlay; (419) 423-2729.

Bunky's Bike Emporium: 626 North Countyline St., Fostoria; (419) 435-8492.

Restrooms

Start/finish: Riverbend Park.

Mile 16.9: City Park on South Vine in Fostoria.

Maps

DeLorme: Ohio Atlas & Gazetteer: Page 30.

23 Logan County Cruise

Campbell Hill, 2 miles east of Bellefontaine, at 1,549 feet above sea level, is the highest point in Ohio. This ride, however, sticks to the flatter areas of Logan County. Perhaps the "high point" of the route is McColly Covered Bridge crossing the Great Miami River.

Start: Southview Park in Bellefontaine.

Length: 30.4 miles.

Terrain: Flat to rolling with a couple of hills.

Traffic and hazards: Mostly light traffic; heavier getting out of Bellefontaine and on SR 117 in Huntsville.

Getting there: Take US 68 to Bellefontaine. Turn west onto Lake Avenue/CR 11. In less than a mile, the park will be on the left.

The Ride

Finding the highest point in the state in the nearly flat glaciated plains of western Ohio is a bit of an anomaly. Geologists explain that the region gets its hills from an outcrop of Devonian rock forming a rock island or outlier. Don't ask, because it gets even more complicated.

Maybe those hills provided a good outlook over the surrounding area—maybe not. But for some reason, in around 1777 the Shawnee war leader Blue Jacket built a settlement here known as Blue Jacket's Town. That town was destroyed in Logan's Raid, conducted by the Kentucky Militia in 1786 at the start of the Northwest Indian War. The expedition was led by Benjamin Logan, namesake of the county. Blue Jacket and his followers relocated northwest to the Maumee River.

Bellefontaine is the county seat. It was named after the French word for "beautiful spring" since several limestone springs once existed in the area. If you like trivia,

McColly Covered Bridge

here it is: In 1901, Bellefontaine became the first community in the United States to have a street paved with concrete, which had just been invented. Bellefontaine also has the world's shortest street, McKinley Street, which is about 20 feet long. Now on to the bike ride.

Experience town traffic for a couple of miles until you leave the city behind; be careful going under the narrow underpass at the start of the route. Soon the traffic quiets down. You'll pass a vineyard and ride through woods. At mile 6.9 it looks as if you're going to run smack into US 33, but the road you're riding on bends right and becomes CR 39. In Huntsville, Lims Street/SR 117 is busy but has a shoulder.

The next little community is Lewistown (named after another Shawnee leader, Captain John Lewis). It is a gathering of a few houses, a post office, and a church.

On CR 60 the route is near the Great Miami River; look for herons and egrets. Soon you will come to a scenic overlook of the McColly Covered Bridge. Built in 1876 for $3,103, it has undergone several renovations. The last was in 2000. The cost? $700,000!

On this part of the ride, you'll notice horse manure on the roads—you might see a horse and buggy; this is Amish country. The traffic will pick up, and the houses will get closer together as you return to Bellefontaine.

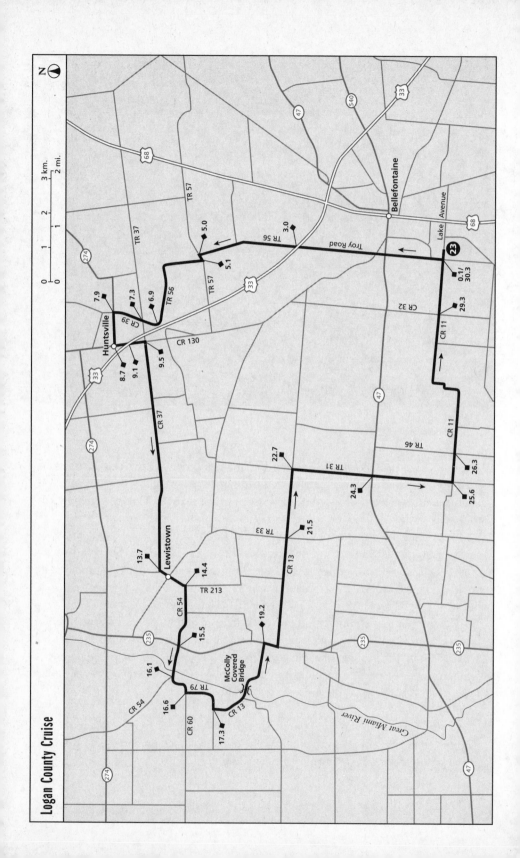

Logan County Cruise

Miles and Directions

0.0 Turn left from Southview Park onto Lake Avenue/CR 11.

0.1 Turn right onto Troy Road by the Belletech Corporation.

1.0 Cross Auburn Avenue and in short order Chillicothe, Sandusky, and Williams Avenues (not shown on map).

2.3 Troy Road becomes TR 56.

3.0 Pass under US 33.

5.0 Jog left onto TR 57.

5.1 Turn right, back to TR 56.

6.9 The road bends right and becomes CR 39.

7.3 Cross TR 37.

7.9 Take a left onto SR 274.

8.2 Arrive in Huntsville.

8.7 Turn left onto Lims Street/SR 117.

9.1 Cross over US 33.

9.2 Continue straight on CR 130.

9.5 Turn right onto CR 37.

13.7 At the T turn left onto CR 54 and ride through Lewistown. In less than a mile you will cross Williams, Main, and Elbridge Streets (not shown on map).

14.4 Bear right, remaining on CR 54 when TR 213 goes left.

15.5 Cross SR 235.

16.1 Turn left onto CR 60.

16.6 Cross the bridge and turn left onto TR 79.

17.3 Go left onto CR 13—loose gravel alert.

18.3 Ride through McColly Covered Bridge.

19.2 Jog right onto SR 235 and then left back to CR 13.

21.5 Cross TR 33.

22.7 Turn right onto TR 31.

24.3 Cross SR 47.

25.6 Take a left onto CR 11.

26.3 Cross TR 46.

29.3 Cross CR 32.

30.3 Cross Troy Road by Belletech.

30.4 Arrive back at the start.

Local Information

Logan County Convention and Tourist Bureau: 100 South Main St., Bellefontaine; (888) LOGAN-CO (564-2626); www.logancountyohio.com.

Attractions

Ohio Caverns: 2210 SR 245 East, West Liberty; (927) 465-4017; www.ohiocaverns.com. Known as "America's Most Colorful Caverns," the Ohio Caverns are open year-round and feature an exquisite display of stalactite and stalagmite formations.

Piatt Castles: 10051 Road 47, P.O. Box 497, West Liberty; (937) 465-2821; www.piatt castles.org. Listed on the National Register of Historic Places, Castle Mac-A-Cheek and Castle Mac-O-Chee were built in the late eighteenth century. The castles interpret over 200 years of history. They feature ornate woodwork, frescoed ceilings, antiques, and hands-on activities for children.

Restaurants

Vicario's Pizza and Pasta LLC: 825 North Main St., Bellefontaine; (937) 599-4511; www .vicariospizza.com. Since 1977; they have a varied menu, but pizza is what they're known for.

Homecoming Family Restaurant: 1330 North Main St., Bellefontaine; (937) 592-7961.

Accommodations

Whitmore House: 3985 SR 47 West, Bellefontaine; (937) 592-4290. A lavish, Victorian-style home offering an escape to simpler times. A full breakfast and evening snack are included in the stay.

Myeerah's Inn Bed and Breakfast: 2875 Sandusky St., Zanesfield; (937) 593-0000. This three-bedroom inn located in the quaint village of Zanesfield was once a stagecoach stop. It is furnished with Ohio antiques and features a hearty French country breakfast.

Bike Shops

Bob's Bike Shop: 11897 Sunrise Ave., Lakeview (near Indian Lake); (937) 843-6827; www.bobs bikeshop.net.

Restrooms

Start/finish: Southview Park.

Maps

DeLorme: Ohio Atlas & Gazetteer: Page 50.

24 Prospect Ramble

This is a loop ride attached to a popular out-and-back bicycle ride along the Scioto River. A man we met in Prospect said, "There's nothing out there but farmers and cows" when we asked him about traffic on the roads. He was right.

Start: Prospect Community Park in Prospect, which is near Marion.

Length: The entire route is 37.6 miles. The ride along the river is an out-and-back, so you could turn around at any time. The loop without the out-and-back is 17.0 miles.

Terrain: Mostly flat.

Traffic and hazards: Light except for 0.1-mile jogs on US 36 and SR 37.

Getting there: From US 23 take SR 47, also called Prospect Mount Vernon Road, west into Prospect, about 6 miles. Turn left onto fifth Street and follow it across Park Avenue and into the park.

The Ride

Blue chicory blooms were covered with yellow cabbage butterflies when we rode this route in late summer. Along River Road turkey vultures were sunning themselves on the metal barn roofs. The river was muddy from recent heavy rains.

After exiting the park, cross the railroad tracks and turn right onto High Street by the grain silos. You are immediately in farm country: fields of corn and beans and yes, cows.

Prospect Norton Road T's into a road with no road signs—turn right. Signage farther on indicates Almendinger Road, aka TR 129. When you cross into Delaware Township, the road becomes North Section Line Road/TR 8. Whatever you call it, the road is flat and smooth.

Hedley Road zigzags right and then left. As you approach the community of Radnor, there's a cemetery with a lychgate on the right. The lychgate was designed to commemorate early settlers of Radnor who emigrated from Wales. Traditional in England and Wales, lychgates are covered gateways used to shelter coffins until clergymen arrived for burial. The Radnor lychgate has two openings: a larger one designed for horse-drawn vehicles and a smaller one for mourners. Radnor has a post office, school, and museum, but we could not find a restroom. Cross SR 203 and pass the Radnor Elevator, with commodity prices written in marker on the door window.

When you come to River Road, by the beautiful farm, go left for the longer ride along the river or turn right for the shorter loop, which follows the river back to Prospect.

My favorite part of this ride was along the Scioto River; it is alongside the road for almost the entire out-and-back section. The upper Scioto begins in west-central Ohio and flows southeast to the confluence of the Olentangy River in Columbus. At

more than 231 miles in length, the Scioto is one of the longest rivers in the state. It eventually empties into the Ohio. Although the Scioto and its tributaries have been impacted by agriculture and urbanization, it is still beautiful.

The upper Scioto River watershed is rich in Native American history; the best-known group to reside in the area was the Mound Builders of the Hopewell culture. Also, the famous bicycle touring classic, the Tour of the Scioto River Valley, better known by its acronym, TOSRV, runs along the Scioto River valley between Columbus and Portsmouth.

On Klondike Road watch for the ball field on the left. That was our turnaround place. Traffic begins to get congested from this point on. Retrace the route back to the farm on River and Radnor Roads. Then continue straight on River Road for the return to Prospect. It changes to Gast Road in Prospect. Turn left onto SR 203 in Prospect, then turn right onto Walnut Street, which becomes Park Avenue.

Miles and Directions

0.0 Exit the park by turning right onto Park Avenue. Cross Sixth, Sugar, and Eighth Streets.

0.3 Turn right onto High Street by the green silos. The road becomes Prospect Norton Road out of town.

1.8 Cross Gooding Road.

2.8 Cross Smeltzer Road.

4.3 At the T turn right onto Almendinger Road/TR 129. (There is no street sign at the turn.)

4.8 Cross Norton Road. When you cross the county line, the road you're on becomes North Section Line Road/TR 8.

6.7 Turn right onto Price Road.

7.1 Go left on Hedley Road.

8.6 At the T go right onto Radnor Road.

9.2 Come into Radnor and pass the cemetery.

9.8 Cross SR 203.

11.7 Turn left onto River Road. **Option:** For the shorter loop ride, turn right onto River Road and rejoin the main route at mile 32.3.

16.2 Jog left onto SR 37, then turn right onto Hodges Road.

16.9 Turn right onto Warrensburg Road.

17.3 Go left onto Warren Road when Warrensburg goes right.

18.8 Jog left on Marysville Road/US 36 and then turn right onto Klondike Road.

22.1 On the left is the ball field turnaround—go back the way you came on Klondike.

25.3 Jog left on US 36, then turn right onto Warren Road.

26.9 Turn right onto Warrensburg Road.

27.3 Go left on Hodges Road.

◀ *Hedley Road scene*

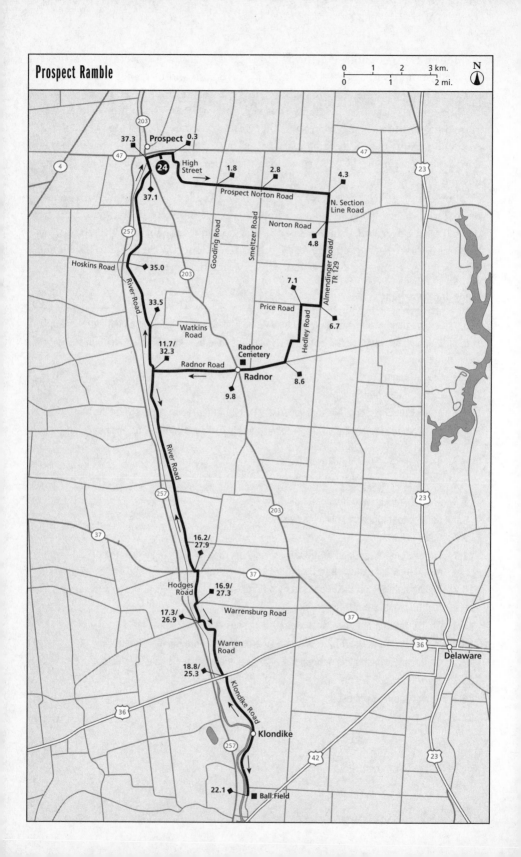

Prospect Ramble

0   1   2   3 km.
0   1   2 mi.

N

203

37.3 **Prospect** 0.3

47

4   **24**   High
                     Street

37.1

257

Hoskins Road   35.0

203

33.5

Watkins
Road

11.7/
32.3

Radnor
Cemetery

Radnor Road

Radnor

9.8

1.8   2.8   4.3

47   23

Prospect Norton Road

N. Section
Line Road

Norton Road

4.8

7.1

Price Road

6.7

Hedley Road

8.6

Gooding Road

Smeltzer Road

Almendinger Road/
TR 129

River Road

River Road

257

203

37

16.2/
27.9

Hodges   16.9/
Road   27.3

17.3/
26.9

Warrensburg Road

Warren
Road

18.8/
25.3

Klondike Road

36

257

Klondike

42   23

37

37

36

Delaware

22.1   ■ Ball Field

27.9 Jog left on SR 37, then turn right onto River Road.

32.3 Cross Radnor Road.

33.5 Bear left on River Road when Watkins Road goes right.

35.0 Cross Hoskins Road.

37.1 Turn left onto Prospect Delaware Road/SR 203, which becomes South Main Street.

37.3 Go right on Walnut Street.

37.4 Cross Elm, South East, and fourth Streets. Walnut becomes Park Avenue.

37.6 Reach the end.

Local Information

Marion County Convention and Visitors Bureau: 1713 Marion-Mt. Gilead Rd., Marion; (740) 389-9770 or (800) 371-6688; www.visitmarionohio.com.

Delaware County Convention and Visitors Bureau: 44 East Winter St., Delaware; (740) 368-4748 or (888) DEL-OHIO (335-6446); www.visitdelohio.com.

Restaurants

Pastimes Ice Cream: 115 North Elm St., Prospect; (740) 494-2450.

Pierces Pizza: 205 Battle St., Prospect; (740) 494-2817. This family-owned business has terrific pizza.

Accommodations

Lauer House Bed and Breakfast: 7366 Smeltzer Rd., Prospect; (740) 494-4398. A restored farmhouse on an eighty-acre family farm. A great place to get away from the fast pace; less than one car per hour passes the house.

Bike Shops

Rocky's Schwinn Cyclery: 239 East Church St., Marion; (740) 387-7079.

Breakaway Cycling: 17 West William St., Delaware; (740) 363-3232; www.breakawaycycling.com.

Restrooms

Start/finish: Prospect Community Park.

Maps

DeLorme: Ohio Atlas & Gazetteer: Page 41.

25 Alum Creek Challenge

Biking from Alum Creek State Park, this route winds down past Hoover Reservoir and through the funky little village of Galena, with its creeks and coffeehouses. It meanders through scenic farmland, past a geological kame, if you happen to care about things like that, and then travels back toward Alum Creek.

Start: Alum Creek State Park Mountain Bike Trails System, Phase 2 parking lot, near Delaware.
Length: 52.5 miles.
Terrain: The whole gamut: long flat stretches, pleasant rolling farmland, and some hills.
Traffic and hazards: Traffic around the park is moderate, with the "avoid rush hour" mantra. SR 37 is busy, but the distance is short. The route traverses many rural roads with light traffic; however, this is a rapidly expanding area and things change by the minute. Clover Valley Road had some very short stretches of gravel. The roads around Pagetown are rough, and the pavement stops for a short stretch on CR 15.

Getting there: From I-71 take exit 131 to US 36. Go west about a mile to Africa Road; turn left. The parking lot is a couple of miles down on the right at 2028 Africa Road.

The Ride

The starting point for this ride is a picnic area along Alum Creek Reservoir with a pleasing view of the lake. Layers of history are here. About 2,000 years ago the Adena culture lived in the area. Several mounds had to be excavated before the creek was dammed to form the reservoir and the valley was flooded. Long after the Adena peoples had left but long before the valley was flooded, the Delaware Indian tribe lived in several villages along the creek. They cultivated a 400-acre cornfield in the heart of present-day Delaware.

The Delaware Indians were gone by the time slaves, following the Underground Railroad, traveled the path along Alum Creek, which is now Sycamore Trail. The slaves (more than 40,000 passed through Ohio on their way to freedom) waded in the creek to elude pursuing trackers. This route travels out and back along Africa Road, which received its name from the fact that thirty slaves, freed in North Carolina, settled near friendly homeowners in this area.

The start of the ride is in suburbia. Turning from Africa Road onto Cheshire Road, you'll pass Cheshire Market, if you want to stop for supplies. Farther along, as you approach Galena on Dustin Road and just past the railway overpass, look on the right for the access to the Hoover Scenic Walkway. This unpaved 0.5-mile trail traverses an old railroad bridge over Little Walnut Creek.

Continuing on the bike route, there's a great view of the Hoover Reservoir from the bridge. Just across that bridge the first road to the right is Front Street. If you turn right (the bike route goes straight), an eighth of a mile down the road is a parking lot

Around the bend heading toward town

and access to the boardwalk. This lake and its mudflats are an important migratory bird stopover and are popular bird-watching spots.

Enter Galena, founded in 1809 by Gilbert Carpenter, who found the creeks perfect for establishing mills. It's now home to Jules Java and Grill and the Mudflats Bar and Grill, popular stopovers for bicyclists.

From Galena you can see the bridge over Big Walnut Creek; cross it and you're on Sunbury Road. After a couple of turns, you will be on SR 37 for a very short distance; there is heavy traffic and no shoulder. Soon you're back in a rural area where the route passes through fertile agricultural land and interesting glacial deposits.

From Clover Valley Road you can see the Ohio Bicentennial Barn on School Lane Road. Just past that road, if you look to the right, you'll see a kame, which is a hummocky mound of layered sand and gravel deposited by meltwater flowing over the ice and pouring its sediment load into the holes and crevasses along the glacial ice margin.

Ride through the little town of Condit, where we found a country store with refreshments and a restroom. On Condit Road you'll pass the Walnut Creek Missionary Baptist Church, which looks as if it has seen some history.

In Pagetown turn left onto CR 15—you have to look for the sign. It's an intersection with houses on three corners and a field on the fourth. A later road sign identified

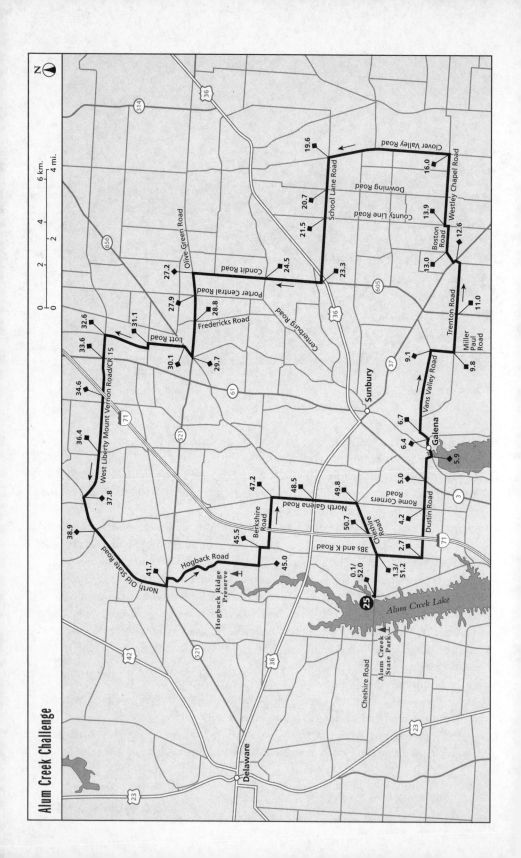

Alum Creek Challenge

this as Morrow West Liberty Road, but the maps call it West Liberty Mount Vernon Road. Whatever you call it, the road is rolling and rough. In fact, the pavement stops a short distance before the road T's into Morrow CR 24—no road sign.

Here the route gets a little hilly; cross back into Delaware County and the road signs reappear. On Hogback Road (you gotta love that name) you're riding a very scenic route along the creek. In about a mile and a half, you'll come to Hogback Ridge Preserve, but just before that, on the right, you can see four osprey nesting platforms along the creek. Osprey, a striking black-and-white bird sometimes called a fish hawk, nest on those platforms. The preserve, on the left, is thirty-seven acres of protected land with a 1.5-mile trail. The McCoy Nature Center in the preserve offers interpretive displays and a wildlife observation deck in addition to restrooms and water.

As you head back toward Alum Creek Park, you will again ride through suburbia with its accompanying traffic.

Miles and Directions

0.0 From the parking lot turn right onto Africa Road.

0.1 Turn left onto Cheshire Road.

1.3 Go right onto 3B's and K Road.

2.7 Turn left onto Dustin Road.

4.2 Cross Rome Corners Road.

5.0 Cross SR 3.

5.9 Turn left at the T onto Old 3C's Highway.

6.1 You're now on Columbus Street as you enter the village of Galena.

6.2 Cross the bridge and bear right onto Sunbury Road.

6.4 Turn left onto Vans Valley Road.

6.7 Bear right, still on Vans Valley, when Joe Walker Road continues straight.

9.1 Turn right onto Miller Paul Road.

9.8 Go left onto Trenton Road.

11.0 Cross SR 605.

12.6 Turn left onto SR 37.

12.7 Turn right onto Ross Road.

13.0 Turn right onto Boston Road.

13.8 Turn left onto County Line Road.

13.9 Turn right onto Westley Chapel Road.

16.0 Hang a left onto Clover Valley Road.

19.6 Turn left onto School Lane Road.

20.7 Cross Downing Road.

21.5 Cross County Line Road, where the road you're on becomes Meredith State Road.

23.0 Cross SR 3/US 36.

23.3 Turn right at the T onto Condit Road.

23.5 Cross North Old 3C's Highway.

24.5 Cross Centerburg Road.

27.2 Turn left at the T onto Olive Green Road.

27.9 Cross Porter Central Road.

28.8 Cross Fredericks Road.

29.7 Turn right onto SR 656.

30.1 Take a left onto Lott Road.

31.1 Jog left onto Chambers Road.

31.2 Turn right, back to Lott Road.

32.6 Turn left onto West Liberty Mount Vernon Road/CR 15.

33.6 Cross SR 61.

34.6 Cross I-71.

36.4 Continue on CR 15.

37.8 Turn left at the T onto Worthington New Haven Road/CR 24.

38.9 Cross Myers Ashley Road, and the road you're on becomes North Old State Road.

41.7 Turn left onto SR 521.

41.9 Turn right onto Hogback Road.

43.5 The Hogback Ridge Preserve has trails, water, and restrooms.

45.0 Turn left at the T onto Howard Road.

45.5 Go right onto 3B's and K Road.

45.8 Turn left onto Berkshire Road.

47.2 At the T turn right onto North Galena Road.

48.5 Cross SR 37/US 36.

49.8 Turn right onto Cheshire Road.

50.7 Cross over I-71.

51.2 Cross 3B's and K Road.

52.0 Turn right onto Africa Road.

52.5 Turn left back into the parking lot.

Local Information

Delaware County Convention and Visitors Bureau: 44 East Winter St., Delaware; (740) 368-4748 or (888) DEL-OHIO; www.visitdelohio.com.

Attractions

Alum Creek State Park: 3615 South Old State Rd., Delaware; (740) 548-4631; www.ohiostateparks.org.

Hoover Reservoir: Galena; (614) 645-3305. Offers boating, fishing, sailing, bird-watching.

Preservation Parks, Hogback Ridge Preserve: 2656 Hogback Rd., Sunbury; (740) 524-8600.

Restaurants

Old Bag of Nails: 66 North Sandusky, Delaware; (740) 368-8083. Eat, drink, enjoy yourself.

Accommodations

Welcome Home Inn: 6640 Home Rd., Delaware; (740) 881-6588 or (800) 381-0364; www.welcomehomeinn.com.

Bike Shops

Breakaway Cycling: 17 West William St., Delaware; (740) 363-3232; www.breakawaycycling.com. Stop in for information on other routes in the area and tips on where to find the best ice cream.

Rocky's Schwinn Cyclery: 239 East Church St., Marion; (740) 387-7079.

Restrooms
Start/finish: At the park.
Mile 6.1: In Galena.
Mile 43.5: Hogback Ridge Preserve.

Maps
DeLorme: Ohio Atlas & Gazetteer: Page 52.

26 Scioto County Classic

Scioto County is among the most picturesque counties in the state, with its erosion-carved valleys and wooded hills. On this ride you can travel from the bottom of those valleys to the top of the hills and on a scenic byway along the Ohio River valley. Or you can choose only the gently rolling out-and-back along Rocky Fork Creek. Bikers come from all over the area for this short and sweet ride.

Start: Shawnee State Park Mackletree picnic area.

Optional start: If you choose to ride only the 17.4-mile out-and-back section, you could start from the Brush Creek Township Community Park on SR 348. It's 0.5 mile south of the intersection of SR 348 and SR 73 in Otway.

Length: 57.8 miles or the 17.4-mile out-and-back (also other options).

Terrain: Rolling to hilly; the out-and-back is gently rolling.

Traffic and hazards: Moderate traffic on narrow, winding SR 125 and on US 52. Light traffic elsewhere.

Getting there: From SR 125 turn west (it only goes one way) onto Mackletree Road in Shawnee State Forest. Travel 0.3 mile to the picnic area by Roosevelt Lake. For the optional start, the Brush Creek Township Community Park is on SR 348 about a half mile south of Otway, which is at the intersection of SR 348 and SR 73.

The Ride

Scioto County is at the confluence of the Ohio and Scioto Rivers. The 63,000 acres of Shawnee State Forest and Shawnee State Park encompass a part of the former hunting grounds of the Shawnee Indians. The name Shawnee means "those who have silver," as the tribe conducted trade in this precious metal. Shawnee State Forest is the largest of Ohio's nineteen state forests. This route goes through impressive stands of oak, hickory, sassafras, buckeye, black gum, pitch pine, and Virginia pine. Because of the ridges and because the view from the highest points shows a gentle blue haze caused by moisture from the thousands of acres of forest, the area is sometimes called "Ohio's Little Smokies."

The state forest is known for its diversity of flora and fauna. Nature-loving junkies flock here for the wildflowers, birds, and butterflies. I rode this route one fall and the

Flowers in the mist along Rocky Fork Road

roadsides were a riot of colorful joe-pye weed, ageratum, jewelweed, and sunflowers. I saw wild turkeys around several bends in the road.

This ride is a mix-and-match. The whole ball of wax is just shy of 60 miles. If you like the aerobic challenge of hills, this is your baby. If you feel like easy and flat, take the shorter ride along Rocky Fork Creek. You could start from the Mackletree picnic area, ride the out-and-back, and backtrack to the picnic area. Or continue along SR 125 and bail out when you come to Mackletree Road. The options are everywhere; look at the map and plan your route.

The ride starts with a meander through a scenic woodland area and then begins to climb. A downhill takes you to SR 125. Choose here if you want to take the out-and-back on Rocky Fork Road or continue on SR 125. The out-and-back follows Rocky Fork Creek and crosses over it several times. You will pass a white country church and crossroads with names like Tick Ridge and Big and Little Spruce Road. You can turn around when you come to SR 348 or continue into Otway where SR 348 T's into SR 73, if you are in need of refreshments or a restroom. There's also a covered bridge alongside SR 348 near that intersection.

Continuing east on SR 125, the route is scenic; you will pass the entrance to the state park lodge, have good views of Turkey Creek Lake, and then come to the Turkey Creek Nature Center (restrooms). When you come to Mackletree Road, you could bail out and return to the picnic area.

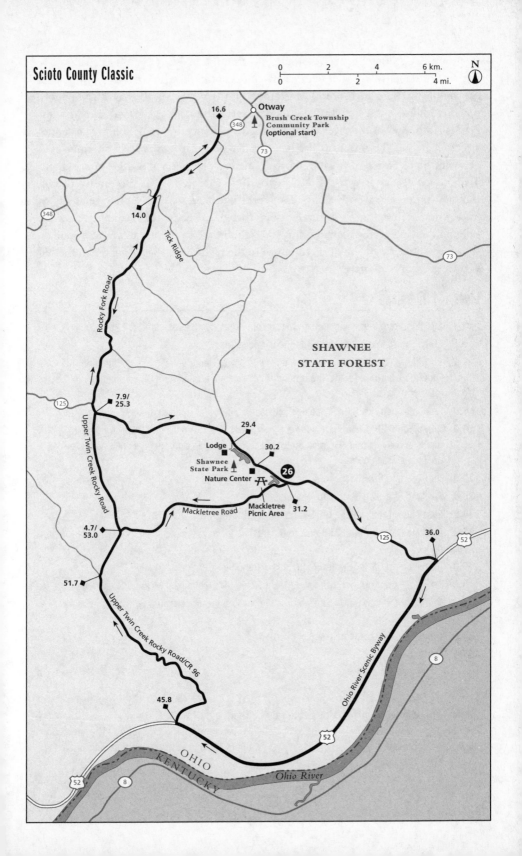

Scioto County Classic

0   2   4   6 km.

0   2   4 mi.

N

16.6

Otway
Brush Creek Township
Community Park
(optional start)

348

73

348

14.0

Tick Ridge

Rocky Fork Road

SHAWNEE
STATE FOREST

125

7.9/
25.3

29.4

Upper Twin Creek Rocky Road

Lodge

30.2

Shawnee
State Park

26

Nature Center

31.2

4.7/
53.0

Mackletree Road

Mackletree
Picnic Area

125

36.0

52

51.7

8

Upper Twin Creek Rocky Road/CR 96

Ohio River Scenic Byway

45.8

52

52   OHIO

8   KENTUCKY

Ohio River

Continuing along SR 125 the route goes through the state forest. The road is rolling and a little narrow, edged with farms, clusters of homes, and of course, woodland. Nearing Friendship, turn onto US 52, the Ohio River Scenic Byway. This highway is gently rolling and scenic. Traffic is moderate; the shoulder comes and goes. You just get brief glimpses of the river but can sense its presence by the tree line that nestles against its edge. The terrain is flat but edged with great hills when you come into Shawnee State Forest. Pass McKendrie Cemetery before turning right onto Upper Twin Creek Rocky Road/CR 96. The return to Mackletree Road is mostly a climb through more deep woods alongside Upper Twin Creek. You'll cross several stream fords. These are interesting stream crossings that give drivers, hikers, and bicyclists the option of staying on the road or going through the stream if the water is not too high. It's a pleasant ending to the ride to return to the picnic area by gliding down the hill you went up at the start.

Miles and Directions

0.0   Turn right from the picnic area on Mackletree Road, riding away from SR 125.

4.7   At the T turn right onto Upper Twin Creek Rocky Road.

7.9   Jog left onto SR 125, the Ohio Byway Scenic Scioto Heritage Trail, then go right onto Rocky Fork Road. **Option:** To skip the out-and-back section, turn right on SR 125 and rejoin the route at mile 25.3

14.0   Bear left when Tick Ridge goes right, cross the creek, and bend to the right.

16.6   Turn around. **Side-trip:** Turn right on SR 348 and ride 1.1 miles into Otway for refreshments and a restroom. Go past the Brush Creek Township Community Park, which is an optional starting point.

25.3   Turn left onto SR 125.

29.4   Pass the Shawnee State Park entrance.

30.2   Pass Turkey Creek Nature Center; there are pit toilets here.

31.2   Pass Mackletree Road. **Bail-out:** Turn right and return to the picnic area to cut short your ride.

36.0   Go right onto US 52 toward Rome. This is the Ohio River Scenic Byway.

45.8   Take a right onto Upper Twin Creek Rocky Road/CR 96 just past McKendrie Cemetery.

51.7   Turn right and stay on Upper Twin Creek Rocky Road by the stream ford (a sign indicates CR 96.6).

53.0   Go right onto Mackletree Road.

57.8   Reach the finish.

Local Information

Portsmouth-Scioto County Visitors Bureau: 341 Front St., Portsmouth; (740) 353-1116; www.ohiorivertourism.org.

Attractions

Shawnee State Park: 4404 SR 125, West Portsmouth; (740) 858-6652. The state park offers hiking, swimming, fishing, and more.

Restaurants

Shawnee State Park Lodge, O-Hee-Yuh Restaurant: 4404B SR 125, West Portsmouth; (740) 858-6621 ext. 414.

Accommodations

Shawnee State Park Lodge: 4494B SR 125, West Portsmouth; (740) 858-6621; Lodge rooms and cottages.

Restrooms

Start/finish: There are latrines at the picnic area.
Mile 17.7: On the side-trip in Otway.
Mile 30.2: Turkey Creek Nature Center.

Maps

DeLorme: Ohio Atlas & Gazetteer: Page 77.

27 Fremont Ramble

This ride is in Great Black Swamp territory. Start out on the North Coast Inland Trail and cycle through Fremont farmland, cross over the scenic Sandusky River, and see Old Fort on this peaceful route; Native Americans referred to this area as *jungquendendah* ("place of peace").

Start: Biggs-Kettner Memorial Park in Fremont.
Length: 27.5 miles.
Terrain: Flat to rolling.

Traffic and hazards: Traffic is light to moderate—it's on country roads and the cars go fast.

Getting there: From I-75 take exit 179 to US 6 for 24 miles toward Fremont. Stay straight to go onto Hayes Avenue. In 2.8 miles turn left onto Front Street. In 0.4 mile turn right onto West State Street/US 20. In 1 mile turn right onto Saint Joseph Street and follow it to the end. This is the location of the Biggs-Kettner Memorial Park and the Fremont Community Recreation Complex (restrooms) at 601 Saint Joseph Street. When you pull in, the complex is to the right (west) and the park is to the left in the southeast corner of the parking lot. The park connects to the North Coast Inland bike path, and the ride starts out on the trail.

The Ride

Biking in northwestern Ohio, you will notice that it is much more sparsely settled than other parts of the state. In part that's because of the Great Black Swamp. For thousands of years the swamp covered thousands of square miles. It was wild and majestic and almost impenetrable. The swamp's wheel-sucking mud, the buzzing, biting mosquitoes, and a malarial illness called ague put fear into the hearts of the pioneers. They avoided it. Eventually, however, all of the surrounding land was settled. Those pioneers finally figured out how to drain the land. They did such a good job that the landscape was changed forever, and now folks are trying to figure out how to restore some of it.

A gaggle of geese along the Fremont Ramble

The coming of the iron horse certainly helped to get that swamp tamed. The Toledo, Norwalk and Cleveland Railroad was established in 1851 as the final link between New York and Chicago. In the late 1970s rail transportation slowed as companies switched to trucks on the new interstate highway system. The train route was abandoned. Today the North Coast Inland Trail brings a new kind of transportation to the railroad corridor. While this route travels only a short distance on the trail, there's always another day . . .

Take the access road to the bike trail and go left. Exit the trail on Finefrock Road and go right. Follow winding rural roads past charming old farm homes—some are a little tired looking, but all are tidy. Cross into Seneca County. Seneca County Line Road is TR 113 on the road signs, but it's also CR 62 on some maps.

The route gets rolling in Seneca County—you can swoop down a hill and gain enough momentum to get to the top of the next hill. It goes through Knobby's Prairie and Sugar Creek Wildlife Areas and crosses over Sugar Creek. On CR 33 the route goes past Steyer Nature Preserve and across Abbotts Bridge. Expect a great view of the Sandusky State Scenic River.

The Sandusky flows 130 miles in a unique "L" shape. It is one of the longest rivers within the Lake Erie Watershed. Its valley was once home to the Seneca and Wyandot Indians. There were four forts along the river's banks, including Fort Stephenson, where the Americans won a decisive victory in the War of 1812. One cannon, "Old

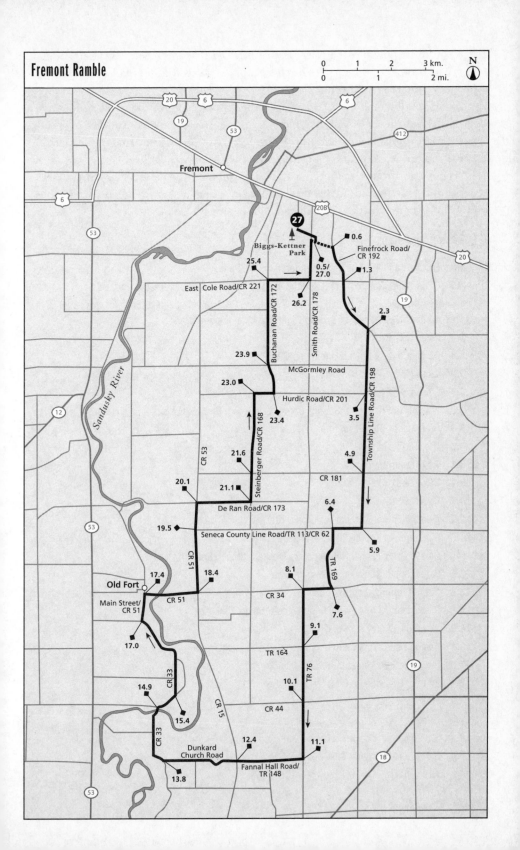

Fremont Ramble

0   1   2   3 km.
0   1   2 mi.

N

Fremont

27

Biggs-Kettner Park

0.6

Finefrock Road/
CR 192

25.4

0.5/
27.0

1.3

East Cole Road/CR 221

26.2

2.3

Buchanan Road/CR 172

Smith Road/CR 178

23.9

McGormley Road

23.0

Hurdic Road/CR 201

Township Line Road/CR 198

23.4

3.5

CR 53

Steinberger Road/CR 168

21.6

4.9

CR 181

20.1

21.1

6.4

De Ran Road/CR 173

19.5

Seneca County Line Road/TR 113/CR 62

5.9

CR 51

TR 169

17.4

18.4

8.1

Old Fort

CR 51

CR 34

7.6

Main Street/
CR 51

9.1

17.0

TR 164

TR 76

CR 33

10.1

14.9

CR 44

CR 15

15.4

CR 33

12.4

11.1

Dunkard
Church Road

13.8

Fannal Hall Road/
TR 148

Sandusky River

Betsy," was the only heavy artillery at the fort. Old Betsy still stands at the site of the fort, which is now home to the Birchard Library and is near the start of this ride in Fremont on Croghan Street.

Soon you'll come into Old Fort, pass the school, and cross the river again. Then head back north, enter Sandusky County, and return to the bike path but on a different route. After turning left onto Smith Road, you will soon come to the railroad tracks and the access road back to Biggs-Kettner Memorial Park; go left.

Penny and I rode this route on a hot, late summer day; cicadas chirped, swallows dived, and brown-eyed Susans were in bloom. Then we got caught in a ferocious thunderstorm and had to take refuge beside a barn.

Miles and Directions

0.0 Exit the parking lot at Biggs-Kettner Memorial Park.

0.5 Cross Smith Road/CR 178 and the railroad tracks, then go left (east) onto the trail.

0.6 Exit the trail and go right onto Finefrock Road/CR 192. It is the first road you cross after Smith Road; there's a big radio tower ahead on the left.

1.3 Cross Cole Road/CR 221.

2.3 Go right onto Township Line Road/CR 198.

3.5 Cross Hurdic Road/CR 201.

4.9 Cross CR 181.

5.9 At the T turn right onto Seneca County Line Road/TR 113/CR 62.

6.4 Go left onto TR 169 and past Cleveland Farms.

7.6 The road T's into CR 34; turn right.

8.1 Go left onto TR 76.

9.1 Cross TR 164.

10.1 Cross CR 44.

11.1 Take a right onto Fannal Hall Road/TR 148.

11.6 Ride through Knobby's Prairie Wildlife Area

12.4 Cross CR 15. Fannal Hall becomes Dunkard Church Road.

12.9 Ride through Sugar Creek Wildlife Area

13.8 At the T turn right onto CR 33.

14.8 Pass Steyer Nature Preserve and cross Abbotts Bridge

14.9 At the next T stay right on CR 33.

15.4 Bear left on CR 33 when TR 145 continues straight.

17.0 Turn right onto Main Street/CR 51 in Old Fort.

17.4 Turn right, staying on CR 51.

17.5 Cross Fort Street.

17.6 Cross the Sandusky State Scenic River.

18.4 Go left onto CR 51 when CR 34 continues straight.

19.5 Cross Seneca County Line Road; CR 51 becomes CR 53.

20.1 Turn right onto De Ran Road/CR 173.

21.1 Take a left onto Steinberger Road/CR 168.

21.6 Cross CR 181.

23.0 At the T turn right onto Hurdic Road/CR 201.

23.4 Go left onto Buchanan Road/CR 172.

23.9 Cross McGormley Road.

25.4 Turn right onto East Cole Road/CR 221.

26.2 Go left onto Smith Road/CR 178.

27.0 Exit the bike path, cross the railroad tracks, and go left on the access path back to the park.

27.5 Return to the parking area.

Local Information

Fremont/Sandusky County Convention and Visitors Bureau: 712 North St., Suite 102, Fremont; (419) 332-4470; www.sanduskycounty.org.

Restaurants

Whitey's Diner: 216 East State St., Fremont; (419) 334-9183. "Nothing could be finer than to eat at Whitey's Diner," the menu promises. Open for breakfast, lunch, and dinner; homemade soups and pies. Good food.

The Depot: 117 North Monroe St., Fremont; (419) 332-5510. Family run, good pizza and subs.

Accommodations

Blessings Bed and Breakfast: 903 Birchard Ave., Fremont; (419) 333-STAY (7829).

Farrell House Lodge at Sunnybrook Trout Club: 1104 Fremont Ave., Sandusky; (419) 625-8353; www.farrellhouselodge.com. Tucked away on 130 acres of scenic woodland that are preserved as a nature conservancy.

Bike Shops

Fremont Cycle and Fitness Center: 107 North Ohio Ave., Fremont; (419) 332-4481; www.fremontcycleandfitness.com. Visit this bike shop for information on the Flatlanders Bicycle Club, which recommended this route, and information on other rides in the area.

Restrooms

Start/finish: Fremont Community Recreation Complex.

Maps

DeLorme: Ohio Atlas & Gazetteer: Page 31.

28 Huron-to-Milan Cruise

Leave from the picturesque town of Huron on the shore of Lake Erie and at the mouth of the Huron River. Enjoy this great rolling route out along the Huron River to the historic and scenic village of Milan, birthplace of Thomas Edison. Many roads are rural and quiet, but some are a little busy.

Start: The Lake Front Park in Huron.
Length: 23.5 miles.
Terrain: Typical Ohio—flat to rolling with a couple of hills.
Traffic and hazards: Traffic is heavier around Huron and Milan—avoiding rush hour is a good idea. There are many bumpy railroad cross-ings on River Road. You'll find moderate traffic with no shoulder on SR 113 into Milan and for a short distance on Shaw Mill Road leav-ing Milan. The route travels through two busy intersections—on Church Street crossing US 250/SR 13 as you exit Milan and where Mason Road crosses US 250.

Getting there: Take US 6 into Huron, and at the Donut Shop turn north onto Center Street—going toward the lake. This takes you to the Lake Front Park, which is at Park and North Center Streets.

The Ride

Huron was an early Native American village; the French established a trading post there in 1749. The town has a history of shipbuilding, fishing, and ice harvesting. Huron was an important freshwater port on the Great Lakes; currently farm commodities, limestone, and iron ore are received and shipped from the port.

The Lake Front Park has, obviously, a great view of Lake Erie. Take a good look before you leave so you're not tempted to rubberneck as you wend your way through the narrow, winding streets. At the stop sign carefully turn left onto Cleveland Road. Bear right at the boat ramp (there's a restroom there), and Cleveland becomes Main Street. By the landmark Donut Shop, cautiously cross US 6 West and turn left onto US 6 East. Pass the Pied Piper ice cream shop and enter the sidewalk to cross the bridge; there's a scenic view of the Huron River. Just across the bridge turn right onto River Road. Traffic eases as you get out of town, and there are some fantastic views of the Huron River (I saw a bald eagle here), but watch those pesky railroad crossings.

At 3.1 miles you'll see parking for the Huron River Marsh, which provides more river views and great birding spots. As you come into suburban Milan Township, the road becomes rolling with a couple of hills. Look for the farm market at the Mason Road jog if you need to refuel. Turn back to River Road and climb the hill. Just ahead on the left, a scenic marker tells about Camp Avery.

You will be traveling through farmland until houses begin to cluster as you approach Milan. SR 113 is busy, but it doesn't take long to get into the village. You could definitely spend some time in Milan. Signage on Edison Drive indicates the

Windmill near Huron

birthplace of Thomas Edison and the Milan Historical Museum, where you can learn about the Milan Canal. It was a ship's canal that carried Great Lakes vessels from Milan to Lake Erie.

Continuing on East Front Street, you'll come to the Milan Square, a neat little park. On Park Street, still on the square, look for the Milan Township Hall. Just next to it is a memorial bell, and there are public restrooms behind it. Back on SR 113, called Church Street in town, you cross a busy highway. Shaw Mill Road is a little congested when it starts out up a steep winding incline, but you are soon back in more rural country. Shaw Mill does not announce when it becomes Whittlesey Avenue, but you will see that it has when you turn onto Schaefer Road. Cross the Huron River, then swoop down and climb another hill.

On Lovers Lane bike past the 295-acre Milan Wildlife Area. Gifted to the state in 1932, the area hosted a raccoon propagation facility until 1952. I guess they realized we didn't need any more raccoons.

It's not obvious from maps, but Kelly Road T's into Mason Road just before the US 250 intersection, where you will find fast food and restrooms.

You'll know you're near the sanitary landfill on Hoover Road when you see the gulls soaring overhead. After that you'll soon be back to Huron.

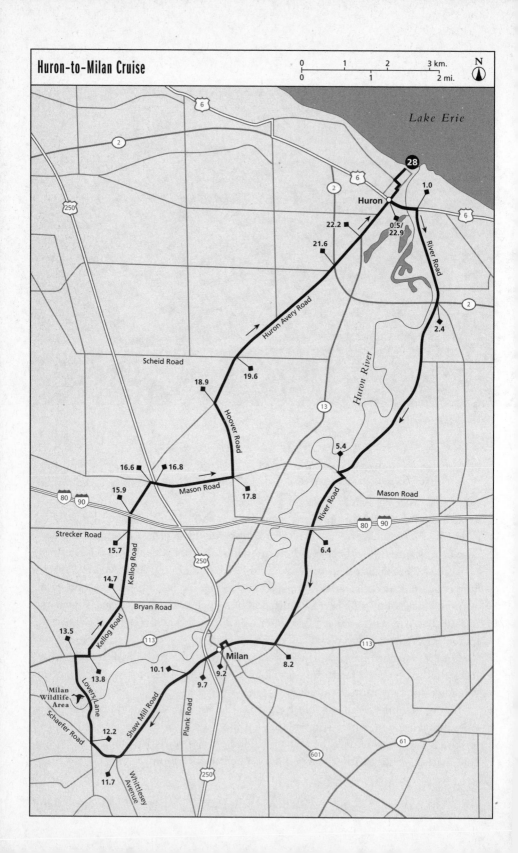

Miles and Directions

0.0 From the Huron Lake Front Park on Park Street, turn right onto Center Street.

0.07 Cross South Street.

0.19 At the stop sign carefully turn left onto Cleveland Road West.

0.21 Cross Williams Street.

0.24 Bear right at the Boat Basin; you're now on Main Street.

0.4 Cross Mill Street.

0.5 Cross US 6 West and turn left onto US 6 East (also called Cleveland Road East).

0.9 Enter the sidewalk to cross over the bridge; scenic view of the Huron River.

1.0 Turn right onto River Road—just across the bridge.

2.4 Go under SR 2.

5.4 Turn left onto Mason Road and go under the underpass, then jog right, back onto River Road.

6.4 Cross under I-80/I-90.

8.2 Turn right at the T onto SR 113 (called Church Street in Milan).

8.9 Turn right onto North Edison Drive. After 0.01 mile, at the stop sign, turn left onto East Front Street. **Side-trip:** Continue straight on Edison past Front Street. Thomas Edison's Birthplace Museum and other places of interest are just ahead.

9.1 Turn left onto Park Street.

9.2 There's a public restroom next to the Milan Township Hall just behind the bell.

9.2 Turn right onto East Church Street.

9.6 Cross North Huron Street.

9.7 Cross US 250/SR 13 and continue straight onto Shaw Mill Road.

10.1 At the stop sign bear right up the hill when Plank Road goes left.

11.4 Shaw Mill Road becomes Whittlesey Avenue.

11.7 Turn right onto Schaefer Road.

12.2 Go right onto Lovers Lane.

13.5 At the T turn right onto SR 113.

13.8 Take a left onto Kellog Road.

14.7 Cross Bryan Road.

15.6 Beware the rumble strips.

15.7 Cross Strecker Road.

15.9 Pass through a narrow underpass beneath the Ohio Turnpike.

16.6 At the T just before the intersection, turn right onto Mason Road.

16.8 Cautiously cross US 250 and continue straight on Mason Road.

17.8 Turn left onto Hoover Road.

18.9 At the T turn right onto Huron Avery Road.

19.6 Cross Scheid Road.

21.6 Cross SR 2.

22.2 At the stop sign bear left, now on Main Street, when Mud Brook Road goes right.

22.8 Cross Standard Street.

22.9 Cross US 6.

23.0 Cross Mill Street.

23.1 Turn left onto Cleveland Road West.

23.3 Go right onto Center Street.

23.4 Cross South Street.

23.5 Turn left onto Park Street.

Local Information

Lake Erie Shores and Islands Welcome Center-West: 770 Southeast Catawba Rd./SR 53, Port Clinton; www.shoresandislands.com.

Milan Chamber of Commerce: 3 North Main St., Milan; (419) 499-4909; www.milanohio.com.

Huron Chamber of Commerce, Inc.: 509 Huron St., Huron; (419) 433-5700; www.huron.net.

Attractions

Edison Birthplace Museum: 9 North Edison Dr., Milan; (419) 499-2135; www.tomedison .org. Thomas Alva Edison, America's greatest inventor, held 1,093 patents including those for the phonograph and the light bulb. The museum, operated by family members, includes many of Edison's early inventions, documents, and family mementoes.

Inland Seas Maritime Museum: 480 Main St., Vermilion; (440) 967-3467 or (800) 893-1485; www.inlandseas.org. A key attraction of Ohio's north coast, this museum contains one of the world's largest collections of Great Lakes historical maritime artifacts, documents, ship records, and original artwork.

Restaurants

Donut Shop: 501 Main St., Huron; (419) 433-7117. Open mornings only.

Pied Piper: 502 Huron St., Huron; (419) 433-2601. A classic ice-cream drive-in founded in 1952.

Lemmys Eatery Shoppe: 2027 Cleveland Road West, Huron; (419) 433-5501. Home-style cooking.

Accommodations

Captain Montagues Bed and Breakfast: 229 Center St., Huron; (419) 433-4756 or (800) 276-4756; www.captainmontagues.com. This beautifully restored bed and breakfast, just 2 short blocks from Lake Erie, was built in the late 1870s by the local lumberyard owner and master shipbuilder of the day, John Wickham. It features beautiful wood throughout and has been featured in many local and national magazines.

Angel Welcome Bed and Breakfast: 2 Front St., Milan; (419) 499-0094; www.angelwelcome .com. Enjoy charming surroundings and warm hospitality just steps from the historic Thomas A. Edison birthplace. Stroll by antique and specialty shops, restaurants, and tree-lined streets of Victorian homes.

Bike Shops

Bicycle Bill's Fitness Center: 5523 SR 60 South, Vermilion; (440) 967-2453; www.bicycle bills.com.

Restrooms

Mile 0.24: At the Boat Basin on Main Street in Huron.

Mile 9.18: In Milan next to the Milan Township Hall.

Mile 16.7: At the Marathons gas station and McDonalds.

Maps

DeLorme: Ohio Atlas & Gazetteer: Page 32.

29 Lexington Ramble

See Amish farms, rock ledges, and gorgeous scenery on this route—maybe even a bald eagle. While this is a mostly comfortable ride, there are a few hills to test your mettle.

Start: The Lexington staging area of the Richland B & O bike trail.
Length: 27.0-mile figure-eight loop.
Terrain: Flat to rolling with a couple of energizing hills.
Traffic and hazards: Traffic is moderate but cars move along—especially during rush hour.

You'll cross a couple of busy intersections; there's some traffic on US 42, but it has a comfortable shoulder. Look for another very short but busy stretch on SR 97. The Amish buggies have created wheel-catching ruts on some roads.

Getting there: From I-71 take exit 165 to SR 97 north toward Lexington—about 3 miles. It turns left onto US 42 just before Lexington. In town turn right onto Plymouth Street. In 0.5 mile watch for the very small Richland B & O bike trail sign on the right. Wind back the driveway to the staging area, which is behind the village of Lexington's water department. The address is 152 Plymouth Street, Lexington.

The Ride

The Richland B & O Trail, an 18.3-mile paved trail, is built on the railroad bed of the former Baltimore & Ohio Railway. It connects Mansfield, Lexington, Bellville, and Butler. The trail and this route traverse some of the most scenic parts of north-central Ohio. Once you're off the bike trail at the start of this ride, a couple or three hills will have you panting, but overall this jagged figure-eight loop is pleasantly rolling, in an area of the Appalachian foothills known for its skiing.

Start out on the bike path, then cross under a highway, pass behind the local bike store, and exit the bike path onto a sort of driveway just before the Ohio Public Works Commission. The ride starts in a light industrial area but quickly opens to farmland.

The landscape goes from suburban to rural and back again. Ride through Pebble Creek Golf Course and then a section of typical golf-course-style homes. When you begin to notice wash hanging on lines, signs for shoe repair and country stores, and farmhouses not connected to utility wires, you'll know that you're in Amish country.

If you are a cemetery prowler and like to investigate old headstones, prowl through the Old Center Huntsman Cemetery. If you avoid cemeteries whenever possible, still take a very short side-trip to the right for a spectacular view of the valley.

You may feel as if you are riding through molasses on the steady but gradual climb into Johnsville. It has genuine small-town atmosphere. Hersche's Country Side Restaurant, Apple Pie Inn, and the Bellville B & M restaurant are both biker friendly and provide restrooms and food including great apple or cherry pie a la mode.

Lexington Ramble

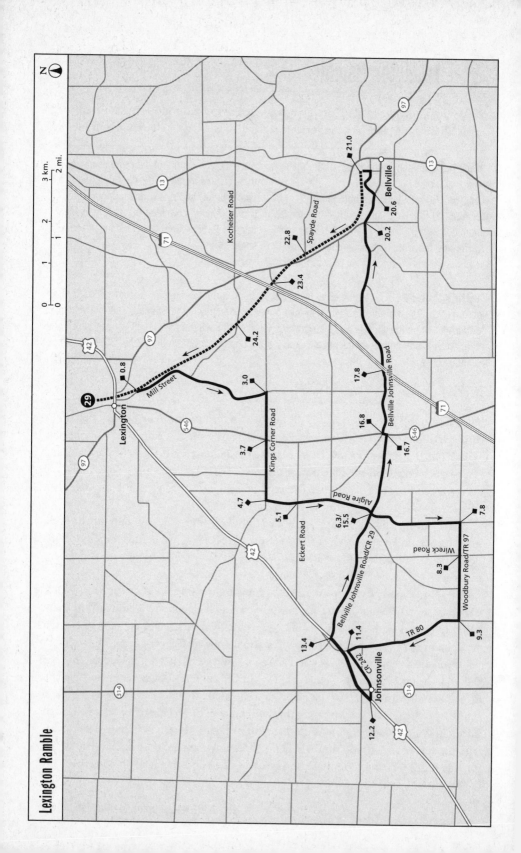

Mill Street hill

Continuing on US 42, which has a shoulder, enjoy a great gliding downhill, although motorists will be speeding along beside you. Ride a long stretch along Bellville Johnsville Road broken with a short jog on SR 546. Most of this road is very scenic and rural; expect to see Amish kids and farmers working the fields with horses.

Traffic is heavy on a very short stretch of SR 97 before you turn left onto Fry Road, which immediately seems to become Ogle Street and then shoots you left onto Flower Street—you'll see the bike path ahead. Ride alongside the bike path for a couple of hundred feet until you come to a short paved entrance to the left. The route continues to the left on the bike path, but don't miss the side-trip that goes right into Bellville and the Pumpkin Hollow Antiques Mall, where you'll find restrooms, food, and of course, antiques.

From there follow the bike path back to Lexington. It travels along SR 97 for a stretch and then crosses it; for goodness' sake, be careful. I walked across. The rest of the path is quiet and scenic with some good birding opportunities.

Remember to watch for the Lexington staging area to the left after you ride under the highway, although riding farther on the bike trail is an option.

Miles and Direction

0.0   Exit the parking lot and turn right (south) onto the bike trail. Ride under the highway; Y-Not Fitness and Cycling is off to the right.

0.8   Just past the bike shop, exit the bike path right before the Ohio Public Works Commission by turning right onto a short road/driveway.

0.9   At the end of the short road/driveway, turn left onto Mill Street.

3.0   Turn right onto Kings Corner Road.

3.7   Cross SR 546—this is a busy road.

4.7   Turn left onto Algire Road and ride through the golf course.

5.1   Cross Eckert Road.

6.3   Cross Bellville Johnsville Road. You'll be coming back on this road.

7.8   Turn right onto Woodbury Road/TR 97.

8.3   Cross Wireck Road by the Old Center Huntsman Cemetery. (Note: Take a 0.1-mile side-trip to the right for a great view.)

9.3   Turn right onto TR 80—you have to look for the sign.

11.4 Turn left when the road T's onto CR 242. It's not marked, but if you look to the right, you will see US 42.

12.0 Come into Johnsville, where you'll find several options for food and restrooms.

12.2 Turn right onto US 42. Hersche's Country Side Restaurant is to the left.

12.5 Apple Pie Inn has good food plus great pie a la mode.

13.4 Go right onto Bellville Johnsville Road/CR 29.

15.5 Cross Algire Road.

16.7 At the T jog left into SR 546.

16.8 Turn right, back onto Bellville Johnsville Road.

17.8 Cross over I-71.

20.2 The road T's into SR 97; turn right.

20.6 Go left and down the hill onto Fry Road, which immediately becomes Ogle Street.

20.9 Turn left on the downhill from Ogle Street to Flower Street.

21.0 Turn left into the entrance to the bike path, and go left on the bike path to continue the route. **Side-trip:** Go right a couple of hundred feet on the bike path to Pumpkin Hollow Antiques Mall for shops, restrooms, ice cream, and Tuscan Village Restaurant.

22.8 Carefully cross Spayde Road—watch for cars turning left from SR 97.

23.0 Cross busy SR 97.

23.4 Cross Alexander Road and go under the highway.

24.2 Cross Kocheiser Road. Then pass the village of Lexington wastewater facility.

27.0 Turn left back to the staging area.

Local Information

Mansfield and Richland County Convention and Visitors Bureau: 124 North Main St., Mansfield; (800) 642-8282; www.mansfieldtourism.com.

Attractions

Malabar Farm: 4050 Bromfield Rd., Lucas; (419) 892-2784; www.malabarfarm.org.

Historical Ohio State Reformatory: 100 Reformatory Rd., Mansfield; (419) 522-2644.

Restaurants

Apple Pie Inn: 7398 North US 42, Mount Gilead; (419) 362-1337. On the route.

Pueblo Grande Inc.: 275 East Main St., Lexington; (419) 610-1998.

Accommodations

The Buckhorn Inn: 8702 Ross Rd., Lexington; (419) 884-3500. A restored farmhouse situated on eighty acres of gently rolling hills.

Bike Shops

Y-Not Fitness and Cycling: 64 East Main St., Lexington; (419) 884-6135; www.ynotcycling.com.

Restrooms

Start/finish: At the staging area.

Mile 12.0: In Johnsville.

Mile 21.0: In the Pumpkin Hollow Antiques Mall.

Maps

DeLorme: Ohio Atlas & Gazetteer: Page 43.

30 Licking County Cruise

Wind along Raccoon Creek on the T.J. Evans Recreation Trail and ride through tall woods full of birdsong. Leave the bike path and ride through a beautiful ravine walled with ferns. Return by way of the picturesque town of Granville, home to two historic inns, and sample some Velvet ice cream made in nearby Utica.

Start: Licking County Family YMCA, Newark.

Length: 37.9 miles.

Terrain: Flat on the bike path, rolling with some hills on the roads.

Traffic and hazards: Off the bike path, traffic is light to moderate; Caswell Road is a narrow, winding climb. The route goes on busy SR 37 for a very short distance, and there's a sidewalk. The area around Granville is busy.

Getting there: From SR 79 in Newark, turn west onto Church Street. The YMCA is at 470 West Church Street. Go to the rear of the parking lot near the Mitchell Family Recreational Center. Take the bike path out of the northwest corner of the parking lot (when you're facing the building, it is on the left).

The Ride

Licking County is one of Ohio's largest counties. Glassmaking industries have always played a role here. The county is also the home of the largest complex of ancient geometric earthworks in the world. While you won't see the earthworks on the ride, it passes near them. Visitors from ancient cultures traveled to the area some 2,000 years

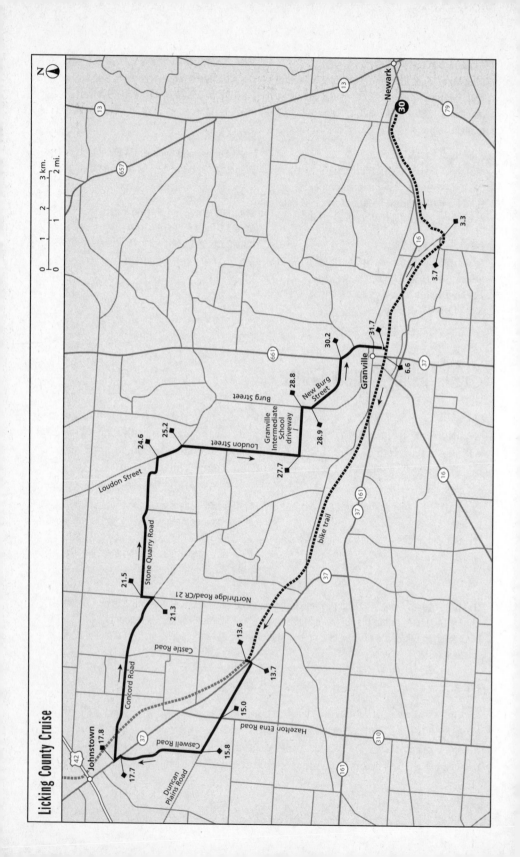

Licking County Cruise

Stretching sculpture along the bike path

ago to trade things like copper, mica, and seashells for local natural resources such as multicolored flint. So you can just bet that they walked over the lands we're biking over today.

This ride is on the edge of the Appalachian plateau, which means hills. The flattest place to ride is on the T.J. Evans Recreation Trail, so we took advantage of that for part of the route. At the start of the ride, look for the outdoor swimming pool—that's the clue that you're going the right way on the bike path. Shortly you'll pass an interesting swinging bridge to the left. Don't turn right at the sculpture of the girl stretching. Ride over the Squire Whipple Bridge behind Cherry Valley Lodge; it is one of four of its kind left from the 1850s.

Cross the highway on the southern edge of Granville and stay on the bike path. The route exits the path on Castle Road; immediately cross SR 37 and continue straight on Duncan Plains Road (there is an option to stay on the bike path a bit longer). Pass a sawmill on the climb up Caswell Road. Come up to SR 37 by the Johnstown Police Department and Chamber of Commerce. There is a family restaurant in Johnstown if you're hungry.

On Concord Road (traffic is not heavy, but the cars go fast), you'll cross the bike path again. After a short stretch on Northridge Road (ditto the remarks about Concord), ride into the ravine on Stone Quarry Road. This is a beautiful, scenic area—the creek is at bedrock here. And yes, the quarry is in a deep valley. Climb out of the valley, add on some miles, and then turn left into the school driveway—there is a sign and it's more like a road than a driveway. Ride past the school and exit onto Burg Street. Traffic is a bit heavier coming into Granville. There is a bike path on which to ride for a short section.

Soon you'll come back into Granville (this time on the northern edge), home of Denison University. The route passes the historic Granville and Buxton Inns, both amazing, with great restaurants. Granville was founded in 1805 by New Englanders looking for fertile farmland. The Ohio Canal, Cleveland to Portsmouth, passed east of Granville; however, a feeder canal was built and Granville thrived. The Granville historic district has more than one hundred buildings on the National Register of Historic Places. The town is full of interesting, locally owned shops. Several of them sell ice cream.

Just out of town go down a hill and rejoin the bike trail for the pleasant return to the YMCA.

Miles and Directions

0.0 Follow the bike path from the parking lot, staying parallel to Church Street, not going right and up the hill.

0.1 Pass an outdoor swimming pool on the right.

0.5 Go left under the tunnel toward Cherry Valley Road.

3.3 Continue straight (another path goes right) and cross the bridge.

3.7 At the T turn right and cross the Squire Whipple Bowstring Truss Bridge. Just after the bridge continue straight when another trail bears left.

6.6 In Granville the Certified gas station to the left has restrooms. Cross SR 37/SR 661 and continue on the bike path.

13.6 Exit the bike path and turn left onto Castle Road (A sign announcing Baker's Acres farm is a landmark on the right). **Option:** Stay on the bike path approximately 3.5 more miles and rejoin the route at mile 18.3 by turning right onto Concord Road.

13.7 Cross Johnstown Alexandria Road/SR 37 and continue straight onto Duncan Plains Road.

15.0 Cross Hazelton Etna Road/SR 310.

15.8 Turn right onto Caswell Road.

17.7 Go left onto SR 37. There is a sidewalk and a shoulder.

17.8 Take a right onto Concord Road.

21.3 Turn left onto Northridge Road/CR 21.

21.5 Go right onto Stone Quarry Road.

24.6 At the T turn right onto Loudon Street.

25.2 Bend to the right, still on Loudon, when Dry Creek Road continues straight.

27.7 Turn left into the Granville Intermediate School driveway. Pass the school.

28.8 Exit the driveway and turn right onto Burg Street.

28.9 Go left onto New Burg Street when Burg continues straight.

30.2 Pass Granville High and Middle Schools. At Pearl Street enter the bike path on the right.

30.5 Continue into Granville on Pearl Street when the bike path ends; there is a sidewalk.

30.9 Cross East College Street.

31.0 In Granville cross Broadway and continue on South Pearl Street. (The Granville and Buxton Inns are here. Turn right onto Broadway for a public restroom and ice cream at Whit's.)

31.7 Go left onto the bike path.

34.0 Just past the tunnel take the bike path to the left.

34.3 Go through two tunnels.

34.5 Just past the bridge continue straight when another path goes left.

37.9 Return to the parking lot.

Local Information

Greater Licking County Convention and Visitors Bureau: 455 Hebron Rd./SR 79, Heath; (740) 345-8224 or (800) 589-8224; www.lccvb.com.

Attractions

The Dawes Arboretum: 7770 Jacksontown Rd. SE, Newark; (740) 323-2355 or (800) 44-DAWES (443-2937); www.dawesarb.org. More than 1,700 acres with 8 miles of hiking trails and a 4-mile auto tour.

The Newark Earthworks: 455 Hebron Rd./SR 79, Heath; (740) 344-1919 or (800) 600-7178; www.ohiohistory.org. Explore 2,000-year-old earthworks that served as both a cathedral and astronomical observatory for people known to archaeologists as the Hopewell culture.

Ye Olde Mill: 11324 Mount Vernon Rd., Utica; (740) 892-3921 or (800) 589-5000; www.velveticecream.com. Produces more than six million gallons of Velvet ice cream a year in six states. Free factory tours, a restaurant, and, of course, an ice-cream parlor.

Restaurants/Accommodations

The lodge and both inns are on the bike route. All three have excellent restaurants.

Cherry Valley Lodge: 2299 Cherry Valley Rd., Newark; (740) 888-1212 or (800) 788-8008; www.cherryvalleylodge.com. The lodge offers incredible dining and fantastic amenities. It is also an arboretum and botanical garden. There's an indoor water resort and spa.

Buxton Inn: 313 East Broadway, Granville; (740) 587-0001; www.buxtoninn.com. Ohio's oldest inn has provided travelers with comfort since 1812. Casual and fine dining.

Granville Inn: 314 East Broadway, Granville; (740) 587-3333 or (888) 472-6855; www.granvilleinn.com. Historic manor inn has been a landmark since 1924. Award-winning restaurant.

Bike Shops

The Bike Corral: 407 West Church St., Newark; (614) 345-4708.

Franklin Frames and Cycles: 7179 Reform Rd., Newark; (740) 763-3838.

Restrooms

Start/finish: At the YMCA.

Mile 6.6: Certified gas station on the bike trail in Granville.

Mile 31.0: Public restroom at the Village Hall, 141 East Broadway in Granville.

Maps

DeLorme: Ohio Atlas & Gazetteer: Page 53.

31 Thornville-to-Somerset Challenge

This is a short yet ambitious route traveling from the little village of Thornville through the scenic hills of Perry County and into the Somerset Village Square. There it rambles past the historic courthouse and the monument in honor of General Philip Henry Sheridan, the only equestrian Civil War statue in Ohio.

Start: Municipal ballpark in Thornville.
Length: 25.9 miles.
Terrain: Heart-pumping hills, swooping valleys.
Traffic and hazards: Traffic is moderate for a good part of the route, yet there are some very pleasant rural roads. Some roads are narrow, and you must use caution because of the hills. TR 383 has loose gravel. Traffic on SR 757 and SR 13 is fairly heavy; there is a sidewalk along 13.

Getting there: Thornville is in Perry County north of Lancaster. Take SR 204 into Thornville and turn south onto Church Street. Turn left onto Park Drive. The ballpark is at Park and Thornhill Drives.

The Ride

Find the little village of Thornville, then stop in at the Inn-Town Restaurant for a hearty breakfast before you start pedaling; you're going to need the energy on this go-getter ride. Park at the ballpark and, on your bike, head back the way you came. Turn left onto Church Street, which becomes Zion Road, then hang a right onto Bruno Road. On the way up the first hill, notice the Ohio Bicentennial barn on the right. Enjoy that grand sweep of a view at the top and the wind in your face as you soar down.

Turn left onto the first crossroad you come to, High Point Road; there may not be a road sign. Pass the beautiful 1808 Zion Reformed Church with the stained-glass windows. Its story is on the roadside Ohio Historical Marker.

When you cross Zion Road/CR 30, bend around to the right of the white church. In just over a mile, keep a lookout for TR 383 off to the right. It's a little one-laner, narrow and winding. Watch the loose gravel! Keep going until the road T's onto SR 757. Keep a heads-up on this hilly, narrow-shouldered road.

The next T you come to is near Somerset; traffic is heavy, but there is a sidewalk and it's not far to Somerset. Chill out a little in the Somerset Village Square on the traffic roundabout. This old German town has a lot of history and some interesting craft shops. You'll see the 1829 Courthouse, and who can resist the man-on-a-horse statue in the square. It's General Philip Henry Sheridan, nicknamed "Little Phil," a Union general in the Civil War, who grew up in Somerset. US 22 is Main Street here. There are a couple of non-chain restaurants on Main Street in town.

Leave town on US 22, which has a wide shoulder. This is a part of Zane's Trace, the first road cut out of the wilderness in the Northwest Territory in the late 1700s. Colo-

Bruno Road hill

nel Ebenezer Zane and his brothers followed Native American footpaths to build the road, which is intermingled with what is now the National Road and US 40.

This section of the ride is more low-traffic. A half mile after the T onto Rush Creek Road, that road jogs to the left onto Pleasantville Road. When Rush Creek goes off to the right, continue straight on Pleasantville. After a short jog on SR 256, return to Bruno Road. You will cross High Point Road and then return to Thornville the same way you rode out.

Miles and Directions

0.0   Head back out Park Drive the same way you drove in.

0.1   Turn left onto Church Street.

0.2   Church Street becomes Zion Road/CR 30.

0.6   Turn right onto Bruno Road.

2.7   At the top of the hill at the four-way stop sign, turn left onto High Point Road.

3.8   Cross SR 13.

4.7   Cross TR 37.

5.6   In Ziontown, cross Zion Road/CR 30. Do a slight jog to bend around to the right of the church, still on High Point Road.

6.0   Cross TR 25.

6.8   Turn right onto TR 383, a one-lane road that starts out down a hill—gravel alert!

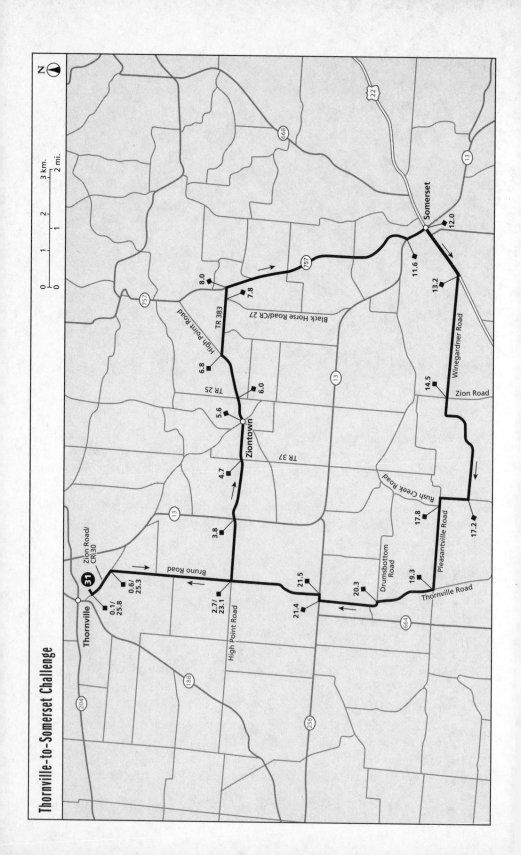

Thornville-to-Somerset Challenge

7.8 Black Horse Road/CR 27 comes down from the right and TR 383 ends; continue straight, now on Black Horse.

8.0 Turn right at the T onto SR 757.

11.6 Turn left at the T onto SR 13—heavy traffic, sidewalk available.

12.0 Turn right onto US 22, which has a shoulder. Look for restaurant and restroom options.

13.2 Turn right onto Winegardner Road, which will bend to the left and then back to the right.

14.5 Cross Zion Road.

17.2 Turn right at the T onto Rush Creek Road.

17.7 Bend to the left, now onto Pleasantville and Rush Creek Roads.

17.8 Take a slight left, staying on Pleasantville Road when Rush Creek breaks to the right.

19.3 Turn right onto Thornville Road.

20.3 Bear left and remain on Thornville when Drumsbottom Road goes right.

21.4 Turn right onto SR 256.

21.5 Turn left onto Bruno Road.

23.1 Cross High Point Road.

25.3 Turn left onto Zion Road at the T.

25.7 Zion Road becomes Church Street.

25.8 Turn right onto Park Drive.

25.9 Arrive back at the ballpark.

Local Information

Perry County Chamber of Commerce: 121 South Main St., New Lexington; (740) 342-3547; www.perrycountyohiocofc.com.

Events/Attractions

Buckeye Lake State Park: 2905 Liebs Island Rd., Millersport; (740) 467-2690. Ohio's oldest state park, Buckeye Lake is known for picnicking, swimming, boating, skiing, and fishing.

Thornville Backwoods Festival: 8572 High Point Rd., Thornville; (740) 246-4709; www.thornvillebackwoodsfest.com. One of Ohio's finest arts-and-crafts festivals. Always the third weekend in September.

Restaurants

Inn-Town Restaurant: 7 South Main St., Thornville.

Anthony's Pizza: 107 West Main St., Somerset; (740) 734-1522.

The Little Phil Inn: 102 East Main St., Somerset; (740) 743-2330.

Clay Haus Restaurant: 123 West Main St., Somerset; (740) 743-1326; www.clayhaus.com. The finest in German and American dining in a historic building. It is reported to be haunted by any number of spirits.

Accommodations

Zane Trace Inn: 129 West Main St., Somerset; (740) 743-9230; www.zanetraceinn.com. Country life at its finest. Ohio's premier scrapbook retreat.

Bike Shops

Southside Cycling: 2924 Maysville Pike, South Zanesville; (740) 453-7550.

Restrooms

Start/finish: At the Inn-Town Restaurant in Thornville.

Mile 12.0: In Somerset.

Maps

DeLorme: Ohio Atlas & Gazetteer: Page 63.

32 Albany Challenge

Meandering through the foothills of the Appalachians, this route boasts glorious scenery: woods and farmland, creeks and ponds. In spring the wildflowers coat the hills. In autumn the color is vibrant, as it is throughout the unglaciated portions of Ohio, and that's the locale of this ride. Expect exhilarating hills and ravines.

Start: Albany Village Park in Albany near Athens.
Length: 35.7-mile figure-eight loop.
Terrain: If you like hills, this is your ride.

Traffic and hazards: Traffic is mostly light—a little busier close to Albany and during rush hour on the state routes. The cars tend to go fast on the country roads, which are narrow and winding, and did we mention hilly?

Getting there: From US 50/SR 32 in Albany, take State Street/SR 681 west. It is less than a mile to the park. Turn right on SR 681, now Washington Road. When 681 goes left, continue straight on Washington Road. Turn left onto Lee Street, then right onto Broad Street, and the park is right there on the right.

The Ride

Coming from southwestern Ohio, where hills are little to middle-sized with flatlands in between, the hill-to-hill-to-hill riding of southeastern Ohio always gives me pause. I've even been known to walk up a few, but the scenery is so gorgeous I don't mind. I don't know if it is the scenery or something in the air, but many cyclists thrive on those hills—Athens County and the surrounding area is a hotbed of bicycling activity.

This route is taken from a series of five self-guided Athens, Vinton, and Meigs County tours called "Tom's Trillium Tour" (these and other self-guided tours are available at www.athenscyclepath.com—just follow the link). In the spring redbud, dogwood, and wildflowers make the hills look like a watercolor painting. In fall the color is breathtaking.

This loop ride begins in Albany, in the southwest corner of Athens County, then meanders briefly into Vinton and Meigs Counties. Many of the road signs on this route are placed what in my part of the state would be considered sideways. It can be confusing until you get used to it.

As you pedal away from the park in Albany, the traffic gradually eases. After crossing Baker Road, you'll begin to get a feel for the beauty of this area—the woods, beautiful farms, and open country. The road is winding and scenic with some little hills.

Sunflowers on the way ▶

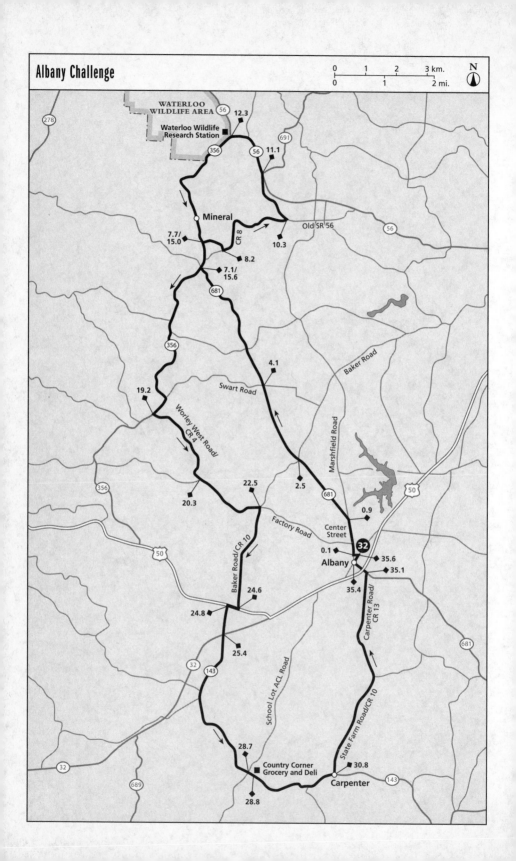

Albany Challenge

WATERLOO
WILDLIFE AREA

Waterloo Wildlife
Research Station

12.3
11.1
10.3

278
56
691
356
56
Old SR 56
56
50

Mineral

7.7/
15.0
8.2
7.1/
15.6

CR 8

681

356

4.1

Swart Road

Baker Road

19.2

Worley West Road/
CR 4

20.3

22.5
2.5

681

0.9

Marshfield Road

Factory Road

Center
Street

356

50

32

Albany
0.1
35.6
35.1
35.4

Baker Road/ CR 10

24.6
24.8
25.4

Carpenter Road/
CR 13

32
143

School Lot ACL Road

State Farm Road/ CR 10

28.7
28.8

Country Corner
Grocery and Deli

30.8

681

Carpenter
143

32

689

CR 8 is still scenic, but also narrow, winding, and uphill. Heads up! Old SR 56 has a speed limit of 55 miles per hour but not too many cars. It's got some thigh-busting hills.

You'll ride through the Waterloo Wildlife Research Management Station, the office and laboratory of the Ohio Division of Wildlife's forest wildlife research. The wooded areas are used for squirrel research. There's also a wild turkey management unit on the site. If you're a bird junkie, eighty species of birds can be seen here, including ruffed grouse.

Pass SR 681 on the left, and in a short distance take a brief meander into Vinton County, the least populated of Ohio's eighty-eight counties—beautiful country. Return to Athens County and you'll see a few more homes.

Next the route drops down into Meigs County. Meigs has 57.2 miles of Ohio River shoreline, but you won't get even a glimpse of river on this route. In Valley Ford you will see the Country Corner Grocery and Deli, which has farm-fresh, locally produced milk and other refreshments but no restroom. Cross Leading Creek and you'll see signage for the Carpenter Inn and Conference Center.

In Carpenter, just over the crest of a hill, turn left onto State Farm Road. Before you know it you'll notice a few more houses and cars as you return to Albany and wind your way back to the park.

Miles and Directions

0.0 Exit the park and go left on Broad Street, then right onto Lee Street.

0.1 Turn right onto Center Street/SR 681.

0.9 Bear left on SR 681 when Marshfield Road goes straight.

2.5 Cross Baker Road.

4.1 Cross Swart Road.

7.1 SR 681 ends. Turn right onto SR 356.

7.7 Turn right onto Mineral Road/CR 8.

8.2 Bear left on CR 8 when Lovers Lane goes right.

10.3 At the T turn left onto Old SR 56.

11.1 At the T turn left onto SR 56.

12.3 Turn left onto SR 356 when SR 56 goes right. Pass the Waterloo Wildlife Research Management Station.

14.2 Come into Mineral, which is a few houses and a church.

15.6 Continue straight when you pass SR 681 to the left.

19.2 Turn left onto Worley West Road/CR 4.

20.3 Enter Athens County and the road becomes Factory Road.

22.5 Turn right onto Baker Road/CR 10.

24.6 At the T turn right onto US 50.

24.8 Turn left onto SR 143 toward Middleport.

25.4 Carefully cross SR 32—it's four lanes.

25.6 Enter Meigs County.

28.7 Cross School Lot ACL Road.

28.8 Pass Country Corner Grocery and Deli, which has drinks and sandwiches but no restrooms.

30.8 Enter Carpenter, and just over the crest of a hill, turn left onto State Farm Road/CR 10.

33.3 Cross into Athens County. The road changes to Carpenter Road/CR 13.

35.1 Turn left onto State Street/SR 681. Cross US 50.

35.4 Turn right onto Washington Road, which is still SR 681. When SR 681 turns left, continue straight on Washington Road.

35.6 Turn left onto Lee Street.

35.7 Turn right onto Broad Street. The end.

Local Information

Athens County Convention and Visitors Bureau: 667 East State St., Athens; (740) 592-1819 or (800) 878-9767; www.athensohio.com.

Events/Attractions

Ohio Pawpaw Festival: Lake Snowden, Albany; (740) 698-6060; www.pawpawfest.com. This is the biggest and best pawpaw celebration in the world! Join pawpaw fanatics from around the country at the peak of the season each September for a day filled with pawpaws, pawpaw foods, pawpaw beer, pawpaw music, pawpaw art, pawpaw history, pawpaw people, and much more.

Athens Farmers Market: 1000 East State St., Athens; (740) 593-6763; www.athensfarmers market.org. Open every Saturday year-round and Wednesdays during the warmer months. This market is called one of the nation's best by *Audubon* magazine.

Restaurants

Deputy's Pizza and Subs: 5329 Washington Rd., Albany; (740) 698-4911. Near the start of the ride.

Dairy Queen: 2384 Blizzard Lane, Albany; (740) 698-2384.

Accommodations

Carpenter Inn and Conference Center: 39655 Carpenter Dyesville Rd., Carpenter; (740) 698-2450 or (800) 644-2422. Referred to as "a world of comfort and tranquility," the inn is situated on 250 acres of rolling hills. It is located near the bike route.

Bike Shops

Cycle Path: 104 West Union St., Athens; (740) 593-8482; www.athenscyclepath.com. This bike shop is an excellent resource for bike routes in the area.

Restrooms

Start/finish: None at the park, but there are gas stations and fast-food places nearby.

Maps

DeLorme: Ohio Atlas & Gazetteer: Page 73.

33 Athens Quilt Barn Cruise

Called a Patchwork Tour, this quilt barn tour combines hills, quilts, and weathered barns. The route passes five of the Athens County Quilt Blocks and the Bicentennial Barn, all in the hills of Athens County; there is a flat stretch on the Hockhocking Adena Bikeway.

Start: The Hockhocking Adena Bikeway at the Athens Community Center.
Length: 29.5-mile loop.
Terrain: Hilly with some invigorating climbs.
Traffic and hazards: Heavy traffic for short distances on West Union Street and Richland Avenue—there's no shoulder but there are sidewalks. The route crosses US 50/SR 32, a busy four-lane highway, twice. Traffic is moderate to light on other roads, which are narrow, winding, and hilly.

Getting there: Take US 50/US 33 into Athens and turn east onto East State Street. The community center is about a quarter mile down on the right. It sits back off the road, and the only sign is on the building. The route starts on the Hockhocking Adena Bikeway, which can be accessed from the back of the parking lot of the Athens Community Center, 701 East State Street, Athens. Locals refer to the garden spot on the bikeway where the ride begins as "the Stanley Triangle."

The Ride

Resting in the Appalachian foothills, Athens County is a cool place full of arts, crafts, agriculture, and interesting people. *Mother Earth News* listed it as one of the "Twelve Greatest Places You've Never Heard Of."

Wanting to promote the artistic and agricultural aspects of the county as well as its Appalachian heritage, a group of individuals, artists, and organizations devised the Quilt Barn Project. They painted quilt squares on more than twenty old and weathered barns, reminiscent of the way logos were once painted on barn sides.

The ride hangs mostly in the suburban area surrounding Athens and wanders through some farmland. It starts and ends on the bikeway, which stretches along the Hocking River for 19 miles from Athens to Nelsonville. Gaslights make the section along the Ohio University campus scenic, but beware—you risk getting your car towed if you park there.

Starting out on the bikeway, ride along the Hocking River and get a great view of the Athens skyline. Exit the bikeway by the Habitat House/mini-park by turning left onto West Union Street, which is busy. Elliotsville Road starts out up a hill and keeps going. The first quilt barn, showcasing the Appalachian Sunburst Block, is on the right. This restored barn was built with sandstone and slate from an 1880s barn. Continue on Elliotsville and look for Ernie when you pass Sesame Street.

There's a scenic overlook when you turn right onto Stage Coach Road, and— don't get bored—the road is briefly flat. On Ervin Road you ride alongside the

Dairy Barn Arts Center

railroad tracks for a while and next to an interesting drop-off before crossing the tracks. Marion Johnson Road crosses US 50/SR 32—a busy four-lane highway. But before you cross, keep going for a tenth of a mile to see the Athens County Bicentennial Barn. Then backtrack, cross the highway, and continue on CR 80, which soon becomes Hebbardsville Road.

When you're on Harner Road, you could turn left to continue the route and skip the Passion Flower Block, but you'd be missing a great barn. It is a unique design created by artists from Passion Works Studio, which offers opportunities for people with developmental disabilities in collaboration with professional artists and community members. The Passion Flower is the official flower of Athens. The barn itself was built in 1845. That's a natural gas pumping facility you pass on Sams Road.

Back on Fisher Road you'll pass the Corn and Bean Block: Athens County has over 510 farms averaging 160 acres. Surrounded by farmland, this barn was erected as a milking barn in the late 1880s.

Wind around, cross the highway, and double back toward Athens. Go slow on the brick road that runs in front of the Dairy Barn. Built in 1914, the Dairy Barn is listed on the National Register of Historic Places. It sits on thirty-six acres of land and was at one time a working dairy barn for the state asylum. The barn was slated to be demolished, but nine days before that was scheduled to happen, Harriet and Ora Anderson petitioned the governor and eventually the barn became a community art

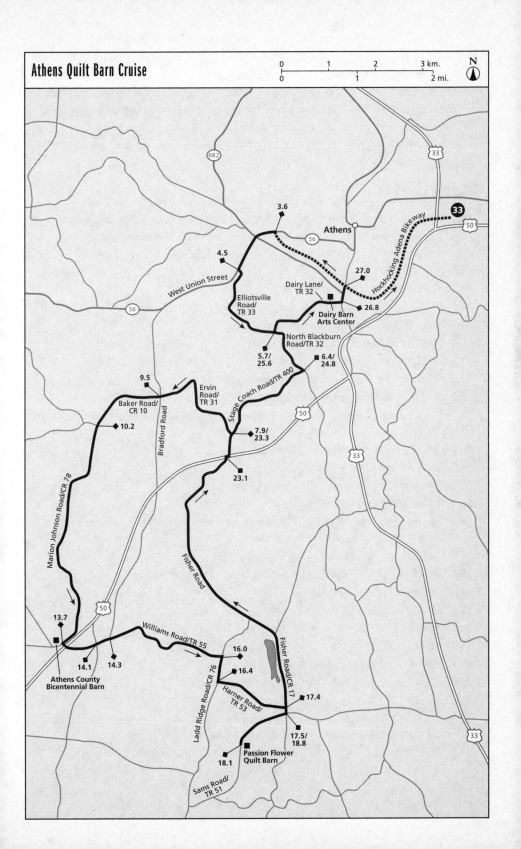

Athens Quilt Barn Cruise

0   1   2   3 km.
0   1   2 mi.

N

682

33

US 50

3.6

Athens

56

27.0

Hockhocking Adena Bikeway

33
50

4.5

West Union Street

Dairy Lane/
TR 32

26.8

56

Elliotsville
Road/
TR 33

Dairy Barn Arts Center

North Blackburn
Road/TR 32

5.7/
25.6

6.4/
24.8

9.5

Ervin
Road/
TR 31

Stage Coach Road/TR 400

50

Baker Road/
CR 10

Bradford Road

33

10.2

7.9/
23.3

23.1

Marion Johnson Road/CR 78

Fisher Road

50

13.7

Williams Road/TR 55

16.0

Fisher Road/CR 17

14.1

14.3

16.4

Athens County
Bicentennial Barn

Ladd Ridge Road/CR 76

Harner Road/
TR 53

17.4

17.5/
18.8

18.1

Passion Flower
Quilt Barn

33

Sams Road/
TR 51

center. The Dairy Barn Star Block (yellow) and the Quilt National Block (blue) are on opposite ends of the building. It is definitely worth your while to stroll through the Dairy Barn.

Turning onto Richland Avenue is a traffic challenge; cross the bridge on the walkway, and just on the other side there is a quick turn to the right, before the first traffic light, and a short, steep downhill to take you back to the bike path for the return to the Stanley Triangle.

Miles and Directions

0.0   From the Athens Community Center turn right onto the Hockhocking Adena Bikeway.

3.6   Exit the bikeway and turn left onto West Union Street/SR 56. Restrooms and water are available here.

4.5   Turn left onto Elliotsville Road/TR 33.

4.6   At the Y bear right; you're still on Elliotsville Road.

4.8   The Appalachian Sunburst Block is on the right. Keep going.

5.7   Bear right onto North Blackburn Road/TR 32.

6.4   Turn right onto Stage Coach Road/TR 400.

7.9   Turn right onto Ervin Road/TR 31.

9.5   Cross Bradford Road; Ervin becomes Baker Road/CR 10.

10.2   Bear left onto Marion Johnson Road/CR 78.

13.7   You are going to cross US 50/SR 32, then continue straight on CR 80. That barn just ahead is the Athens County Bicentennial Barn.

14.1   The road becomes Hebbardsville Road/CR 19.

14.3   Turn right onto Williams Road/TR 55.

16.0   Turn right at the T onto Ladd Ridge Road/CR 76.

16.4   Go left onto Harner Road/TR 53.

17.4   Turn right onto Fisher Road/CR 17. **Option:** Turn left onto Fisher Road to continue the route and skip the Passion Flower Quilt Barn.

17.5   Turn right onto Sams Road/TR 51.

18.1   The Passion Flower Block is on the left; turn around and backtrack.

18.8   Turn left onto Fisher Road/CR 17.

19.0   The Corn and Bean Block is on the right.

23.1   Cross US 50/SR 32 and continue straight onto Ervin Road/TR 31.

23.3   Turn right onto Stage Coach Road/TR 400; you've been here before.

23.7   Continue straight when Cornell Road goes left.

24.8   At the T go left onto North Blackburn Road/TR 32.

25.6   Turn right onto Dairy Lane/TR 32.

26.1   Stop at the Dairy Barn Arts Center. Go around the barn to see both the Quilt National and the Dairy Barn Star quilts. There are restrooms inside.

26.8   Turn left onto Richland Avenue. This is a busy intersection. Get onto the walkway and ride across the bridge.

27.0 Just across the bridge by the OHIO UNIVERSITY INFORMATION sign, before the first traffic light, turn a sharp right, ride down a short, steep hill, and bear a slight left onto the bikeway.

29.5 End at the community center.

Local Information

Athens County Convention and Visitors Bureau: 667 East State St., Athens; (740) 592-1819 or (800) 878-9767, www.athensohio.com.

Events/Attractions

Ohio Pawpaw Festival: Lake Snowden, Albany; (740) 698-6060; www.pawpawfest.com. This is the biggest and best pawpaw celebration in the world! Join pawpaw fanatics from around the country at the peak of the season each September for a day filled with pawpaws, pawpaw foods, pawpaw beer, pawpaw music, pawpaw art, pawpaw history, pawpaw people, and much more.

Athens Farmers Market: 1000 East State St., Athens; (740) 593-6763; www.athensfarmers market.org. Open every Saturday year-round and Wednesdays during the warmer months. This market is called one of the nation's best by *Audubon* magazine.

Restaurants

Casa Neuva: 6 West State St., Athens; (740) 592-2016; www.casanueva.com. An innovative worker-owned cooperative promoting local food.

Athens has a typical college town's unique array of restaurants.

Accommodations

The Cabin at Chimney Lake Bed and Breakfast: 8776 Mine Rd., Athens; (740) 592-4147 or (888) 592-4147; wwwbigchimney.com. A log house nestled in the woods overlooking a lake and the hills beyond.

Bike Shops

Cycle Path: 104 West Union St., Athens; (740) 593-8482; www.athenscyclepath.com. This bike shop is an excellent resource for bike routes in the area.

Restrooms

Start/finish: At the community center.
Mile 3.6: The mini-park as you exit the bike path.
Mile 26.1: The Dairy Barn Arts Center.

Maps

DeLorme: Ohio Atlas & Gazetteer: Page 73.

34 Cambridge Challenge

This is an out-and-back ride from Cambridge through Salt Fork State Park to the lodge and back. It's a reasonably rolling ride—okay, there are a few hills—but this is hill country. You will enjoy beautiful, scenic views of Guernsey County and Salt Fork Reservoir.

Start: On East Pike Road/US 40 just east of Cambridge.
Length: 28.7-mile out-and-back with an optional 3.6-mile side-trip.
Terrain: Guernsey County is unglaciated, and that means hilly. However, this ride covers some of the flattest land to be found. Read: rolling with some long, lovely flat stretches—especially on Endley Road—and hills.
Traffic and hazards: Old National Road/CR 450 is narrow with hairpin turns and loose gravel. There is some traffic on US 22, but there's a wide shoulder.

Getting there: From I-77 take exit 46A onto East Pike Road/US 40—go east and you're right there. Or take US 22/US 40, which becomes Wheeling Avenue in Cambridge, east from Cambridge. On Wheeling Avenue cross I-77 (don't follow US 22 when it goes left) and it becomes East Pike. There are a cemetery and several small businesses where you can park. We parked with permission at 10150 East Pike Road, at Security First Capitol Limited Resort Developing.

The Ride

This ride leaves from Cambridge, a pleasant and historic small town. Wheeling Avenue, the main drag, is lined with unique shops and restaurants (also a bakery and ice-cream shop). The route is based on the Cambridge Countryside Ride, which takes place every July. Bicyclists leave from the scenic courthouse and have lots of help to get out of town safely. To avoid the traffic on Wheeling Avenue and US 40, you can drive east out of town a ways—past I-77. Find a place to park and then bike away from Cambridge on East Pike Road.

The ride starts out on US 40, the Historic National Road. Most pioneers reached Guernsey County by traveling on Zane's Trace, a trail carved out of the wilderness in 1796. That route was replaced in 1827 by the Old National Road. Designated by President Thomas Jefferson in 1827, it was the nation's first interstate highway linking the eastern seaboard with the western frontier. It mostly follows US 40. This ride also goes on the Old National Road/CR 450.

Soon after starting out you'll be pedaling uphill; the road surface is rough, the road is narrow and winding, but don't fret. It gets much better soon. Endley Road goes to the right first—don't go that way; wait until it turns left. It is blissfully flat with lots of wildflowers in the spring. If you're lucky, you might see wild turkeys or hear a bobwhite quail.

Just past Zane Road there's a scenic overlook of Guernsey County. I hope the chainsaw-carved bear is still roaring on the west side of the road. Turn onto US 22

Along the lake toward the marina

and start up the long steady hill. The road is wide and smooth; traffic is not bad. Turn left into Salt Fork State Park, and you'll soon come to the park office on the right. There are restrooms there, and you can pick up a park map.

The name Salt Fork is said to come from a salt well used by Native Americans that was located near the southeastern corner of the park. Salt Fork is a scenic blend of rich woodlands and rolling meadows bordering Salt Fork Lake.

Don't miss the side-trip to the marina. It will give you a good view of the lake, which is a reservoir. Continue on Park Road #1 and keep heading toward the lodge. The road is certainly rolling, but the views are great. Pass the beach and the horsemen's area. Turn left onto Park Road #3 and pass the golf course.

Ride up to the lodge and enjoy the view and the amenities. Then turn around and go back.

Miles and Directions

0.0 Leaving from 10150 East Pike Road/US 40, across from the cemetery, turn left.

0.7 Turn left onto Old National Road, also known as CR 450.

1.5 Bear right and stay on Old National Road when Larrick Ridge Road goes left.

2.0 Continue straight when Endley Road goes right.

2.1 Bear left onto Endley Road.

3.6 Stay left on Endley when Zane Road goes right.

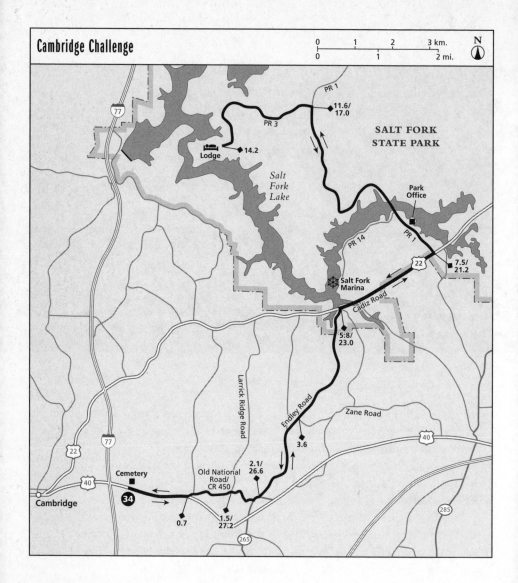

Cambridge Challenge

0   1   2   3 km.
0   1   2 mi.

N

SALT FORK
STATE PARK

Salt
Fork
Lake

Lodge ◆ 14.2

PR 1

PR 3

◆ 11.6/
17.0

Park
Office

PR 1

PR 14

22

◆ 7.5/
21.2

Salt Fork
Marina

Cadiz Road

◆ 5.8/
23.0

Larrick Ridge Road

Endley Road

Zane Road

◆ 3.6

40

2.1/
26.6

Old National
Road/
CR 450

Cemetery

40

34

Cambridge

◆ 0.7

1.5/
27.2

265

285

77

22   77

5.8 At the T turn right onto Cadiz Road/US 22.

7.5 Turn left into Salt Fork State Park and get on Park Road #1.

8.1 Pass the park office—restrooms.

8.5 Continue to follow Park Road #1 past the beach and the horsemen's area. **Side-trip:** Turn left toward Salt Fork Marina on Park Road #14 for a 3.6-mile round-trip, down-and-back scenic tour. There is a restroom at the marina. Continue the ride by turning left back at Park Road #1.

11.6 Turn left toward the lodge on Park Road #3.

14.2 When you reach the lodge, you'll find a restaurant and restrooms.

14.3	Exit the lodge, turning right onto Park Road #3.
17.0	Go right on Park Road #1 toward US 22 and I-77.
21.2	Turn right onto Cadiz Road/US 22.
23.0	Turn left onto Endley Road.
26.6	At the T turn right onto Old National Road.
26.7	Stay on Old National when Endley Road goes left.
27.2	Bear left, still on Old National Road, when Larrick Ridge Road goes right.
28.7	Reach the end of the ride.

Local Information

Cambridge/Guernsey County Visitors and Convention Bureau: Guernsey County Administration Building, 627 Wheeling Ave., Cambridge; (800) 933-5480; www.visitguernseycounty.com. Two free tour brochures, a Cambridge walking tour and a National Road (US 40) driving tour, are available here.

Attractions

Salt Fork State Park: 14755 Cadiz Rd., Lore City; (740) 439-3521; www.ohiostateparks.org. Ohio's largest state park offers fishing, swimming, golf, and more. It has a lodge, Timbers Restaurant, and Trekkers Snack Bar.

The Wilds: 14000 International Rd., Cumberland; (740) 638-5030; www.thewilds.org. A 10,000-acre wildlife conservation center.

Restaurants

Kennedy's Bakery: 1025 Wheeling Ave., Cambridge; (740) 432-2301. Good cookies and other baked goods since 1925. Has placed first, second, and third in the USA Baking Contest.

Accommodations

1511 Clairmont Bed and Breakfast: 1511 Clairmont Ave., Cambridge; (740) 432-8406 or (888) 524-5005; www.1511clairmont.com.

Bike Shops

Southside Cycling: 2924 Maysville Pike, Zanesville; (740) 453-7550.

Restrooms

Start/finish: In Cambridge.
Mile 8.1: The park office.
Mile 14.2: Salt Fork Lodge.

Maps

DeLorme: Ohio Atlas & Gazetteer: Page 55.
A Salt Fork State Park map is available at the park office.

35 Muskingum Valley Classic

This gutsy ride winds through the scenic, hilly, and very hilly northeastern part of the state. It passes the Tappan and Leesville Lake Parks and travels along the Moravian Trail Scenic Byway. At the end of the day, you'll be tired.

Start: Tuscora Park, New Philadelphia.
Length: 66.4 miles.
Terrain: This is unglaciated Ohio and that means hills.
Traffic and hazards: Traffic is heavy getting out of New Philadelphia, but there's a shoulder most of the way. It's also busy on US 250 and on SR 39 from Sherrodsville back to New Philadelphia, where the shoulder is stingy to nonexistent. Throughout the route many of the roads have light traffic, but they are narrow and visibility is limited because of hills and bends.

Getting there: From SR 800/SR 416, which is North Broadway in New Philadelphia, turn west onto Tuscora Park Avenue—you will see signage for the park, which is on the right at 161 Tuscora Park Avenue.

The Ride

This route goes through a section of the Muskingum Valley Conservancy District. This district was organized in 1933 for the purposes of flood control, conservation, and recreation. It comprises 54,000 acres of land and water. The ride traverses a beautiful section of the state replete with lakes, woods, and farmland.

Pack enough water and fuel for a long day. Throw in some Twinkies if you like; you'll burn them off on the hills.

On your way out of New Philadelphia, the 1882 Tuscarawas County Courthouse is on the left. This first part of the ride is urban and not too scenic, but be patient. Before leaving town, you'll pass the Schoenbrunn Village State Memorial—it's the site of the first Ohio town and a living history museum. Also look for the airport where John Glenn learned to fly. When you exit New Philadelphia, you will in short order come upon the first cornfields and hills.

Come into Uhrichsville and then Dennison. The Dennison Depot was the site of a famous World War II servicemen's canteen that served 1.5 million GIs. The depot stands exactly halfway between Pittsburgh and Columbus—100 miles to the east and west, respectively—because that is as far as a steam engine could go before it needed water.

Enjoy the pleasant scenery and the flat stretch along Mount Bethel Road. Climb a big hill or two, be cautious on US 250, and then enjoy another flat section on Reed Road and the quilt barn on the right.

1882 Tuscarawas County Courthouse

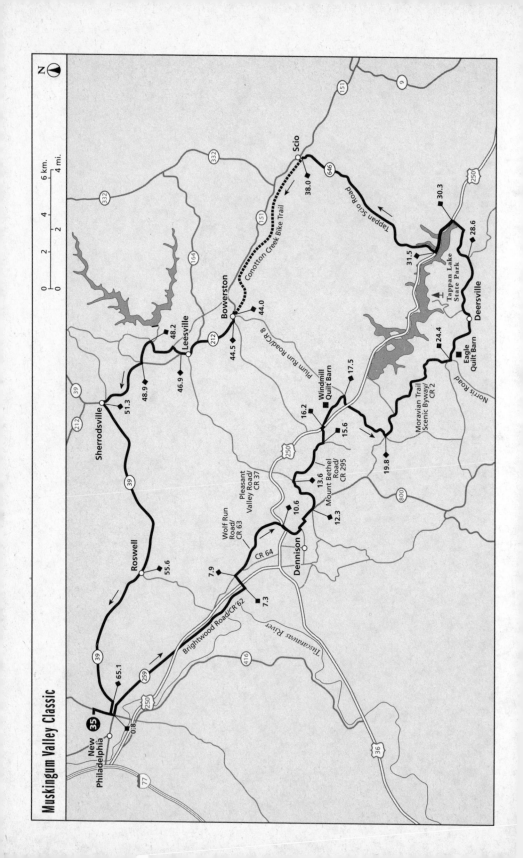

Muskingum Valley Classic

N

0 2 4 6 km.
0 2 4 mi.

New Philadelphia

35

0.8

65.1

259

250

77

39

Roswell

55.6

7.9

7.3

Brightwood Road/CR 62

Tuscarawas River

416

36

Sherrodsville

51.3

39

212

48.9

46.9

48.2

Leesville

212

44.5

Bowerston

44.0

Plum Run Road/CR 8

332

164

332

Conotton Creek Bike Trail

151

Scio

38.0

646

9

151

Tappan Scio Road

31.5

30.3

Tappan Lake State Park

28.6

Deersville

Eagle Quilt Barn

24.4

Moravian Trail Scenic Byway/CR 2

Norris Road

250

800

19.8

17.5

Windmill Quilt Barn

16.2

15.6

Mount Bethel Road/CR 295

13.6

12.3

10.6

Dennison

CR 64

Wolf Run Road/CR 63

Pleasant Valley Road/CR 37

250

Get your breath after the big climb on Plum Run Road and turn left onto the Moravian Trail Scenic Byway. You're biking along a trail used by the Delaware and Wyandot Indians before white settlers came into the region. It became known as the Moravian Trail when Moravian missionaries followed it to establish settlements in the region. The trail was also one of the major stagecoach routes in the area. Ride through Feed Springs, where travelers would pause to feed their livestock at the springs.

The next long climb at least has some flat areas to allow you to catch your breath. You'll come into Deersville. By now you may need refreshment, so visit the Deersville General Store. It has pizza, a deli, and world-famous homemade ice cream. Ride up a steep hill and through the Deersville National Historic District. You'll pass the entrance to Tappan Lake Park on the left. It is about a mile to ride back to the lake (restrooms and concessions are available at the beach in season), but you don't really have to take the trip because you will be going along the lake on US 250. It has a shoulder.

Leave the scenic byway when you turn right onto SR 646. Come into Scio and turn right onto East Main Street. You'll see the Conotton Creek bike path signs; go left. The bike path is a pleasant respite going through wetlands, over bridges, and past sandstone cuts. Watch for wildlife. When you exit the trail at Bowerston, which is really the beginning of the trail, you'll feel as if you are in somebody's backyard. Just follow the little roadway to SR 151.

Highway riding takes you into Leesville, and guess which way you're going; that's right—up. Stay to the right on the loop and get out of town. Azalea Road is a rough-surfaced road taking you to Leesville Lake. Deer Road goes right from Azalea and then left in a couple of tenths of a mile. Go right on Deer for the side-trip to Leesville Lake and Dam, or left to continue the route.

Pedal up and down another hill, wind around in Sherrodsville, and head for home on SR 39. It's narrow, hilly, and winding, and the cars go fast. Ride through Roswell and back into New Philadelphia and to the park. Go somewhere for a really nice dinner. You deserve it.

Miles and Directions

0.0   Exit the park by turning left onto Tuscora Park Avenue and then right onto North Broadway.

0.8   Turn left onto East High Avenue by the courthouse.

1.2   Bear right on US 259 (which is still East High Avenue) when SR 39 goes left.

4.4   Continue straight on Brightwood Road/CR 62.

7.3   Go left onto Johnson Drive and cross US 250.

7.9   Turn right onto East Fork Port Road/CR 64.

8.2   Continue straight on Wolf Run Road/CR 63 when CR 64 goes right.

10.3   Turn right onto Fette Road/CR 35.

10.6   At the T go right onto US 250, also called Cadiz Dennison Road.

10.7 Continue straight onto SR 800.

11.3 The route continues to the left on Center Street. **Side-trip:** Turn right and go less than a mile for a side-trip to the Dennison Depot, which houses a museum, restaurant, and gift shop and lots of history.

11.4 Bend right and cross the railroad tracks; you're now on Jewett Avenue.

11.9 Turn left onto Taylor Avenue/SR 800.

12.0 Turn right onto Johnson Avenue/SR 800 when Taylor Avenue goes straight.

12.3 Turn left onto Pleasant Valley Road/CR 37.

13.6 Take a right onto Mount Bethel Road/CR 295.

15.6 Turn left onto Edie Road.

16.1 Jog right onto US 250.

16.2 Turn left onto Reed Road/CR 503.

17.2 Stop to see the Windmill Quilt Barn.

17.5 Turn right onto Plum Run Road/CR 8.

18.0 Cross US 250.

19.8 Turn left onto the Moravian Trail Scenic Byway/CR 2.

24.4 Bear left around the bend and stay on Moravian Trail when Norris Road goes right.

24.7 The Eagle Quilt Barn is on the right.

26.0 Come into Deersville, where CR 2 is also Main Street. (Out of town it becomes Deersville Ridge Road.)

26.3 The Deersville General Store is on the right. Just ahead, the community building has public restrooms in the back.

26.5 The entrance to Tappan Lake Park is on the left. Ride back about a mile for a look at the lake. Restrooms and concessions are available seasonally at the beach.

28.6 Continue straight onto Deersville Road/SR 55 when Deersville Ridge Road goes right.

30.3 At the T turn left onto US 250.

31.5 Turn right onto Tappan Scio Road/SR 646.

37.7 Caution—hazardous intersection. Continue straight, now on Fowler Road.

37.9 Turn right onto East Main Street.

38.0 Go left onto the Conotton Creek Trail.

44.0 The bike trail ends. Follow the driveway-like road onto Broadway Street.

44.1 Bear right onto Erie Street.

44.2 Turn left onto SR 151.

44.5 Turn right onto Leesville Road/SR 212.

46.4 The road becomes Green Street in Leesville.

46.7 Bear right around the loop.

46.9 Turn right onto Azalea Road.

48.0 Pass Deer Road on the right. **Side-trip:** Turn right onto Deer Road and ride for 2 miles to see Leesville Lake and Dam; then return to the route.

48.2 Turn left onto Deer Road.

48.9 At the T turn right onto SR 212.

50.7 Come into Sherrodsville.

51.3 Turn left onto SR 39 toward New Philadelphia.

55.6 Come into Roswell.

64.8 In New Philadelphia the road becomes Beaver Avenue.

65.1 Turn right onto Pearl Street.

65.3 The road becomes Ray Avenue.

65.7 Turn right onto North Broadway.

66.3 Turn left onto Tuscora Park Avenue.

66.4 Hope your legs can get you to your car.

Local Information

Carroll County Convention and Visitors Bureau: 61 North Lisbon St., Carrollton; (330) 627-0103 or (887) 727-0103; www.carrollcountyohio.com. **Tuscarawas County Convention and Visitors Bureau:** 124 East High Ave., New Philadelphia; (330) 602-2420 or (800) 527-3387; www.ohiotimelessadventures.com.

Attractions

Atwood Lake Resort: 2650 Lodge Rd., Sherrodsville; (330) 343-6780; www.atwoodlakeresort.com. The 1,540-acre lake offers swimming, boating, vacation cabins, and more. The resort and conference center, overlooking the lake, offers fine accommodations and dining.

Restaurants

Bluebird Farm Restaurant, Gift Shop and Toy Museum: 190 Alamo Rd., Carrollton; (330) 627-7980; www.bluebird-farm.com. Great home-cooked specialties. Breakfast and lunch only.

Bike Shops

Ernie's Bicycle Shops: 315 Wabash Ave. NW, New Philadelphia; (330) 343-4056; www.ernies bikeshop.com.

Restrooms

Start/finish: Tuscora Park.
Mile 11.3: At the Dennison Depot on the side-trip.
Mile 26.2: Deersville Community Building—in the back.

Maps

DeLorme: Ohio Atlas & Gazetteer: Page 45.

36 Medina Ramble

Medina County is currently one of the ten fastest-growing counties in Ohio, despite the fact that it has a large agricultural base. This ride traverses that agricultural land while also visiting four small, interesting villages: Chippewa-on-the-Lake, Seville, Creston, and Westfield Center.

Start: Buckeye Woods Park in Medina.
Length: 24.9 miles.
Terrain: Rolling with some doable hills.

Traffic and hazards: Moderate traffic; avoid rush hour.

Getting there: Take I-71 to exit 209 to I-76 East. In about a half mile take exit 2 to SR 3. Follow SR 3 north for about 5 miles to Wedgewood Road/CR 162. Turn left (west). In about 3 miles you'll come to Buckeye Woods Park, at 6335 Wedgewood Road, Medina, on the right. The parking area is near the ball fields.

The Ride

Medina County is in the Western Reserve, a 120-mile strip between Lake Erie and a line about 3 miles south of the present-day US 224. This land once belonged to Connecticut. In 1795 that state sold it to a land company. Small problem was that the Indians still held title to the land west of the Cuyahoga River. The title was not cleared until the Treaty of Fort Industry in 1805. The land company arranged for the surveying of most of the land into townships. To this day the Western Reserve townships differ in size from most townships in the rest of the state.

The staging area for this ride is Buckeye Woods Park, so named for the grove of buckeye trees (Ohio's state tree) growing along the creek in the Schleman Nature Preserve (the bike route returns through the nature preserve).

Be cautious at the start of the ride—expect traffic, and the roads are narrow. In a couple of miles you will come into the village of Chippewa-on-the-Lake, which is on Chippewa Lake, Ohio's largest natural inland lake. The route passes a deli— Goodman's Corner Cupboard—if you're hungry.

Ride on to Seville and go past Leohr Park, which includes a pond, a restored wetland, and a path connecting to downtown Seville—you could follow it if you want to see Seville. If not, ride on and leave town; soon the route crosses over into Wayne County farmland, complete with oil wells.

Ride through Creston, which was a railroad town founded in the late 1800s when the Atlantic and Great Western Railroad came through. That was horse-and-buggy days, this was farm country, and the rail business flourished. There's now a car wash where that original rail line was. Two railroads still run through Creston, and you will cross those tracks. The village has a fifty-acre park with restrooms—go right on Main Street for maybe a block if you need that facility. Out of Creston, return to farmland.

The park is named for the buckeyes growing there

You will see a few privately owned oil wells. Turn right onto Seville Road just before I-71 and ride parallel to the highway for a bit. This section of the ride is rolling.

On Leroy Road you will ride into the village of Westfield Center, home to the Westfield Group. In 1848 the Ohio Farmers Insurance was founded by local farmers. In 1971 it became the Westfield Group. The company is said to have "put the village on the map." It is the largest employer in Medina County.

Settlers from New England came to the region in 1817. Their neighbors were the Wolf and Chippewa Indians. The town was established in 1826 and the village was laid out as a typical New England settlement with a central four-acre green. Stay to the right as you bike around that green and then turn right, past the fire station, still on Leroy Road.

Traffic picks up as you go through Chippewa-on-the-Lake again. The lake is on the right. The end of the ride is a scenic tour through a wetland in the Schleman Nature Preserve. I have seen bald eagles there; you can count on seeing great blue herons, kingfishers, and other water birds. Exit the trail when you see the ball fields.

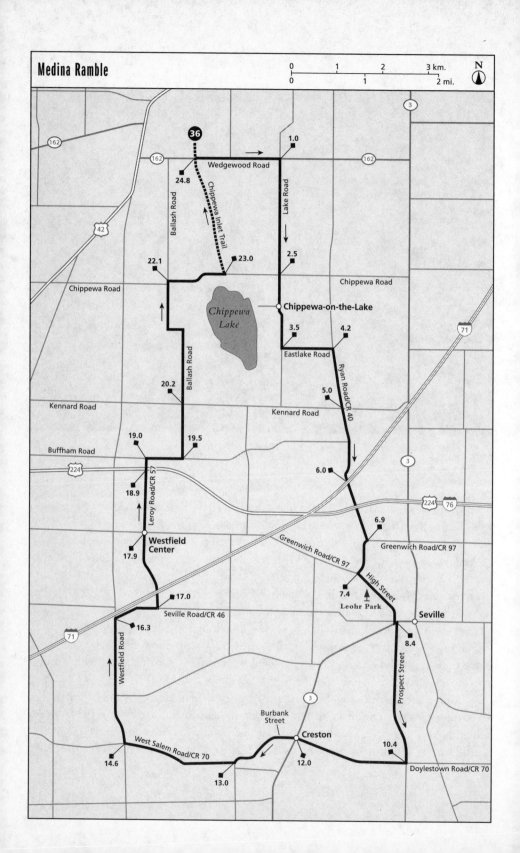

Medina Ramble

0   1   2   3 km.
0   1   2 mi.

N

162

36

24.8

Ballash Road

Chippewa Inlet Trail

Wedgewood Road

1.0

→

Lake Road

162

3

↓

2.5

42

22.1   23.0

Chippewa Road   Chippewa Road

Chippewa Lake

◇ **Chippewa-on-the-Lake**

Ballash Road

↑

3.5   4.2

Eastlake Road

Ryan Road/CR 40

71

20.2

Kennard Road   Kennard Road

5.0

Buffham Road

19.0   19.5

224

↓

6.0

3

18.9

Leroy Road/CR 57

↑

224 **76**

◇ **Westfield Center**

6.9

17.9

Greenwich Road/CR 97   Greenwich Road/CR 97

High Street

17.0

7.4 ▲ Leohr Park

Seville Road/CR 46

Seville ◇

16.3

8.4

71

Westfield Road

Prospect Street

↑

Burbank Street

3

14.6   West Salem Road/CR 70   **Creston**

10.4

12.0   Doylestown Road/CR 70

13.0

Miles and Directions

0.0 Exit the park and turn left onto Wedgewood Road/CR 162.

1.0 Turn right onto Lake Road.

2.5 Cross Chippewa Road in the village of Chippewa-on-the-Lake (there is a deli on the route).

3.0 Bear left when Longacre Lane goes right.

3.5 Go left onto Eastlake Road.

4.2 At the T turn right onto Ryan Road/CR 40.

5.0 Cross Kennard Road.

6.0 Go under I-71.

6.2 Enter Seville.

6.9 At the T turn right onto Greenwich Road/CR 97.

7.4 Turn left onto High Street.

7.7 Arrive at Leohr Park. There's a pond, restored wetlands, and a towpath trail.

8.3 Cross Main Street and at the T take a left onto Pleasant Street.

8.4 Turn right onto Prospect Street—beware the sewer grate.

9.9 Enter Wayne County, and the road you're on becomes Eby Road.

10.4 Go right onto Doylestown Road/CR 70.

11.5 Reach Creston.

11.8 The road becomes Sterling Street.

12.0 Cross Main Street/CR 3, and the road you're on becomes Burbank Street.

12.8 Bend left when Peake Court goes right.

13.0 At the three-way stop sign, turn right onto West Salem Road/CR 70.

14.6 Go right onto Canaan Center Road/CR 51.

15.3 Enter Medina County, and the road you're on becomes Westfield Road.

16.3 Turn right onto Seville Road/CR 46, just before I-71.

17.0 Take a left onto Leroy Road/CR 57.

17.1 Cross I-71.

17.2 Enter Westfield Center.

17.9 Go right around the village green on Park Circle, crossing Greenwich Road, then continue right on Leroy past the Westfield Fire Station.

18.9 Cautiously cross US 224.

19.0 At the T turn right onto Buffham Road.

19.5 Take a left onto Ballash Road.

20.2 Cross Kennard Road.

22.1 Turn right onto Chippewa Road.

23.0 Go left into the nature preserve and onto the Chippewa Inlet Trail.

24.8 Cross Wedgewood Road.

24.9 Watch for the ball fields and then exit the bike trail.

Local Information

Medina County Convention and Visitors Bureau: 124 West Lafayette Rd., Medina; (330) 722-4405 or (800) 860-2943; www.visitmedinacounty.com.

A PDF file of Medina County bike routes is available at www.co.medina.oh.us/bikemap.pdf; (330) 723-3641; e-mail: medinaco@co.medina.oh.us.

Attractions

America's Ice Cream and Dairy Museum: Housed at historic Elm Farm, 1050 Lafayette Rd., Medina; (330) 722-3839; www.elmfarm.com. Visitors are shown the history of ice cream through toys, dippers, and collectibles. Also has a premium ice-cream parlor.

Restaurants

Dan's Dogs—A Hotdog Eatery: 111 West Liberty St., Medina; (330) 723-3647.

Thyme, The Restaurant: 716 North Court St., Medina; (330) 764-4114; www.thymetherestaurant.com. Fine dining in a casual atmosphere.

Accommodations

The Spitzer House Bed and Breakfast: 504 West Liberty St., Medina; (330) 725-7289 or (888) 777-1379; www.spitzerhouse.com. Ranks in the top 3 percent of bed-and-breakfasts and country inns in the United States and Canada.

Bike Shops

Century Cycles: 1079 North Court St., Medina; (330) 722-7119.

Restrooms

Start/finish: Buckeye Woods Park.
Mile 7.7: Leohr Park.

Maps

DeLorme: Ohio Atlas & Gazetteer: Page 34.

37 Oberlin-to-Vermilion Cruise

What a ride! Leaving from the college town of Oberlin and traveling to Vermilion, which calls itself "a small town on a Great Lake," it passes through Kipton, whence comes the saying "on the ball" (read on). The route is very scenic, with great views of the Vermilion River; you can easily take a side-trip for a Lake Erie view.

Start: Splash Zone, a Lorain County Metropark in Oberlin.
Length: 35.2 miles.
Terrain: Take your pick: There are nice flat sections, mostly at the start and end; some areas are rolling; and the roads around the Vermilion River have some hills.

Traffic and hazards: Many roads are rural with light traffic. There is moderate traffic near Oberlin and Vermilion. The roads tend to be narrow. There's slow but heavy traffic on US 6 for a brief section in Vermilion. Gifford Road has a steep downhill with curves.

Getting there: Take US 20 into Oberlin. Go north on SR 58 for a little more than 2 miles. Turn left onto Hamilton Street, and Splash Zone is on the left at 95 West Hamilton Street, Oberlin.

Boats in a Lake Erie marina
COURTESY OF LORAIN COUNTY CVB

The Ride

Oberlin and Vermilion both have lots of quaint shops and interesting eateries. A map is available at the Oberlin Heritage Center on South Professor Street for a 4.5-mile bike tour of Oberlin. But Mother said, Don't ride on the sidewalks!

This ride, which begins and ends on the Lorain County Metroparks bike trail, follows part of the Back Roads & Beaches route, and you will see signs indicating that route.

Leaving from Splash Zone, head left on Hamilton Street until you see the bike path signs. A short access path takes you to the main trail—go left.

The ride starts out through a country club and the suburbs, with light traffic and narrow roads. When you get to Vermilion Road, look for Millers Orchard on the left. In season their peaches are to die for.

If you don't want to ride through Vermilion, go straight onto North Ridge Road when Vermilion Road goes to the right. Rejoin the route at mile 19.9 by going left onto Gore Orphanage Road, the first crossroad you come to after leaving Vermilion Road.

If you do ride into Vermilion, take some time to enjoy it. You can detour down any one of many side streets to view Lake Erie. If you continue straight on Liberty Avenue beyond where the route turns from Liberty onto West River Road, you'll find restaurants and a park with restrooms.

On West River Road, wind around and cross a couple of little streets and railroad tracks before getting into the country again. And it is very pretty country; you'll cross the Vermilion River. The entrance to the bike path is to the left just past Haigh Road. The path goes through the Kipton Community Park. The Kipton Depot was the site of a train wreck in 1891. The crash occurred because a conductor's watch had stopped for four minutes. The railroad company enlisted a jeweler, Webb C. Ball, to investigate. He instituted a railroad industry timekeeping program, and his accuracy led to the saying "Get on the ball."

The bike path winds through scenic countryside. It breaks when you spill out onto Hamilton Street for a brief section on a well-marked bike lane. Go left onto Pyle Amherst Road and turn right—back to the bike path. Exit on the access path and return to Splash Zone; SR 58 is a short distance past the access, so if you cross it, you've gone too far—unless, of course, you want to keep riding. The bike path continues on for a tour through Oberlin and ends in Elyria.

Miles and Directions

0.0 Exit the Splash Zone parking lot and go left on Hamilton Street.

0.6 Turn right onto the access trail to the bike path.

0.8 Turn left (west) toward Pyle Amherst Road on the main trail.

1.1 Exit the bike path and turn right onto Pyle Amherst Road.

2.1 Cross West Lorain Street/Cleveland Oberlin Street.

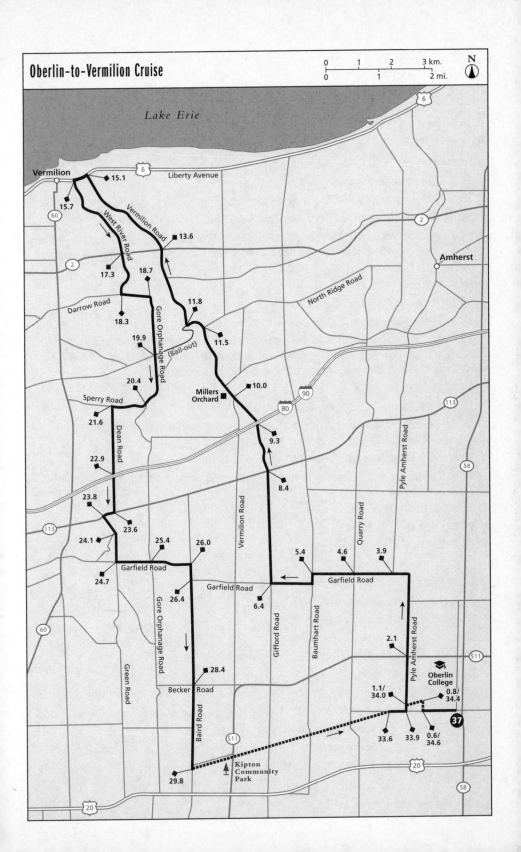

3.9 Continue straight on Garfield Road when Pyle Amherst goes right.

4.6 Cross Quarry Road.

5.4 Jog left onto Baumhart Road and then go right, back to Garfield.

6.4 Go right onto Gifford Road.

8.4 Cross SR 113.

8.6 Caution—steep downhill, dangerous curves.

9.3 Cross over the Ohio Turnpike.

10.0 Take a right onto Vermilion Road.

10.3 Take a break and visit Millers Orchard on the left.

11.5 Bear left, staying on Vermilion, when North Ridge Road goes right.

11.8 Bear right and stay on Vermilion Road. North Ridge Road goes straight. **Bail-out:** Skip the ride through Vermilion by continuing straight on North Ridge and rejoining the main route at mile 19.9.

13.6 In Vermilion bear left and cross over SR 2.

15.1 At the T turn left onto Liberty Avenue/US 6.

15.3 Huggy's Coffee Shop (and ice cream) is on the right.

15.7 Turn left onto West River Road. Bend around to the left and cross the railroad tracks. **Side-trip:** Continue straight on Liberty for a couple of blocks to find restaurants, a park with restrooms, and opportunities for a close-up view of Lake Erie.

17.3 Cross SR 2.

18.3 At the T turn left onto Darrow Road.

18.7 The road bends a hard right and becomes Gore Orphanage Road. You won't know that until you see the road sign at the next intersection.

19.9 Cross North Ridge Road; rejoin the route if you skipped the ride through Vermillion.

20.4 At the T turn right onto Sperry Road, which is Morse Road to the left, but don't count on seeing a road sign.

21.6 Go left onto Dean Road.

22.9 Cross the Ohio Turnpike.

23.6 Jog right onto Milan Elyria Road/SR 113.

23.8 Take a left onto Green Road.

24.1 Continue left on Green when Clary Road goes right.

24.7 Turn left onto Garfield Road.

25.4 Cross Gore Orphanage Road.

26.0 At the T turn right onto Baird Road.

26.4 Continue straight on Baird when Garfield goes left.

28.4 Cross Becker Road.

29.8 Turn left onto the bike path (not on Haigh Road, which is just before the bike path).

30.4 Pass Kipton Community Park—there is a restroom.

33.6 Exit the bike path and turn right onto Hamilton Street.

33.9 Turn left onto Pyle Amherst Road.

34.0 Turn right to get back on the bike path.

34.4 Go right on the bike path access.

34.6 Exit the bike path and turn left onto Hamilton Street.

35.2 Return to the Splash Zone parking lot.

Local Information

Lorain County Convention and Visitors Bureau: 8025 Leavitt Rd., Amherst; (440) 984-5282 or (800) 334-1673; www.visitloraincounty.com. Available here are a route map and information about the Back Roads & Beaches tour, a bike and multisport journey through Lorain County. In addition to road biking, there are opportunities for mountain biking, canoeing, kayaking, swimming, and hiking.

Restaurants

Oberlin Inn Garden Restaurant: 7 North Main St., Oberlin; (440) 775-1111 or (800) 376-4173.

Granny Joe's Ice Creamatorium: 5598 Liberty Ave., Vermilion; (440) 967-3663. Breakfast, lunch, great ice cream. In Vermilion's historic Harbour Town district, it's been featured on the *Jay Leno Show.*

Huggy's Coffee Shop: 5024 Liberty Ave., Vermilion; (440) 967-7575. A stop for ice cream on the route.

Accommodations

Oberlin Inn: 7 North Main St., Oberlin; (440) 775-1111 or (800) 376-4173. Within walking distance to downtown Oberlin. You can bike to Splash Zone, the start of the ride.

Bike Shops

Dale's Bike Shop: 43239 Oberlin Elyria Rd., Oberlin; (440) 774-7433; www.dalesbikeshop.com.
Bicycle Bill's Fitness Center: 5523 South Street, Vermilion; (440) 967-2453; www.bicyclebills.com.

Restrooms:

Start/finish: Splash Zone.
Around mile 15: Vermilion
Mile 30.4: Kipton Community Park.

Maps

DeLorme: Ohio Atlas & Gazetteer: Page 33.
Back Roads & Beaches map available at Lorain County Convention and Visitors Bureau.

38 Geauga County Cruise

Headwaters Park includes East Branch Reservoir at the headwaters of the east branch of the Cuyahoga River. This ride begins at the park, travels along a few miles of the wooded Maple Highlands Trail, goes on roads through hills and valleys in beautiful countryside on to Thompson Ledges Park, and then returns to the starting point.

Start: Headwaters Park, East Branch Reservoir, Chardon.
Length: 35.6 miles.
Terrain: Rolling to hilly.

Traffic and hazards: Most roads are rural with light to moderate traffic. US 6 has heavy traffic. Rock Creek Road/SR 166 and Chardon Windsor Road are also busy.

Getting there: From US 322 near Claridon, turn south onto Old State Road/SR 608. The park is not quite 2 miles down on the left at 13365 Old State Road, Chardon; it is a staging area for the Maple Highlands Trail. There's a parking lot to the right just as you turn into the park; that's the one nearest the trailhead. Drive to the end of the access road for the restrooms.

The Ride

Geauga County is the state's top maple syrup–producing county, earning it the title of Ohio's Sweetest County. It's also home to the second-largest Amish community in the state; *wilkum* is the Amish word for "welcome," and that's a word you will see often.

Thousands of years ago retreating glaciers scraped across Ohio's Appalachian plateau and left behind rich topsoil, sandstone ledges such as those at Thompson Ledges Park, and valleys that became the headwaters of the Grand, Chagrin, and Cuyahoga Rivers, which all flow out of Geauga County. You'll be biking over the ledges and into those valleys on this ride.

Start out on the pleasantly shaded bike path as it winds through a section of beech-maple forest with a scattering of hemlock, tulip, and cherry trees. Exit onto Stillwell Road and enjoy a scenic trek alongside the river. Then it's onto Kile Road, which is rolling. Pass the Hambden Orchard Wildlife Area. You'll see signage indicating that snowshoe rabbits have been released in that area. There is some evidence that those rabbits are reproducing now; that is, after all, what rabbits tend to do.

After a busy stretch along US 6, Clay Street is pleasantly rolling and rural. The hills start to get longer and more insistent on Dewey Road.

Many New England settlers came to Geauga and left their mark on the landscape. Those settlers, Geauga's pioneers, believed strongly in a central green surrounded by the community's most valuable institutions—church, school, and government—and often supplemented by the homes of prominent families and primary businesses. You'll see this when you ride into Thompson. Thompson Road becomes one-way along the green, so you have to turn right and circle the park before resuming the

Gazebo on the green in Thompson

route on Thompson Road. The green is a pleasant park with a gazebo. Stocker's on the Park offers down-home food.

Just past the square you will come to Thompson Ledges Park. These ledges have long been known for their natural beauty, with caverns, fissures, springs, and a striking view. There are hiking trails.

Just past the park the road travels downhill alongside one of the ledges. Turn onto Ledge Road and climb back up; there are great views here. On the return ride you will retrace part of the route from Dewey Road to Clay Street, then continue on Clay instead of turning on US 6. On the right you'll see the Nassau Observatory (named after the observatory director, John Nassau, not that place in the Bahamas). This observatory was part of Case Western Reserve University and was used for research until light pollution dimmed the starlight. The Geauga Park District acquired it, and the 'scopes are now used for student education and public programs.

Turn onto Chardon Windsor Road and then back to Kile, and from Stillwell return to the bike path.

Miles and Directions

0.0 Turn right onto the Maple Highlands Trail—the only way it goes.

2.0 Cross Mayfield Road/US 322.

2.8 Exit the trail and go right onto Stillwell Road, the next road after Mayfield.

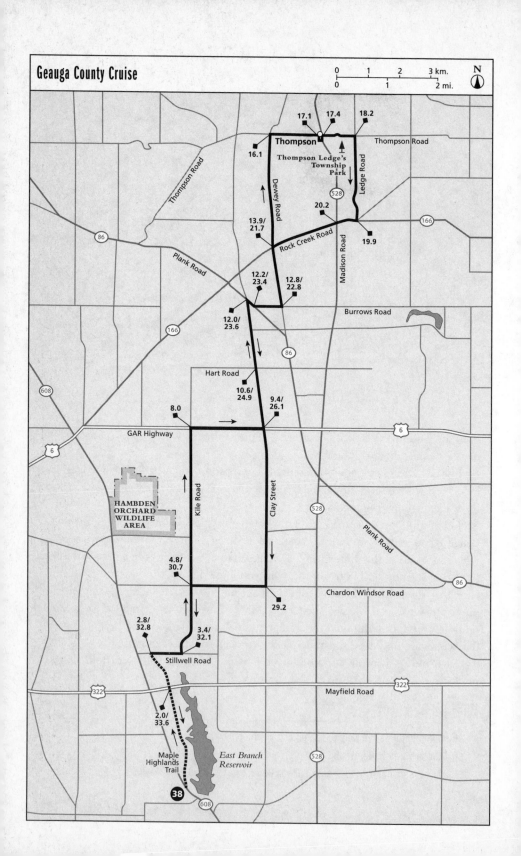

Geauga County Cruise

3.4 Turn left onto Kile Road.

4.8 Cross Chardon Windsor Road. Pass Hambden Orchard Wildlife Area.

8.0 Turn right onto US 6/GAR Highway, heading east toward Montville. Traffic is heavy.

9.4 Take a left onto Clay Street.

10.6 Cross Hart Road.

12.0 Hang a right onto Plank Road.

12.2 Go left onto Burrows Road.

12.8 Turn left onto Dewey Road.

13.9 Cross Rock Creek Road/SR 166.

16.1 Go right onto Thompson Road.

17.1 Turn right onto Madison Road/SR 528. (Thompson Road is one-way through Thompson. Circle Thompson Township Park and then continue right on Thompson Road.)

17.3 Pass Stocker's, a restaurant on the green, which has a restroom.

17.4 Turn right onto Thompson Road.

17.9 Reach Thompson Ledges Township Park.

18.2 Hang a right onto Ledge Road.

19.9 Turn right onto Rock Creek Road/SR 166.

20.2 Cross Madison Road/SR 528.

21.7 Turn left onto Dewey Road.

22.8 Go right onto Burrows Road.

23.4 At the T turn right onto Plank Road.

23.6 Turn left onto Clay Street.

24.9 Cross Hart Road.

26.1 Cross US 6/GAR Highway.

29.2 Turn right onto Chardon Windsor Road.

30.7 Go left onto Kile Road.

32.1 Turn right onto Stillwell Road.

32.8 Go left onto the bike trail.

33.6 Cross US 322.

35.6 Exit the trail, then turn left and return to parking lot.

Local Information

Geauga Tourism Council: 14907 North State Rd., Middlefield; (440) 632-1538 or (800) 775-TOUR (8687); www.tourgeauga.com.

Attractions

This is maple syrup country. Buy locally made maple syrup products at JMJ Enterprises and Sugar Valley Maple Products, 15864 Nauvoo Rd., Middlefield; (440) 785-0005.

Restaurants

Mary Yoder's Amish Kitchen: 14743 North State St./SR 608, Middlefield; (440) 632-1939. Authentic Amish cooking; everything is homemade. Don't miss the gift shop.

Cogan's Village Eatery: 13816 West Center St., Burton; (440) 834-8062.

Maxx Doogan's: 602 South St., Chardon; (440) 285-8222; www.maxxdoogans.com. Maxx Doogan's advertises "the best burgers in Ohio."

Known for their Slider Buckets, they also offer chicken, steak, sandwiches, salads, and a full drink menu.

Accommodations

Punderson Manor Resort and Conference Center: 11755 Kinsman Rd., Newbury, in Punderson State Park; (440) 564-9144; www .pundersonmanorresort.com. Punderson Manor rests among giant maples and pine trees on the shoreline of Lake Punderson. The full-service restaurant provides a lake view.

Red Maple Inn: 14707 South Cheshire St., Burton; (440) 834-8334 or (888) 646-2753; www.redmapleinn.com.

Bike Shops

Mountain Road Cycles: 109 South St./SR 44 (on the Square), Chardon; (440) 279-0374; www.mtnroadcycles.com.

Restrooms

Start/finish: Headwaters Park.
Mile 17.3: Stocker's on the Park Restaurant.

Maps

DeLorme: Ohio Atlas & Gazetteer: Page 26.

39 Harpersfield Cruise

Enjoy two covered bridges, ride through picturesque wine country, and take a tour on the Western Reserve Greenway Trail; all that, plus ride past the oldest tavern in Ashtabula County. Life is good.

Start: Harpersfield Covered Bridge, Ashtabula County Metropark.
Length: 32.0 miles.

Terrain: Flat to rolling with some hills.
Traffic and hazards: Mostly light; heavy on SR 534, but it has a berm.

Getting there: From I-90 take exit 218 and head south on SR 534. In about 0.2 mile turn right (south) on Harpersfield Road/SR 154. It's just over a half mile to the bridge. You can park on the north end, which is an Ashtabula County Metropark.

The Ride

In the late summer and early fall, the tang of ripening grapes is in the air along this Grand River Valley tour. The rich and fertile soils of the region are perfect for producing great grapes; Ashtabula County produces 65 percent of the grapes grown in Ohio. Twenty local wineries are in the area, and the route passes several of them.

It begins at the Harpersfield Covered Bridge, built in 1868, which spans the Grand River. At 228 feet, this two-span Howe truss bridge is the second-longest covered bridge in the state. The great flood of 1913 washed away the land at the north end of the bridge, and the steel span was attached. The bridge is on the National Register of Historic Places. You can park at the Ashtabula County Metropark at the north end. Take the walkway across the bridge and continue on Harpersfield Road.

Vineyard on SR 534

Turn right onto SR 534, and you will soon pass wineries with tour options. You're out of traffic and into farmland on scenic Footville Richmond Road. At about mile 9.0, you will pass Morgan Swamp, a Nature Conservancy property. This self-sustaining swamp ecosystem is one of the largest privately protected wetlands in the state. It's a fantastic wildlife area with numerous rare species recorded.

At the intersection of Footville Richmond Road and Main Street, if you look to the right, you can see a local restaurant called The Pasta Oven. It's pretty much the village hangout including the local liars' table; it also has good food and restrooms.

In Rock Creek, Footville Richmond Road changes to Water Street—stay on Water Street. Just out of town turn left onto Jefferson Street. In a short distance, voila, it transforms back to Footville Richmond Road. At mile 12.8 turn left onto the Western Reserve Greenway Trail. This rail-trail runs parallel to SR 45 and is part of the Great Ohio Lake-to-River Greenway, a 100-mile trail that will eventually stretch from Lake Erie in Ashtabula to East Liverpool along the Ohio River. It is well maintained and scenic. Interesting information about local Underground Railroad activity is posted along the way.

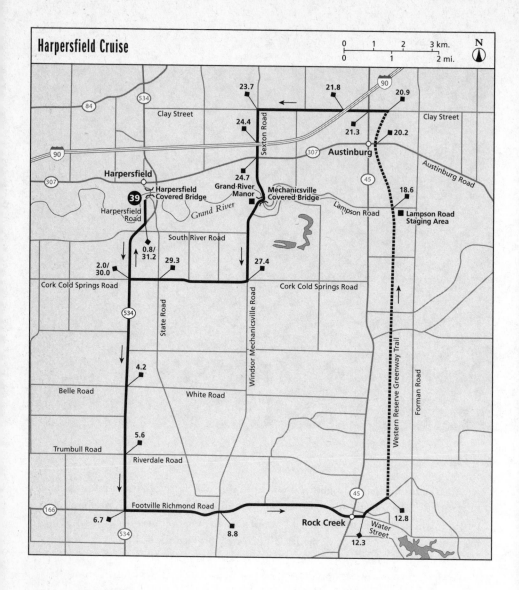

At the Austinburg Road crossing, you can see a mini-mart just to the left. Continue on and pass Jewels Dance Hall. When you see the metal truss bridge up ahead, look for the exit off to the left. Take it to Clay Street and continue left. You'll come to a busy intersection—cross cautiously. There is fast food available. On Sexton Road the route crosses over I-90 and then SR 307. Sexton Road becomes Windsor Mechanicsville. There is signage for Mechanicsville Covered Bridge and Ashtabula County's oldest tavern. You're on a roll—keep going.

Ride through the Mechanicsville Bridge. This 1867 bridge over the Grand River is believed to be the county's oldest covered bridge. It was renovated in 2003. Look inside at the big arch—it was rotting. What's interesting is that you can see where they meshed new boards with the old to preserve a large part of the original arch. These Ashtabula County people know the value of their old bridges and work to preserve them. Notice the hay forks in the window? Betty Morrison, Covered Bridge Festival director, told me they were put there to create interest—something unique. That's what attracts people to the bridges; they are all different.

If you hear music while you're coming through the bridge, just keep going and you'll come to the source. The Grand River Manor, founded in 1847, advertises "Good food, cold beer, lousy service." Penny and I, in need of water, bellied up to the bar and got our water bottles refilled, ice included. We were invited back for the annual clam bake.

On the way home now, the route returns to SR 534, but only for a short distance before returning to Harpersfield.

Miles and Directions

0.0   Leave the covered bridge via Harpersfield Road.

0.7   Turn right onto SR 534.

1.0   Cross South River Road.

2.0   Cross Cork Cold Springs Road.

4.2   Cross Belle Road (to the right) and White Road (to the left).

5.6   Cross Trumbull Road (to the right) and Riverdale Road (to the left).

6.7   Turn left onto Footville Richmond Road.

8.8   Cross Windsor Mechanicsville Road.

11.7   Enter Rock Creek.

11.8   Footville Richmond Road becomes Water Street.

12.3   Turn left onto Jefferson Street (in a short distance it will be Footville Richmond Road).

12.8   Go left onto the Western Reserve Greenway Trail.

18.6   Reach the Lampson Road staging area; restrooms are available.

20.2   Cross Austinburg Road—notice Jewels Dance Hall on the left.

20.9   Just before the King Metal Bridge, take the exit on the left and turn left onto Clay Street.

21.3   Cross SR 45.

21.8   Cross I-90.

23.7   Take a left onto Sexton Road.

24.4   Cross over I-90.

24.7   Cross SR 307. The road you're on becomes Windsor Mechanicsville Road. Follow the sign to Ashtabula's oldest tavern.

25.6   The road bends right—continue straight, then go right through the Mechanicsville Covered Bridge.

25.7   Pass Grand River Manor: "Good food, cold beer, lousy service."

27.4   Turn right onto Cork Cold Springs Road.

29.3   Cross State Road.

30.0 Go right onto SR 534.

31.0 Cross South River Road.

31.2 Turn left onto Harpersfield Road.

32.0 Reach the finish.

Local Information

Ashtabula County Convention and Visitors Bureau: 1850 Austinburg Rd., Austinburg; (440) 275-3203 or (800) 337-6746; www.visit ashtabulacounty.com.

Events/Attractions

Geneva on the Lake State Park—Lodge and Conference Center: 4888 North Broadway, Geneva; (440) 466-7100 or (800) 801-9982; www.thelodgeatgeneva.com. The lodge and the adjacent state park are both on Lake Erie. The park offers fishing, swimming, and boating; the lodge has all of the amenities including a full-service restaurant overlooking the lake. Two dozen wineries are in the area.

Ashtabula County Covered Bridge Festival: Ashtabula County Fairgrounds, 25 West Jefferson St., Jefferson; (440) 576-3769; www.covered bridgefestival.org.

Restaurants

Mary's Diner: 666 East Main St., Geneva; (440) 466-6393. A fifties-style diner; great food.

Ferrante Winery and Ristorante: 5585 SR 307, Geneva; (440) 466-8466; www.ferrantewinery .com. Restaurant and wine sales.

Accommodations

Geneva on the Lake State Park: See above.

Polly Harper Inn: 6308 South River Rd., Geneva; (440) 466-6183; www.pollyharperinn .com. Rises above acres of vineyards that roll toward the Grand River Valley.

Bike Shops

BJ Baker Bicycle Sales and Service: 996 West Prospect Rd., Ashtabula; (440) 997-3486.

Restrooms

Mile 11.7: Rock Creek.

Mile 18.6: Lampson Road staging area.

Mile 25.7: Grand River Manor tavern.

Maps

DeLorme: Ohio Atlas & Gazetteer: Page 26.

40 Ashtabula County Covered Bridge Cruise

Ashtabula County, the second-largest county in Ohio, is known for its covered bridges. This cruise visits seven of those bridges on a route that travels through gorgeous rural vistas.

Start: The Graham Road Covered Bridge Metropark near Jefferson.
Length: 37.4 miles.
Terrain: Flat to rolling in with some hills.

Traffic and hazards: Mostly light traffic. You will encounter some cars in the residential areas including in Jefferson, which has a sidewalk. There's heavier traffic for 0.2 mile on SR 46; it has a wide shoulder.

Getting there: From SR 167 south of Ashtabula, turn north onto Stanhope Kelloggsville Road, then in 2 miles turn right onto Graham Road. Graham Bridge Metropark is just ahead on the right. There is a small gravel parking lot. The bridge is closed to motor traffic.

The Ride

Amazing; at one time this ride would have been in Connecticut. When the original royal land grants were awarded in the seventeenth century, the boundaries of Connecticut were established as extending "from sea to sea." Northern Ohio is directly west of Connecticut. In 1786, Connecticut gave up its claims to western lands except for a part of northeastern Ohio called the Connecticut Western Reserve. Eventually that too became Ohio, and "Connecticut" was dropped, but this area is still called the Western Reserve.

Lots of streams meander through the Western Reserve, resulting in lots of covered bridges. Over time many were lost to fire, flooding, and pure neglect. Around 1982 the county realized their value and began a massive campaign to preserve the historic covered bridges and even to build new ones. They celebrate their covered bridges every year with the Ashtabula County Covered Bridge Festival, always the second full weekend in October.

This ride starts at an old bridge with a story. The Graham Road Bridge was originally in the southern part of the county. It got washed out in the 1913 flood. The bridge was rescued and for reasons unknown moved to the Graham Road crossing. Albert Benson helped rebuild it. The county checked its safety every summer, recalled Bill Benson, grandson of Albert, by driving a truckload of rocks across and watching how badly the bridge sagged. By 1970 it was worn out and needed to be replaced. Bill Benson did not want to see the old bridge destroyed, so he donated a third of an acre of his yard to house the bridge, which, while it no longer spans a creek, is now the centerpiece of a metropark.

When you pass Caine Road early on this ride, look left to see the Caine Road Covered Bridge. This new bridge spanning the Ashtabula River was built in 1986 in

Netcher Road Covered Bridge, built in 1998

honor of Ashtabula's 175th anniversary. This part of the ride is flat; it could also be a barn tour—you'll see some beautiful examples of barn architecture.

On South Denmark Road you'll come to the third bridge, appropriately called the South Denmark Road Covered Bridge. It is a Town lattice bridge and spans Mill Creek. The 1890 bridge was bypassed in 1975.

The fourth bridge is unique and new. The Netcher Road Covered Bridge was built in 1998, funded by an Ohio Department of Transportation Timber Grant. It graces the cover of the Ashtabula County map. Its beauty is more than skin deep: It will hold two semi-trailer trucks.

Ride into the village of Jefferson, named after President Thomas Jefferson. It has a village park, a vintage train, a historic depot, and the world's only perambulator museum. If you're hungry, turn right onto North Chestnut Street for a side-trip to the Jefferson Diner or one of the other local restaurants. As you continue the ride out of town, you will pass the Ashtabula County Fairgrounds, home of the Ashtabula County Covered Bridge Festival.

Turn right onto Doyle Road and ride right through the 1868 Doyle Road Covered Bridge spanning Mill Creek. A laminated arch was added to this bridge when it was renovated in 1987. When renovations are undertaken, the engineers try to maintain the architectural design of the bridges while strengthening them to carry school buses, milk trucks, and motor homes.

On Griggs Road you will be heading toward the Ashtabula County Airport. Be cautious riding through the narrow train trestle. Plymouth Gageville Road is rolling; maybe even hilly. On Benetka Road you can see the Ashtabula River even before you come to the Benetka Road Covered Bridge. This beautiful bridge was built in 1900 and renovated in 1985.

Turn right onto Plymouth Ridge Road; don't follow the Covered Bridge Driving Tour. The route continues to be rolling but will pancake out again around Kelloggsville. On Stanhope Kelloggsville Road look left when you pass Root Road for the last bridge of the trip. This 114-foot bridge crosses the Ashtabula River. It was raised 18 inches when it was rehabbed in 1982–83.

Turn left on Graham Road and return to the Graham Bridge Metropark.

Miles and Directions

0.0 Start from the Graham Road Covered Bridge.

0.3 Turn left onto Stanhope Kelloggsville Road.

1.3 Look to the left to see the Caine Road Covered Bridge—Caine Road is gravel.

2.1 Cross SR 167.

4.1 Turn right onto South Denmark Road when Stanhope-Kelloggsville goes left.

6.5 Cross SR 193.

7.5 Cross Clay Road. You're now on the Ashtabula County Covered Bridge Driving Tour.

7.8 The South Denmark Road Covered Bridge is just to the left of the road.

8.7 Cross over SR 11.

10.8 Look to the right to see the Netcher Road Covered Bridge—this bridge is on the cover of the Ashtabula County map.

10.9 The road T's into East Jefferson Street and Garrett Road; turn left onto East Jefferson and enter the village of Jefferson.

11.6 Cross Spruce Street and Sycamore Street soon after; pass the feed mill on the left.

12.3 Cross the Ashtabula, Carson and Jefferson Scenic Line railroad tracks and then Market Street.

12.7 Cross North Chestnut Street/SR 46. Restrooms are available at the BP gas station to the left, and there are several restaurants on this street. The Jefferson Diner is to the right.

13.2 Turn right onto Poplar Street just after crossing Elm Street.

13.8 At the T turn left onto Beech Street/SR 307.

14.3 Turn right onto Doyle Road.

15.2 Ride through the Doyle Road Covered Bridge.

16.5 Turn right onto Clay Street.

17.6 Turn left onto SR 46.

17.8 Turn right onto Griggs Road, heading toward the Ashtabula County Airport.

19.2 Cross SR 11 and ride through the narrow bridge/train trestle.

20.4 Bend left onto Brown Road.

22.9 Brown becomes Plymouth Road.

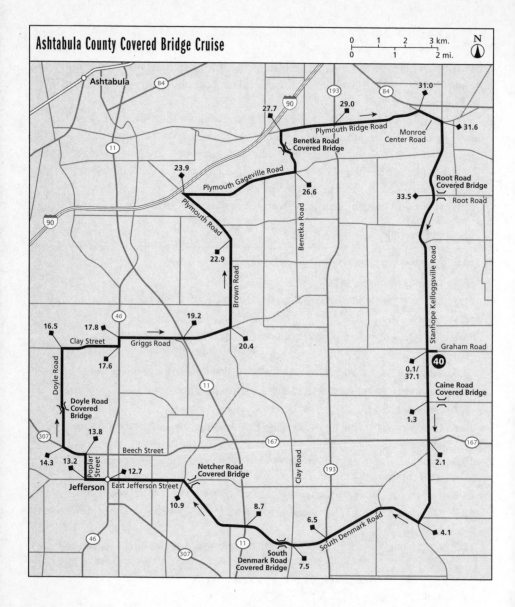

Ashtabula County Covered Bridge Cruise

0	1	2	3 km.
0		1	2 mi.

N

23.9 Turn a hard right onto Plymouth Gageville Road just before I-90

26.6 Turn left onto Benetka Road.

27.3 Come to the Benetka Road Covered Bridge, which crosses the Ashtabula River.

27.7 At the T turn right onto Plymouth Ridge Road, riding in the opposite direction of the Covered Bridge Driving Tour.

29.0 Cross SR 193.

31.0 At the T turn right onto Monroe Center Road.

31.6 Turn right onto Stanhope Kelloggsville Road.

33.5 Pass the Root Road Covered Bridge to the left.

37.1 Turn left onto Graham Road.

37.4 Finish at the bridge.

Local Information

Ashtabula County Convention and Visitors Bureau: 1850 Austinburg Rd., Austinburg; (440) 275-3203 or (800) 337-6746; www.visit ashtabulacounty.com. A Covered Bridge Driving Tour map is available.

Events/Attractions

Geneva on the Lake State Park—Lodge and Conference Center: 4888 North Broadway, Geneva; (440) 466-7100 or (800) 801-9982; www.thelodgeatgeneva.com. The lodge and the adjacent state park are both on Lake Erie. The park offers fishing, swimming, and boating; the lodge has all of the amenities including a full-service restaurant overlooking the lake. Two dozen wineries are in the area.

Ashtabula County Covered Bridge Festival: Ashtabula County Fairgrounds, 25 West Jefferson St., Jefferson; (440) 576-3769; www.covered bridgefestival.org. In October.

Restaurants

Jefferson Diner: 20 North Chestnut St., Jefferson; (440) 576-1977. Mouth-watering home-cooked meals complete with homemade breads and soups. Pies to write home about.

Deli in the Rye: 35 South Chestnut St., Jefferson; (440) 576-3434.

Accommodations

The Michael Cahill Bed and Breakfast: 1106 Walnut Blvd., Ashtabula; (440) 964-8449; www .cahillbb.com. Comfortable, spacious lodging in a landmark home that has been integral to the harbor neighborhood since 1887.

Bike Shops

BJ Baker Bicycle Sales and Service: 996 West Prospect Rd., Ashtabula; (440) 997-3486.

Restrooms

Mile 12.7: In Jefferson.

Maps

DeLorme: Ohio Atlas & Gazetteer: Page 27.

Index of Rides by Name

About the Author

Celeste Baumgartner rode a blue fat-tire Schwinn-type bike complete with a basket and coaster brakes as a kid, packing picnic lunches and exploring the country with friends. Then she got too grown up for such nonsense. Years later she started to bike again with her kids, boldly moving onto a bike with three gears and dropped handlebars—woo-hoo! She wrote a bicycling column for the local paper for more than fifteen years and actually got paid to ride a bike. She has moved through a progression of bikes, currently riding a recumbent with enough gears to run an amusement park, and again packs a lunch and explores the country with friends. That, she believes, is more important than work of any kind.

Visit the premier outdoor online community ..

FALCON GUIDES®

Search

HOME   ABOUT US   CONTACT US   BOOKS   COMMUNITY   PHOTOS   TRAIL FINDER

UPLOAD YOUR PHOTOS

show us your stuff

Eric Hörst on "Diamond Life" (5.13a) New River Gorge, WV

OUTFIT YOUR MIND

For more than twenty-five years, FalconGuides have led the way to every accessible hiking trail, every climbable route, every key mountain biking area, every national park, every outdoor destination; and have guided, instructed, and educated our customers at every level and around every turn, ensuring a safe, enjoyable, and fulfilling experience in the great outdoors.

○ CHECK IT OUT

GET SOCIAL WITH FALCON

 FOLLOW US ON TWITTER

find us on **facebook**

RECENT BLOG POSTS

Kayaking with Big George - October Edition
Grand Canyon
Portable Composting Toilet
Kayaking With Big George - September Edition.
Grand Canyon Adventure Tours
Grand Canyon Helicopter
Kayaking With Big George - August edition...
magnifica_tion
Ask Tina July 2009
Ask Tina June 2009

more

FEATURED NEW BOOK

THE CYCLIST'S MANIFESTO

by Robert Hurst

EXPERT BLOGS

Pure Photography In Glacier Na
By: Bert Gildart

"A wonderfully whimsical exploration of America's transport choices...A relli...

LYTE GO
GO AHEAD

outfit your mind®

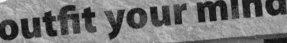

• Chris Sharma
• Beth Rodden
• Dean Potter
• Jason Kehl
• Josh Wharton
• Steph Davis

falcon.com